Do the Hong Kong Chinese experience ghosts, hauntings, spirit mediumship, ESP and other paranormal phenomena just like British and Americans? Or is their culture so different that the ghost accounts in this book will seem bizarre to anyone else?

This classic presentation of cases is based on 3,600 interviews, questionnaires and observations in Hong Kong in 1980/81, updated by recent materials over 30 years later. Interestingly, in spite of clear influences from ancestor worship and Confucian/Taoist/Buddhist culture, parapsychological theories of apparitions from the West also apply to the Chinese cases.

For this 2017 edition, Charles Emmons has revisited his earlier conclusions and added new material that has come to light in the intervening years. This book remains the only major cross-cultural study comparing Chinese with Western ghost experiences.

Chinese Ghosts Revisited

A Study of Paranormal Beliefs and Experiences

Charles Emmons

BLACKSMITH BOOKS

DEDICATION

This book is dedicated to three men who, in the 1960s, both in their scholarly work and in their personal encouragement to me, helped plant the seeds of curiosity and enthusiasm that eventually produced this study: Dr. P. Ward Peterson, Vice President an Professor of Foreign Languages at Gannon University, Dr. John Fleming, Professor of Psychology at Gannon University, and the late Dr. J. B. Rhine of the Foundation for Research on the Nature of Man.

Chinese Ghosts Revisited
ISBN 978-988-13764-4-2

Published by Blacksmith Books
Unit 26, 19/F, Block B, Wah Lok Industrial Centre,
37-41 Shan Mei Street, Fo Tan, Hong Kong
Tel: (+852) 2877 7899
www.blacksmithbooks.com

Editorial assistance: Kieran Green
Layout by Pete Spurrier

CONTENTS

PREFACE TO THE 2017 EDITION

After the 1982 edition of *Chinese Ghosts and ESP: A Study of Paranormal Beliefs and Experiences* came out, I had mixed feelings. Although I believed that it was a significant book (and I certainly enjoyed doing it), it was generally ignored by sociologists and anthropologists. This is hardly surprising, given what I know about the sociology of normal science by now. I also experienced some mildly snide and joking comments from colleagues in other fields. For example, one psychologist commented, when there was a reception for me and my book at Gettysburg College, "Oh, it's a hardback. With a subject like that, you'd think it would be a paperback." I still don't know whether that was a consciously or unconsciously demeaning comment.

On the other hand, Scott Rogo, the parapsychologist, whose writings I greatly admired, wrote a review in which he called *Chinese Ghosts* "a refreshing change from the nonsense." That comment made the whole project worthwhile. In other words, most (popular) books about ghosts were ridiculous, but my analysis was not. I also got a good review and a personal letter of encouragement from another prominent parapsychologist, Karlis Osis.

Let me hasten to add that some popular books on ghosts are much better than others. For example, Mark Nesbitt (1991 and later) has written a whole series about *Ghosts of Gettysburg*, for which he used me as an academic, theoretical source. I also provided some cases for him that had been collected by me and my students at Gettysburg College. Mark and I appeared in two television programs with the same title (*Ghosts of*

Gettysburg) that have been shown on cable TV networks dozens of times, leading to hundreds of people communicating with both of us about their own experiences. Most of Mark's cases are first-hand reports thoroughly researched mostly by him, although some are evidently folklore but still worth reading about.

For many years after that, I told myself and other people who dared to study the paranormal that my book and others like it (serious but also accessible books on paranormal topics) would be recognized as valuable (as well as interesting) in 200 years. I am happy to say that it has not taken two centuries for *Chinese Ghosts* to gain wider acceptance. Through my association with groups like Exploring the Extraordinary (based mainly in the UK), the Society for Scientific Exploration, and the journal *Paranthropology*, I have been amazed to discover that the book is considered a classic in some circles. This was apparent when I interviewed sociologists and others in the UK in 2008 for our book *Science and Spirit*. There is a movement, especially among young scholars doing ethnographic research, to take people's paranormal and spiritual experiences seriously.

Here is an example of one such young scholar, Christopher Laursen, who wrote the following on July 7, 2012:

"From June 1980 to January 1981, Dr. Charles F. Emmons, a sociologist from Gettysburg College, Pennsylvania, and his wife at the time, Chee Lee, embarked on a seven-month project to poll Hong Kong residents on their beliefs and experiences in regards to ghosts. Influenced by similar large-scale surveys conducted by the Society for Psychical Research in the late nineteenth century of 17,000 Britons, Charles and Chee did extensive telephone polls of over 1,500 people and distributed nearly 2,000 questionnaires to secondary school students, asking about their views on the topic. Emmons' academic colleagues were far from encouraging, telling him that Chinese people would not wish to speak on the subject, especially to a Westerner. But one sociologist Emmons spoke with had done a small-scale survey in Hong Kong using Chinese student interviewers and only encountered no more than 15% refusal from those asked to participate. [As it turned out, we got a 90% completion rate.]…

"The incredible survey was documented in Emmons' book, and contains a wide range of Chinese ghost experiences. He wrote that the survey revealed the universal nature of paranormal phenomena including ghosts, ESP and reincarnation, but it also was 'entwined with mysteries of Chinese culture: ghost fear, ancestor worship, and lore about tree spirits.'" [Laursen goes on to relate ghost cases G002 and G008 from the 1982 book.]

Because of encouraging responses to the book like this one thirty years after publication, and communications I have received over the years, from China and Hong Kong included, I realized that *Chinese Ghosts* should go back in print, with added commentary and other new materials.

Interestingly there has not been any comparable study done by anybody else in the interim. Indeed it was a huge undertaking at the time with only a small research grant. And of course large funding agencies seldom (never?) touch such topics. Chee Lee deserves enormous credit for the telephone interviewing, something that could probably never be done again, due to the current plague of telemarketing. Indeed, most people I consulted in Hong Kong in 1980 thought it couldn't be done then, as Christopher Laursen points out above, and as you will see in the 1982 preface to the book.

I hope that somebody younger than I will have the energy to do extensive ethnographic interviewing (if not a survey) about first-hand ghost experiences in Hong Kong in the near future. Joseph Bosco (2007) has collected ghost stories (folklore, as opposed to experiences) among young people recently, which I discuss in chapter 13 in this edition.

However, one good thing about doing a general survey was, as somebody pointed out to me recently, that it probably picked up a lot of people who would otherwise have declined to respond (skewing the sample toward experiencers) to a questionnaire that was more specifically about ghosts. That is perhaps why we found only about 4% claiming a ghost experience, in contrast with other studies in the West that have found around twice that percentage. This way, asking a large random sample about a wide range of beliefs, we were unlikely to get as high a percentage of people reporting (or making things up about) ghosts.

My biggest regret is that nobody (including me) has had the resources to do large-scale follow-up surveys like the one in 1980. If so, we might see trends in ghost folklore and ghost stories (which we also studied, along with the first-hand ghost experiences). I wonder if these changed on the way up to 1997, when Hong Kong went back to China, and again since then to match more recent public events and concerns.

All the same, I have added about 10,000 words of new analysis and new cases throughout this edition. There is some new material in each chapter, in addition to this new preface and a new chapter 13 (New Material about Ghosts). When I wrote the 1982 book I was mostly taking the point of view of a sociologist, anthropologist and parapsychologist. By now I have also become a Spiritualist (instead of an agnostic), and I draw on several other books and articles I have written in the meantime.

Hong Kong has changed, and so have I. However, our ghosts are still relevant, as you shall see.

PREFACE TO THE 1982 EDITION

Ever since the cultural upheaval of the radical 1960s, there has been a flowering of what is broadly labeled "the occult" in America (Truzzi, 1972; Heenan, 1973). This revival of interest in paranormal, or "unexplained," phenomena has spread to areas of the world that are influenced by Western popular culture through films like "The Exorcist" and television series like "Project UFO." What must be happening to non-Western cultures, which have their own traditional ghosts and monsters, in the face of imported demons from the supposedly rational West they are trying to emulate?

Hong Kong, a British island-peninsula colony clinging to the southern coast of the People's Republic of China, is the home of nearly five million Chinese caught up in the struggle for achievement in a modern, largely urban economy. What a fascinating context for studying the interplay of Asian and Western systems of paranormal beliefs!

This book is based on a total of over 3,600 interviews, questionnaires, and observations made in Hong Kong from June 1980 through January 1981. The largest number of cases come from a random telephone survey of 1,501 people on Hong Kong Island and from questionnaires completed by 1,989 secondary-school students. [1] Although British and

---

1   Numbers called on the telephone survey were drawn from the 1980 Hong Kong Telephone Directory for Hong Kong exchange "5" by means of a table of random numbers used to select page, column, and number within column. All but about 4% of this exchange are households on Hong Kong Island; the rest are highly urbanized sections of nearby islands (calculation here based on Census and Statistics Dept., 1978: 388-440). The interviewer tried to interview whoever answered the telephone, if he or she spoke Cantonese, unless the respondent

Americans became involved in some of the more significant reports I collected, only speakers of Cantonese were included in the survey and in the school questionnaires. Cantonese is the language usually spoken or at least understood by nearly all Hong Kong Chinese, [2] and Chinese make up about 98% of the population of Hong Kong.

I began the work on the telephone survey with great uncertainty and with some anxiety over the feasibility of the entire study. Five out of six professors I had consulted at colleges and universities in Hong Kong, including four social scientists and one in education, told me in effect, "Surveys of Hong Kong Chinese? Can't be done!" Especially when interviewed by Europeans, Chinese in Hong Kong supposedly clam up in fear of violation of safety and privacy or in suspicion of investigation by the government. Only one sociologist provided any encouragement, saying that he had used Chinese student interviewers on a small-scale survey with only a 10% to 15% refusal rate.

Library research also weighed on the pessimistic side of the issue. Although anthropologists have done good work with participant observation methods in Hong Kong (Freedman, 1977; Johnson, 1977), and significant use has been made of census data and historical materials (Lethbridge, 1978), surveys are rare (cf., however, Chaney and Podmore, 1973).

---

sounded too young to cope; voluntary shifting of the telephone into someone else's hands happened sometimes as well. In the school sample, questionnaires were distributed to students in form-two and form-five classes (analogous to eighth and eleventh grades in the U.S.) of one secondary school in each of four religious affiliations: Buddhist, Catholic, Protestant, and none. No schools refused when asked to participate.

2   Cantonese is the "usual language" spoken by 88.1% of the residents of Hong Kong, and it can at least be understood by nearly all the rest of the Chinese there; less than 2% of residents are primarily speakers of English or of other non-Chinese languages (Economic and Social Commission for Asia and the Pacific, 1974: 23). Cantonese is also the main Chinese language spoken in Kwangtung Province of southeastern China, from which the great majority of Hong Kong families have emigrated.

Not only social scientists but also many Chinese friends told me that if they ever got a telephone call from somebody asking questions like, "Do you believe in ghosts?" they would hang up. Undaunted, my wife, Chee, a native speaker of Cantonese and a sociologist, singlehandedly called 1,668 telephone numbers over a four-month period. I was pleasantly astonished when she achieved a 90% completion rate, with only 7% refusals and 3% disconnected or never answering numbers. [3] My relatively

---

3   It is interesting to speculate on reasons for this surprisingly high completion rate. For one thing, I suspect that the claim by social scientists that interviewing is so difficult in Hong Kong is largely a myth, the function of which is to excuse the lack of survey research work. Second, the design of the survey schedule (questionnaire) probably played a role. In spite of the rather peculiar topic, the first several questions were about whether they celebrated Chinese New Year or other festivals, some of which related to ancestor worship. By the time the belief questions were asked ("Do you believe in ghosts?," etc.), respondents were already involved in a plausible investigation into Chinese customs. Third, Chee seemed to have excellent interviewing technique, sounding both polite and professional. Although I used no other interviewers for comparison, it is clear from changes over time that it could have been much less successful if Chee had not refined her technique along the way. For the first 200 completed interviews, the refusal rate was 15.7%, but it dropped sharply to a fairly level rate of 5.7% for the last 1,300, averaging 7.1% for the total of 1,501 completed interviews (1,501 completed, 119 refusals, and forty-eight disconnected or never-answering numbers). Chee attributes the change to her developing the technique of using slight pressure when people used the typical excuse of saying that they were too busy (which, no doubt, many were): "I'll ask real fast," she said (in Cantonese), and zipped through thoroughly, but quickly, usually in only three or four minutes, unless they had a paranormal experience to relate.

One other indication that the 7% refusal rate was very good comes from a geographer who was doing research on the economic situation of low-income families in Hong Kong. He told me that his interviewers were getting 35% refusals in door-to-door calls, even though his contacts had been established by a missionary society that was taking care of the children of those families in nursery school. He felt that people were especially reluctant to discuss their personal finances, however. On the other hand, a professor in education told me that he had encountered extreme resistance when trying to get Hong Kong Chinese to answer questions on their traditional folk beliefs, questions somewhat similar to mine.

captive-subject sample of secondary-school students [4] responded at the (predictably) even higher rate of 93%.

Although the secondary students provided some interesting insights into an especially important age group, it is the telephone survey that allows generalized statements about Hong Kong. Even the latter is not a completely representative sample, but it is a good approximation.

First, the telephone survey represents the highly urbanized Hong Kong Island, known officially as Victoria, but not the rapidly expanding industrial areas of Kowloon, with its high percentage of recent immigrants, nor the more rural and traditional New Territories, all of which form the larger colony of Hong Kong. One advantage of surveying Hong Kong Island only is that it focuses on the major contact point with Western, urban culture, where the greatest transition in beliefs should be occurring. Yet even on the island, only 58% were born in Hong Kong, nearly 90% of those born elsewhere coming from China (Census and Statistics Dept., 1978: 3). Especially the older respondents on the survey often reported experiences they had had of ghosts or spirit mediums back in their "home town" in China.

Second, a telephone survey is bound to be somewhat biased since not everyone has a phone, especially in the lower social classes. However, a

---

4   The secondary-school students were "relatively" captive subjects in the sense that they were asked by their teachers to fill in the questionnaire and to return it on a specific date. However, it was stated at the top of the questionnaire that they should bring it back blank if their parents were opposed to their doing it. I also instructed the principals to put no pressure on either teachers or students. The returns show that not all types of teachers or students were equally inclined to participate, in spite of the very high overall response rate. Some teachers in form five no doubt felt some reluctance to let outside matters intrude on the heavy work load prescribed for their students who would have to take an exam at the end of the year to determine whether they could attend form six. Three form-five classes returned no completed questionnaires. These three classes are not computed as refusals in the 93% response rate mentioned, because the students were evidently never given the questionnaire. However, if they are added in as non-completions, the completion rate would be 90% instead of 93%. The form-two students had a 97% completion rate, and form-five only 75% (or 91% if the three nonparticipating classes are eliminated from the statistic).

high percentage of households on Hong Kong island have telephones, 87%, only 1.4% of which are unlisted. [5]

There is no completely valid comparison available to check on the representativeness of the telephone survey, but Hong Kong census data, collected in a somewhat different form, give some idea. Among all Hong Kong Island workers, 58% were working class or lower class in 1976, whereas only 46% of main wage earners in the families of telephone respondents were in these same class categories, suggesting a bias toward a high-status sample in the survey, as expected. [6] The age distribution is skewed toward the middle, with the extremes underrepresented. Preteenagers usually did not answer the phone or passed it on an older person; people over age sixty were very underrepresented, only 3.9% of the survey sample but 10.3% of the population of Hong Kong Island by the census (Census Statistics Dept., 1978: 5). The sex distribution was very close, however; males were 47.8% of the survey, and 50.3% by the census (Census and Statistics Dept., 1978: 1). [7]

---

5 Mr. Bosco Liu, public-relations officer for the Hong Kong Telephone Co., Ltd., informed me of the 87% "penetration factor" for Hong Kong Island in a personal interview, June 16, 1980. This is higher than for the colony of Hong Kong in general, in which 84% of residences have telephone lines. The higher the penetration factor, the more likely a random telephone sample is to be representative of whatever the universe is (the universe in this case being households on Hong Kong Island).

6 These comparisons are based on data from the 1976 Hong Kong By-Census (Census and Statistics Dept., 1978: 3). Professional families were 7% of the telephone sample, even less than the 8.5% professional in the census data on workers. However, other middle-class occupations were overrepresented as expected, 46.9% vs. 33.6%. Part of the apparent over-representation of the middle, as opposed to lower class, is probably due merely to the fact that the telephone survey asked about the *main* breadwinner, which would ordinarily give the *highest* status worker in the family, whereas the census counted all workers and not just breadwinners.

7 Such biases overall are probably not very serious, and presumably reflect merely the tendency for certain categories of people to have greater or lesser access to the telephone or to have more or less of a "telephone-answering role." The result will be some distortion in overall statistics – for example, what percentage believe in ghosts – but when comparisons among groups are considered – for

Both the telephone study and the school questionnaire were designed to provide cross-cultural comparisons by replicating a 1978 Gallup poll on paranormal beliefs in the U.S. (cf. Table 1 on page 325; also cf. Emmons and Sobal, 1981a and 1981b). These data on beliefs together with participant observation of practitioners like spirit mediums and fortune-tellers, and the collection of material from popular media presentations, provide the basic for sociological and anthropological analysis. The purpose and theory behind this social / cultural analysis will be explained in greater detail in Chapter 2. The study has another purpose as well, which is to test the plausibility of reports of alleged strange experiences reported in Hong Kong or in the United States by showing parallels in the both societies. Is there, for example, a universal ghost experience that is unaffected by cultural differences and that fits the parapsychological theories of psychical researchers?

In every aspect of this research, there are many individuals and organizations that deserve thanks for their assistance and encouragement. As already indicated, my wife, Chee Lee Emmons, M.A. in sociology, did a masterful job on the telephone survey and also helped as a translator of written material and in other interview and observation situations. Several relatives and friends of Chee's family living in Hong Kong also provided research contacts and general life support and hospitality during our seven-month stay.

Among the many academics with whom I discussed my research before and during the data-gathering stage, Harold Traver, sociology professor at the University of Hong Kong, deserves special thanks for his genuine, friendly interest (and for being the only social scientist to suggest that survey research was feasible in Hong Kong!). Anthropologist Diana Martin shared much of her valuable analysis of spirit mediums and ghost marriage derived from her own research in Hong Kong and Taiwan. Kirsty Hamilton of Radio Three Hong Kong and Aileen Bridgewater

example, differences between age groups on ghost belief – there should be enough in each age group to provide a valid comparison.

of Commercial Radio both gave me important exposure and contacts on their interview / call-in programs. One of these contacts, Thelma Heitmeyer, a well-known yoga teacher in Hong Kong, introduced me to many more people with personal experiences and shared with me her wealth of insight into paranormal topics in Hong Kong.

Dozens of other individuals who gave special reports of their own paranormal experiences or who allowed questionnaires to be distributed in their schools cannot be listed without violating anonymity. Finally, over 3,500 people were kind enough to respond to the phone survey or to the questionnaire.

Organizational support was provided first by Gettysburg College, which granted me a full-year sabbatical leave and presented me with a Faculty Development Grant in partial support of the project. The Centre of Asian Studies at the University of Hong Kong, where I was a Visiting Scholar, supplied not only office space and secretaral assistance but also an exciting intellectual environment. Other parts of the university were cooperative as well, especially the library and the computer center. The Hong Kong Government Information Services supplied very useful files; David J. Roads, Principal Information Officer, and So Kan Ching, librarian, were quite helpful. Again, some organizations cannot be mentioned because of anonymity, such as the four secondary schools that cooperated so well in administering questionnaires to their students.

Note: Cases of firsthand reports are given consecutive three-digit reference numbers representing the order in which they appear in this book, categorized by the following letter code:

E001-E026:	ESP
FT001-FT012:	fortune telling
G001-G127:	ghosts
M001:	monster
P001-P014:	poltergeists and other psychokinetic (PK) effects
R001-R005:	reincarnation
SM001-SM008:	spirit mediums
SP001-SP012:	spirit possession

I

Strange Cases on Exhibit

This chapter is a window on the rest of the book. The cases exhibited here, however, represent only a few of the hundreds of firsthand accounts reported to me in Hong Kong in 1980.

Many of the most significant reports involve ghosts, or "apparitions." Ghosts are by no means always frightening to the people who experience them, but the man who toid me the following recalled it with genuine dread.

G001. The Smokey Ghost

One night I heard someone coming slowly up the stairs. I thought it was a burglar. I picked up a knife, put my left hand on the door knob, and my right hand on the light switch. As I heard the intruder going across the marble floor on the other side of my door, I raised the knife and quickly opened the door. There was no one there!

A few nights later, I was asleep in bed with the door open. I woke up scared when I heard someone coming up the stairs again and across the marble floor outside. Since my bed was against the same wall, I could see through the crack where the door hinges were and into the hall. By telling myself that I was a twenty-two-year-old man and shouldn't be afraid, I got the courage to roll over in bed and look through the crack. Then it came into the room floating sideways, as if being pulled along on a tray. I could vaguely distinguish the facial features. Its expression did not change. It was a thin, grayish light, very smokey but not changing shape. I could see through most of it. It stopped at the foot of the bed, and then started moving in, as if floating forward right through the bed. When it got to my waist, I said, "In the name of Christ, leave me!" Then it backed off, and when it reached the foot of the bed, disappeared. It was petrifying. I was left with pain in that part of my body [up to the waist].

If the next man's memory is accurate, his case, which happened in China, represents the largest number of people to see an apparition at one time in any apparently reliable case I have ever heard or read.

G002. Harvest Homecoming

It was after the harvest, and we had nothing to do. Twenty or thirty of us were sitting and talking on a patio of one house on our street. One person was telling stories, another one singing. About 2 or 3 a.m., we decided to have a snack. All of a sudden a huge guy in a white robe appeared. My aunt yelled, "Look who's here!" and we all saw him walk from one side of the patio to the other and go in the house. We went into the house and asked the woman who lived there who had come in. She was asleep inside, hadn't seen him, and said that nobody had come in. We couldn't find him. But we had recognized him. He was her deceased husband. I don't remember how long ago he had died, but he had died in that house. When he crossed the patio, it took only three or four seconds, and he looked exactly realistic. However, my aunt was immediately afraid when she realized that she had been the first to see the ghost. She got very sick one week later, and died a month later.

Did the ghost really cause the aunt's death? What part do culture and psychology play in such cases? At any rate, reports G001 and G002 illustrate the Chinese fear of ghosts. The apparition in the next report, however, the respondent's mother, seems to have had kindly intentions.

G003. Looking After the Family

Seven days after my mother died, I was half-asleep when I saw her standing beside my bed, looking at me. She called my name twice. I was scared, but not scared, since she was my mother. She stood there for two or three minutes, and I couldn't move. She looked normal but not really that clear, more like a shadowy figure than a real person. She didn't move. All of a sudden she disappeared.

A couple of days later, one of my children, the baby, was sick. I saw my mother following my wife around, carrying some baby clothes while my wife was carrying the sick baby. My mother looked very worried. My wife wouldn't have been able to see her because my mother was behind her. She followed her for a couple of minutes. Again she was shadowy but looked normal otherwise. This time she said nothing. She disappeared all of a sudden again. I haven't seen her since.

G003 raises a number of questions. Is there any significance to when the ghost appeared (seven days after death, a common Chinese theme) or to whom she appeared and in what circumstances? Is it typical for ghosts to look "shadowy" (cf. G001, "The 'Smokey' Ghost")? How could the baby clothes she carried be part of the apparition? Do clothes or other material things have a "spirit," too?

The following apparition, also apparently involving a relative, was experienced by a fifteen-year-old girl in Hong Kong in 1949. Why do you suppose the ghost did not face them? [8] Why was there only half a body?

G004. Encounter in an Alley

My father and I were just leaving the hospital where my sister had died unexpectedly from cholera that day. It was around midnight. There, in an alleyway by two shops, we saw a half-body with no legs, the back toward us, with black hair, not moving. I asked my father who it was, but he just dragged me away. I think it was my sister.

In Chinese culture, important relatives are not limited to the immediate "nuclear" family. Likewise, important family ghosts include a group of ancestors who are worshiped at a family altar. Each ancestor has his or her name written on a wooden tablet before which incense is burned, or sometimes, as in G005 below, an oil lamp.

G005. The Noisy Ancestor

For several nights in a row, I saw the tablet of one of my ancestors moving and making a strange noise, like bamboo knocking against a glass cup. I'm not sure whether it was the doing of a ghost or of a god. But the most suspicious thing is that the strange noise happened every night at about 3:30a.m. I told my mother. She said the oil lamp in front of the tablet usually ran out of oil at that time. So the ancestor thought we didn't respect him and got angry.

If the sixteen-year-old girl who reported the above was actually seeing the tablet move, then the case might be classified as a "poltergeist," literally

---

8   Perhaps the apparition did not want to show her sickly face caused by the cholera ordeal. This is reminiscent of an apparition discussed by Tyrrell (1963: 62, 63) in which the ghost of a woman with cancer of the face entered the room backward with part of her face still hidden by the door.

a "noisy ghost," involving physical movement of real objects. However, I am inclined to call this one an apparition because the unusual noise seemed to come from a nonexistent glass cup.

> *2017: G005 is also an interesting example of how people try to attribute meaning to their ghost experiences. Notice that the girl wonders if it's a ghost or a god. I'm thinking that 3:30 a.m. is around that time when people are most likely to have dreams they can remember or to go into altered states or creative states. I often wake up at about that time having thought of great lecture ideas in my sleep. The girl's mother, who is probably responsible for ancestor worship in the family, thinks about the oil running out.*

So far, all of our ghosts have been human. Case G006, reported by another sixteen-year-old girl, suggests they need not be.

G006. Animal Spirits?

I believe that animals have spirits, too. Facing the hill near our house there used to be a very shabby pig-slaughterhouse. It was like two sheds linked together. I even visited the slaughterhouse; I knew the place well. At noon, I always heard people slaughtering the pigs, and the pigs cried and screamed horribly, and their voices carried far away. I always felt sorry for the pigs and shed tears for them. Later on, the slaughterhouse was torn down because it was too shabby. After one or two months of peacefulness, opposite the hill at night we could hear pigs crying like when they were being slaughtered. It lasted a long time; my brother and I both heard it. My hair stood on end when I heard it. But now we can't hear it any more, because a road was built and cars go by.

> *2017: G006 doesn't seem as strange to me today as it did then, now that I have run across, for example, spirit mediums (Emmons and Emmons, 2003: 38-39) who bring in animal spirits. My favorite*

example is a medium who relayed a message from a cigar-smoking dog. The sitter (person getting the reading) confirmed the validity of the image and said that their milk man used to throw his cigar into their yard, and their former dog used to pick it up and run around with it, appearing to be smoking it.

You may think that this report has the ring of sincerity and truth. On the other hand, you may wonder if teenagers are overly imaginative. The next respondent, a seventeen-year-old girl, shows a self-critical attitude toward her own strange experience which nevertheless made a strong impression.

G007. A Bathroom Ghost

One evening this April or early May, I got up to go to the bathroom. My back was facing the toilet as I pulled the drapes closed. When I turned around to go to the toilet, I saw a blurry figure getting up from the toilet and pulling his pants up with his hands. When I saw that, I quickly ran out. It's my impression that it was not a grownup but a boy around ten years old. At that time, my whole family was home, and it was not too deserted or quiet.

Later on, my classmates analyzed this incident, and they thought that I was very emotional then because I had been preparing for my exams all day and couldn't relax. I could have been going crazy.

At that time I saw only a shadow, but the shape was very clear. I knew right away it was a person wearing clothes, but I couldn't see his face. His head was bending low.

The following case is not the first "collective" apparition, that is, experienced by more than one person at once (cf. also G002, G004, and G006). However, the fact that some but not all of those present saw it poses an interesting paradox. If this apparition was merely a hallucination, why did *several* boys see it? If it was real, why didn't *everybody* see it?

2017: Over the years this has become my favorite case of a partially collective apparition. It is perhaps the clearest demonstration of evidence for an experience that is neither materially real nor just an individual's imagination.

G008. Boy Scout Picnic

In 1973, when I was fifteen years old, I went on a Boy Scout picnic. A whole gang of fifteen or twenty of us were marching along with our leader. I was last in line. It was late in the evening, but there was moonlight. I saw two white spots approaching, self-lit, like two spotlights. When they came close by, I could see that it was a very old couple. They had no expression on their faces, and were not looking at anybody. Both of them were wearing white robes. Their hair was old-fashioned and parted and short, although the woman's hair was longer than the man's. They walked very strangely. First, they would swing their arms together, and then jump, the two of them at the same time. Everybody should have seen the couple, but only five or six of us claimed to have seen them. Our leader did not see them. I was very scared, and turned around to look at them again when they passed by, but they were gone. I'm very sure of what I saw.

Could the old Chinese couple have been a glimpse out of the past, seen by "retrocognition" (literally "knowing backwards") on the part of the more psychically sensitive boys? With the possible exception of the ghost in G003, who seemed concerned about the present health of her grandchild, the other cases might involve retrocognition as well. The next apparition report, however, from a fifty-year-old woman, seems to involve *pre*cognition (seeing the future).

2017: Theoretically there should be no difficulty with there being precognitive apparitions. ESP (psi) should connect without limitation of time or space. If hauntings, like G009, represent an emotional attachment (based on a traumatic event like the fire in this case) of a spirit to a place, it's an interesting question why they would or wouldn't manifest backwards in time. At any rate, this is a rare case in my experience.

G009. Destiny in Bangkok

In 1972, I was returning from England when there were problems with the plane, and we had to stay over in Bangkok. My friend and I stayed in separate rooms in the hotel. Since it was very hot, I went to take a bath. When I opened the bathroom door, I saw a few people in there, some male, some female, all in airline uniforms. At the time, I thought they were regular people, although they didn't move at all. I saw them clearly. But then they disappeared! I was very scared. I shut the door and went to stay with my friend.

Three days later, after I returned to Hong Kong, that hotel had a fire in which a few airline hostesses were burned to death. A pilot with a beard was also killed; I had seen a man with a beard in the bathroom.

If the previous case is a precognitive apparition, the following might be a precognitive dream, a form of extrasensory perception (ESP), although the respondent thinks that there is also something magical about the number two in his life.

E001. The "Lucky" Number

Number two is my lucky number. Two years ago I dreamt that I was on the second floor of the hospital in room two, the second bed. This year it happened.

The next report, from a thirty-year-old mother, is also an ESP dream, either clairvoyant (seeing the event) or telepathic (communicating with another mind), this time simultaneous with the event.

E002. Mother and Infant

My baby was living with a babysitter. One night I dreamt that the baby was spitting up milk. I woke up and tried to use a cloth to catch the milk but realized then that the baby wasn't with me. The next day I called the babysitter and found out that the baby had been spitting up a lot of milk at exactly the same time as my dream.

The following experience, also involving a dream, is categorized as a reincarnation case because that is how it was labeled by the forty-nine-year-old woman who reported it. Can you think of any alternative explanations?

R001. Soul of the Fair-Skinned Girl

The time I was pregnant with my third daughter, I went into labor during my sleep. My husband woke up and told me he was dreaming that a woman floated in through the window. She was naked, and had long hair and very fair skin although she was Chinese. I gave birth to a girl with fair skin. I think it's reincarnation.

Case R001 focuses on the entry of a soul into a new body, but R002, from a thirty-two-year-old woman, allegedly documents the other end of the process.

2017: At the time this case (R002) appeared in 1982 I was not familiar with the pattern of birthmarks indicating a connection to a person in a previous incarnation. For a discussion of Ian Stevenson's studies of birthmarks in reincarnation cases, see Science and Spirit (Emmons and Emmons, 2012: 140-141).

R002. The Recycled Soul

When I was very little in my village in China, a very rich man in his sixties, a neighbor of ours, was very ill and dying. His relatives were all crying, but he said. "Don't cry. I'm going to be reborn in the next village, as a boy again." He died. Then his relatives went to the next village and found a boy born exactly at the time of the old man's death. He even had a mole at the exact same place on his face, and they knew it was him.

The next case involves spirit possession rather than reincarnation. Is this what happens when a soul or ghost temporarily enters a body that is already occupied?

SP001. The Unexpected Guest

As far as I can recall, it happened when I was about ten years old. I saw a ghost-possession case at my adopted father's birthday feast. I was with my adopted father's sister taking shells off shrimps. All of a sudden, her hands started to tremble, and she called my adopted father's name. I was very frightened and screamed. My adopted father and his friends came over to see what was going on. She became very heavy and needed four people to hold her up. They carried her to another room, where she continued to shake. My adopted father held her middle finger, and she started to talk. First, she called his name; then, she asked him to burn her a paper mahjongg set and a paper *cheungsam* [long dress]. She was my adopted father's mother. Finally, his father also came and talked to him, saying that if my adopted mother wanted to see them, they could appear in her dream. The rest I don't quite remember.

Knowing something about Chinese culture certainly helps in understanding this report, not only the fact that people burn paper effigies of articles to send them to their ancestors in the other world (like clothing, or a set of mahjongg, a gambling game) but also the belief that holding a possessed person's middle finger will get the spirit to speak.

The next report, concerning a monster, could use some illumination as well. First, there are separate male and female *po to* trees, each with its own guava-like fruit. The monster here is described as a tree *spirit*, leading one to wonder whether it might be more like a ghost than like a Bigfoot, for example. The expression "three-inch gold embroidered shoes" is the literal Chinese for "bound feet," possessed traditionally by Chinese women. Finally, it should be said that the respondent, a forty-nine-year-old man, sounded perfectly serious.

M001. The Canton Tree Monster

When I was fourteen years old in Canton, I climbed up a male *po to* tree to pick some fruit. Each year, at least three or four people were killed by a monster while they picked these. As I held onto the trunk with one arm, I turned to pick a fruit from a branch, but something kept moving the branch just out of my reach so that I couldn't pick it. Then, I clearly saw that it was the spirit doing it three feet away from me. He was three feet taller than me. But I couldn't see the face because the sun was shining behind him. I just saw the bottom part. The legs were hairy at the bottom, and he had human clothes on. He also had three-inch gold-embroidered shoes. The amazing thing was that the bottoms of the soft shoes were perfectly clean, which means that he didn't come up from the ground, or they would have been dirty. I climbed down without any fruit. I was so scared I almost broke my skull. [His wife noted that he was lucky not to have been killed.] Other people in the village saw the monster, too. Some of the ones who fell out of trees talked a little before they died and said that the *po to* monster had thrown them down.

I hesitate to state that I do not believe any particular firsthand report. However, some reports, like the last one for example, seem less likely than others, either because of a lack of internal consistency or plausibility or because they are not supported by similar reports from others. Fortunately, very few cases fail to fit into consistent patterns.

Now that we have sampled some accounts of ghosts, spirits, and ESP in a Chinese setting, the next chapter will consider how certain theoretical approaches can help make the strange more explainable.

2

PROBLEM AND PURPOSE

The reports in Chapter 1 raise several questions about the nature of paranormal phenomena like ghosts, ESP, and reincarnation. However, these universal mysteries are also entwined with mysteries of Chinese culture: ghost fear, ancestor worship, and lore about tree spirits. The most general problem of this study is how to disentwine the natural (or supernatural!) from the cultural and social. Put another way, the purpose is to determine as much as possible about both the reality (if any) as well as the social functions of such phenomena. For example, what can Chinese ghost reports tell us both about the nature of the ghost experience and about the significance of ghost belief in Chinese culture and society?

It may seem unusual to combine sociology and anthropology with a discipline like parapsychology, which is the study of psychic phenomena, such as ghosts and ESP. After all, parapsychology is directed toward testing the truth of certain claims of the paranormal. Social scientists, by contrast, deal in "social facts": ghosts and sea monsters are socially real if enough people believe in them. Usually, social scientists would not care whether they existed outside the realm of cultural belief or not. There are, however, precedents for using social science as a "filter" that can try to eliminate the need for any paranormal explanation. For example, according to one sociologist who testified before the House Committee on Science and Astronautics in 1968 (Fuller, 1969: 42, 118), some but by no means all UFO reports could be explained by the social process of "collective delusion" (mass hysteria spread by rumor). This is analogous to using astronomy as a filter for UFO reports. J. Allen Hynek (1972, 1977), a professional astronomer and UFOlogist, was able to eliminate about 30% of UFO reports in Project Bluebook from the strange category by identifying them as astronomical phenomena. This kind of analysis provides only negative evidence, of course – that is, it helps eliminate allegedly paranormal cases but cannot prove any on the positive side, nor can it prove that there could never be any legitimately paranormal ones.

What are some social reasons for people to believe in or to report paranormal phenomena (whether they actually exist or not)? One reason, especially in the United States, has been excitement over the occult and the mysterious as portrayed by and diffused through popular media. As Truzzi, a sociologist, suggests (1972), this revival of interest may be relatively superficial. Not everyone who looks at the horoscope in the daily superficial. Not everyone who looks at the horoscope in the daily newspaper, for example, is very serious about astrology. In some other cases, the paranormal may have deeper significance for the social/cultural system. In such cases, the paranormal beliefs form part of a mythology that supports or explains the social system. Ghosts in Chinese culture would be one example. Ghosts (cf. Chapter 3) are at the core of ancestor worship, which in turn represents the traditional unity of the extended family.

Especially in a complex, heterogeneous society, not all type of people share exactly the same beliefs and attitudes. In some cases, the uneven distribution of belief may reflect changes in the society. For example, age groups may differ because younger people are learning a new system. From the perspective of truth testing, it may be suspected that belief in the paranormal is higher in social categories of people who are just more gullible or who need to believe in order to compensate for their marginal position in society. [9]

---

9   This "marginality hypothesis" is generally not supported for the United States, according to Emmons and Sobal (1981a).

On the other hand, suppose that reported experiences of paranormal phenomena like ESP or UFOs turn out to be essentially the same in different societies, perhaps even contrary to what people would be led to expect by their culture. If this should be the case, then we would have some support for the notion that these experiences represent some underlying universal reality. Just passing through this "social filter" would not make a phenomenon any easier to understand; but the more independent and similar reports of ESP or UFOs gathered around the world, the more motivation we should have to take a closer look for patterns that may help generate a theory.

But can these reports be trusted? It is my distinct impression that very few of the respondents in the study were fabricating or significantly distorting their reports of their own firsthand experiences. On the contrary, there was often either a "reluctance to report" [10] (Hynek, 1972) or a stated desire for anonymity. Secondhand and even less direct reports are another matter, often containing at least unintentional distortion (cf Chapters 8 and 9). At any rate, cases that are unique or rare, showing little similarity to phenomena reported by others, can be set aside suspiciously for lack of confirming evidence. [11]

Generating theories to help explain the commonly reported patterns that do occur is no easy task. Almost by definition, paranormal or "unexplained" phenomena have not yet been generally conceded by the scientific establishment to exist, let alone have adequate theoretical explanations if they did exist. However, all of the topics included here have been discussed under the general heading of parapsychological theory:

10   People usually avoid deviant perceptions just as they avoid being associated publicly with deviant behavior. Only after an "escalation of hypotheses" (Hynek, 1972), trying the more normal explanations first, do they admit even to themselves the possibility of strange explanations for their experiences.

11   As this study is primarily sociological, most experiences are reported by anonymous survey. Therefore, "confirming evidence" refers to a set of reports showing a common pattern. Parapsychologists or UFOlogists would usually think more in terms of confirmation based on detailed investigation of the facts in a smaller number of cases.

ghosts, ESP, spirit possession, spirit mediums, reincarnation, and fortune telling. This book provides some reality testing of these phenomena, first to see if they pass through the social filter by being reported similarly in different societies, and second to see if the Hong Kong reports are consistent with parapsychological theory.

2017: It is amusing to me to read this chapter 34 years later. I still like it and agree with it. However, I didn't realize at the time that my position fit into what is now called "experiential source theory" (McClenon, 2002; Hufford, 1982). According to this theory, people all over the world have basically the same types of paranormal and spiritual experiences, but they account for them in different ways and give them greater or lesser attention depending on their culture. Callum Cooper (2011) makes a similar point about ancient Egyptian apparitions being very much like modern ones in terms of the actual experiences reported.

For example, the first thing people in Hong Kong would probably wonder if they saw a ghost would be whether it was a "hungry ghost" (see Chapter 3), maybe one of their own ancestors whom the family was not worshiping properly. In the United States, let's say in Gettysburg, PA, where I live, people would first of all be more skeptical, doubting their own experience more. Then they might wonder if it could be a dead relative (ancestor), but they might also consider it to be a Civil War haunting (and not have any concept of a "hungry ghost"). But these are interpretations, as opposed to experience differences.

The competing theory to experiential source theory is "cultural source theory." This is the standard perspective in most anthropology and sociology of religion, according to which people's paranormal or spiritual experiences are an effect of cultural expectations. In other words, Chinese folk religious beliefs about ghosts should make Chinese people susceptible to having ghost experiences to meet these expectations. If Americans have ghost experiences it's probably because they watch too much TV or listen to ghost lore around the campfire, because there is not much support for ghosts in the religion of most Americans.

What this book tests is whether ghost experiences in a Chinese context are basically the same as in other cultures in spite of the superficial differences in interpretation. Do they show the same characteristics or not? If they do, this would support experiential source theory. If not, this would support cultural source theory.

3

Ghosts in Traditional Chinese Culture

In this chapter, let us set the general framework of traditional Chinese culture that deals with ghosts. More specific and more recent ghost lore will be discussed in Chapters 8 and 9.

Soul and universe

At first glance, there is no single, consistent Chinese view of the soul or spirit, but in fact the various versions essentially stem from the dualism of *yin* and *yang*. Yin is the dark, female principle, associated with earth; yang the light, male principle of heaven.

In some vesions, there seems to be only one soul, as in Hsu's (1967: 144) account of a town in Yunnan Province of southwest China. One informant in Hong Kong, a man deeply into a brand of Taoist thinking, told me that every human has either a *shen* (yang-type) or *guai* (yin-type) soul at death, but not both.

More commonly, humans are thought to have both, a *shen* or *hun*, which is the superior, positive spirit; and a *guai* or *p'o*, which is the inferior, negative spirit (Chan, 1969: 167; Burkhart, 1953:vol. II: 27). Ordinarily, the former returns to heaven and the latter to the earth. However, Willoughby-Meade (1926: 5) notes two versions: one in which the guai, and the other in which the shen stays in the grave until the body decays.

Most Chinese cannot really present "very clear ideas as to how many parts of the soul there are, but there is a vague notion that there is more than one since its presence can make itself felt in more than one place after death" (Elliott, 1964: 29). Breaking up the simple dualism of two places, heaven and earth, is the idea that perhaps a *third* soul "hovers over, or enters into, the ancestral tablet which is inscribed with his name and placed in the family shrine to receive worship from the male members of the family" (Endacott, 1966a: 27). Recall that in case G005 (Chapter 1) a tablet seemed to be moving on the ancestral altar.

Even larger numbers of souls are mentioned. A set of five additional elements beyond *shen* and *guai* has been identified as "subsidiary souls" for five main organs: heart, spleen, lungs, liver, kidneys (Willoughby-Meade, 1926: 5). Potter (1970: 149) in the New Territories part of Hong Kong and Elliott (1964: 28) in Singapore found a system of ten souls. Three are spiritual (*shen*) and associated with the other world, and seven are sensory or emotional and linked to the *guai* (which rapidly fades, some would say).

If the nature of the soul or souls is not crystal clear in everyone's mind, neither is the place they will go after death. Except for those souls or soul elements that will either disintegrate or cling to this world, most will end up in a spirit world.

As early as the Shang Dynasty (1520-1030 B.C.), the universe for the Chinese consisted of the heaven above, humans in between, and the earth (i.e. underworld) below (Christie, 1968: 28), a rather natural cosmology. Potter (1970: 148) describes essentially the same three-layered system in the New Territories: the yin-like hell and purgatory below, the yang heaven above, and earth (the earth of humans) in between. My Hong Kong Taoist informant stressed that the levels of heaven and hell were all part of one system, with earth sandwiched in the middle.

Hsu (1967: 137-142) in Yunnan writes of a boundary between the "World of Man" and the "World of Spirits." After death, one's soul goes beyond this boundary and heads either for the road to the higher or for the road to the lower world of spirits. Buddhism has complicated matters by adding a "Western Heaven" (or Western Paradise) to the old "Supreme Heaven." Just how these two heavens relate to each other is unclear in the cosmology, but the former is more of a pure paradise, and the latter is a parallel of the world of the living complete with a court administration.

In the lower world of spirits there are courts as well, before which some souls may be allowed to reincarnate, according to the Buddhists, as may some from heaven (Hsu, 1967: 145, 146). Some poor souls are so wicked that they can never work their way out of the lower dungeons.

Sometimes, the word "guai" refers specifically to these violent ghosts who are imprisoned in the underworld for their evil deeds, especially murder and theft (Saint Fist Society, no date: 16). Evil ghosts are said to become ugly devils, some smaller and some larger than normal size. Occasionally, evil ghosts appear in the world of the living, as does the King of the Devils, a transformed Buddhist deity, who acts as a warden to keep the devils in line. [12]

Ordinary good souls or ghosts all look like regular humans, according to Taoist and Buddhist conceptions. They will usually be found in heaven but may also appear on earth among the living. One still must be careful when seeing an apparently good ghost, because it may be an evil ghost impersonating a good one. [13] One informant told me that good ghosts eat the food you give them but that evil ghosts survive on the souls of the living.

Another category of ghosts in the broad sense would be the "genies," clever and righteous spirits who live in heaven along with the gods and with the good souls (Saint Fist Society, no date: 16). Genies, like devils, are thought to be rare, whereas good souls are common.

In spite of the great importance attached to ghosts in Chinese culture, not all religious philosophies have accepted them as much as Taoism and Buddhism have. Confucius considered the whole issue beyond human

---

12 A prominent Buddhist monk in Hong Kong told me that the King of the Devils always comes to his exorcisms.

13 Europeans have also believed that devils or goblins, could impersonate particular good ghosts (Glanvill, 1689: 404, 405; Taillepied, 1933: xix, 95).

knowledge, "so his followers dispose of the question on the assumption that the soul merely dissipates itself" (Burkhardt, 1953: Vol. II, 28).

Taoists complained that Confucianists, and another philosophical school called Moists, [14] eroded the belief of ordinary people in ghosts and gods simply by refusing to talk about them (Pao-p'u tzu, 1966a: 49). This parallels the frustration of modern psychical researchers over the refusal of most established scientists to support the investigation of ghosts and ESP. But the Taoists also felt that Confucianists and other sages were just punishing themselves. They could never achieve the immortality of geniehood because they concentrated on human affairs exclusively and ignored "the divine process" (Pao-p'u tzu, 1966b: 201).

The irony of the Confucianist position is that, although they ignored the spirit realm, their emphasis on filial piety helped solidify ancestor worship. And who are the ancestors but the family's ghosts?

Ancestors: ghost relatives

To be sure, there is a hierarchy of social distance from different types of ghosts, and people are of course most intimate with ghosts in the family who are related by kinship or marriage. Somewhat farther out are the souls of nonrelated persons, followed by spirit-world officials, and finally spirits from other societies or cultures (Hsu, 1967: 212, 213, 244). Hsu argues that the middle two categories contain the spirits of which one must be careful and which must be propitiated. Spirits from other societies are too distant and irrelevant, and ancestors can be taken for granted.

Ancestors get more constant attention at the altar, on their birthdays and death days, during certain standard festivals, like the Ching Ming festival in the third lunar month (when graveyards are visited), and sometimes even on a daily basis. They receive offerings of food and flowers, and have incense burned before their tablets on the altar. Sometimes, paper effigies of material goods like mah-jongg sets, houses, and automobiles

---

14   For an outline of the differences between Confucianism and Moism, cf. Chan (1963: 211-213).

are burned to provide them with wants and needs in the parallel world of the spirit.

Ancestor worship is crucial to traditional family centered morality and solidarity. Although it is not considered an organized religion by the Chinese, ancestor worship is in fact a folk religious system. When Indian Buddhism was introduced to China, it came into conflict with ancestor worship by stressing withdrawal from worldly and social affairs (Nakamura, 1964: 269, 270). Karma was based on individual credits built up in past lives, whereas the Chinese worshiped and burned articles for the benefit of their ancestors in the spirit world, who in turn might benefit them. Celibate Buddhist monks had no recognized group of descendants to worship them at all. Buddhism in China, however, was modified to accommodate the culture: karma was conceived as a family matter built up over a chain of lives, and Chinese Buddhists even took up ancestor worship.

Since traditional Chinese kinship has been primarily patrilineal (that is, with relaionship reckoned from father to child) and patrilocal (with households set up near the husband's parents), a woman had to be worshiped by her descendants at an altar in her husband's lineage (Freedman, 1971: 56). This put childless women and separated wives or widows in a dangerous position ritually, since they could not return to their own parents' home either bodily or in spirit, and their worship might be neglected after death.

Sometimes, even nonrelatives have been "worshiped" at the altar like ancestors. It has been argued that this is memorialism or commemoration rather than worship (Freedman, 1971: 154). In one case, Chairman Mao encouraged people to burn paper effigies to heroes of the revolution, whether they were their ancestors or not (Kingston, 1976: 16). This might be called a kind of "state religion" but seems to have been only the form and not the real content [15] or meaning of ancestor worship.

---

15   Chin (1979: 118-200) gives an excellent explanation with many examples of how Mao often used the "particular national form" of traditional Chinese culture to carry the new content of dialectical materialism.

In many other cases, the worship of nonrelatives may show the importance of being worshiped by somebody, even if no relatives are available. One person on the telephone survey said that a former tenant in the house even had a tablet on the altar. Another respondent put up tablets for the wandering spirits of ghosts he continually saw about his flat, not to "commemorate" them but because they might be put to rest by having someone worship them.

Unhappy and evil spirits

What has happened to the souls of dead people who are *not* properly at rest, and what sorts of trouble do they cause, according to traditional Chinese culture? As anthropologist Diana Martin points out, [16] anyone who has not had a full life by Chinese social standards or who has not died a natural death may become a disturbed and even dangerous ghost. Of course, this is a variation on the universal theme that wandering ghosts have suffered a violent death or have had at least some unusual emotional tie to the past that results in an apparition. Specifically in Chinese terms, the factors most likely to produce a troubled spirit are death as a young child, death before marriage, suicide or other violent or unpleasant deaths, improper burial, and improper worship after death.

As a consequence, troubled spirits are expected to produce not only apparitions but physical effects as well.

One tradition has been to look for footprints to see if the soul has returned; even a ladder might be set in place to help the ghost climb over the garden wall (Doré, 1918: vol. II, 146). More likely, people would avoid ghosts or try to set them at rest since they are usually considered dangerous. In his study of Singapore Chinese, Elliott (1964: 28) states that "*kuei* [*guai*] are not considered essentially evil. They merely seek satisfaction of their bodily desires from those who still live an earthly life."

---

16 Diana Martin gave this explanation in a presentation on Chinese spiritualism to an extramural class on "Health Care in Hong Kong," sponsored by the University of Hong Kong, on November 28, 1980.

Unless they are treated properly, however, they may turn into demons, he says.

One fear is that ghosts will cause illness, especially in a younger child, whose soul may be held for ransom by a spirit until imitation paper money is burned by the family. Insomnia is a type of problem that is specifically associated with soul loss for a child. If a culture uses ghosts to explain illness, then it is logical that children will be considered especially vulnerable to ghosts if there are high rates of childhood disease and a high infant-mortality rate. Women may also have difficult child labor due to some disturbed spirit.

Sickness in a family may be attributed to the restless spirit of a dead child. The reason for this is that ancestors must be worshiped by people born later than themselves. Young ancestors have few if any descendants, although, in the case of boy spirits at least, a younger cousin will do. Girls who die before marriage may become dissatisfied spirits and make their families ill, because women are at best temporary members of their parents' family and should be married and have their own offspring to worship them properly.

One irony is that Taoists, in spite of their belief in ghosts and exorcism, sometimes complained that the common folk believed too heavily in ghosts as a cause of illness (Pao p'u-tzu, 1966a: 5; Chan, 1969: 170). The reason for this may be that the Taoists were so involved in using herbs and magical medicine to cure disease, which they say as an imbalance in yin an yang and in the natural elements.

Another common type of ghost fear in traditional Chinese culture has to do with the victims of drowning and suicide. Both stayed on earth as evil ghosts, blocked from the reincarnation process. Those who had drowned could be released by drowning someone else to take their place, a "substitute" (Hsu, 1967: 206). As Maxine Hong Kingston put it (1976: 16), "The Chinese are always frightened of the drowned one, whose weeping ghost, wet hair hanging and skin bloated, waits silently by the water to pull down a substitute." Suicides, according to one version, could not find substitutes but had to wander about until they had used up the time they had been intended to live on earth (Christie, 1968: 113, 114). In another version, they could find substitutes by tempting others to commit suicide (Willoughby-Meade, 1926: 15, 16). [17]

Other miscellaneous evil ghosts [18] were predicted by Taoist priests based on a formula that took into account the day the person died and the person's sex. This information would help one forecast when the ghost would return, to what place, from what direction, what height it would be, and the age and sex of its victims. For example, ghosts of males who had died on certain inauspicious days of the lunar calendar were supposed to return "to the house on the 47th day after death and [kill] little girls of 13 and 14"; and certain female ghosts were to come "from the south, and [kill] pale-faced boys in the third house ... [then] return to the house of death ... [on the] 20th [and 29th days after death]" (Doré, 1918: vol. I, 139-141).

Although a lack of ancestor worship is one way to make a spirit restless, and restless spirits can be dangerous for the living, anthropologists disagree on whether Chinese are afraid of their own ancestors. Hsu (1967: 244, 245) claims they are not: "The ancestral spirits will help their own descendants whenever they can.... They are never offended by their descendants, and they never cause disasters to befall the coming generations." Freedman (1971: 158), on the other hand, states that ancestors can be hostile at times. Certainly, Diana Martin's material about ghosts of dead children causing illness in the family supports Freedman. Moreover, some of my Hong Kong informants said that they suffered illness and bad dreams after forgetting to burn incense for certain close relatives.

---

17   The idea that the souls of people who have died these unpleasant, untimely deaths remain on earth because of barriers to the normal process of death and reincarnation is an interesting alternate explanation that differs from the common view that apparitions of people who have died a violent death occur because of the emotional shock or emotional attachment to unfinished business.

18   The culture of Malaya, with a combination of Malay, Chinese, and Hindu influences, has quite a variety of evil spirits, including those of human origin who have died unpleasant deaths (McHugh, 1959: 19-26).

Nearly everything I have included in this section stresses that Chinese culture views ghosts as a problem. Yet apparitions have also been portrayed as agents of "social control," pointing fingers in order to alleviate problems or bring about justice. [19] In Chinese crime fiction, apparitions and clairvoyant dreams often provided the living with information that brought the murderer before the magistrate (Comber, 1972). Robert van Gulik (e.g., 1963), in the process of Westernizing this genre, would make the apparent apparitions turn out to be natural phenomena by the end of the story in most cases.

The Hungry Ghost Festival and other antidotes

Whether a matter of justice in this world or danger from the next, what can be done to satisfy the spirits and put them to rest? The major ceremony for calling attention to and satisfying the needs of ghosts is the Hungry Ghost Festival. Throughout the entire seventh lunar month, "the hungry ghosts from hell are allowed to escape for a respite on earth" (Elliott, 1964: 34). Some analysts emphasize that only the disturbed, neglected ghosts return, that is, those who have not had offerings of food and paper effigies made to them or who have died a violent death (Endacott, 1966b: 31). However, on the eve of the full moon, on the fifteenth day of the seventh month, offerings are made specially and specifically to one's own ancestors (Hsu, 1967: 31; Burkhardt, 1953: vol. II, 53). Families in Hong Kong not only make offerings on their altars but also take bundles of paper effigies down to the sidewalks to burn.

---

19   Ghost reports and lore collected by the Anglican clergyman Glanvill (1689) in the seventeenth century often have apparitions giving a specific moral message or warning. The sixteenth-century French Capuchin monk, Father Taillepied (1933: 95), wrote that ghosts usually appeared to people who had known them well and would be disposed to carry out their wishes. These wishes generally involved some mission of morality or justice. Of course, the main reason for communication between ghosts and the living in Chinese culture has been for the ancestors to complain about problems relating to ancestor worship rather than worldly justice.

Great care is taken to provide food and entertainment for the miscellaneous wandering spirits throughout the month of festivities in order to curb their mischief (Elliott, 1964: 34). A public altar is even set up for anonymous ghosts who have died with no worshiping descendants (Kehl, 1971). Men scatter rice and sprinkle water around during the festival's parade to keep the ghosts satisfied and to keep them from bothering the spectators; rice offerings must be given mixed with prayers, since rice alone would become fire in the mouths of people in the underworld (Kehl, 1971).

These precautions are similar to the use of firecrackers that Hsu (1967: 161) reports at funerals to scare off uninvited homeless ghosts or to providing paper coins to buy them off. The tendency to fend off or to bribe dangerous ghosts stands in contrast to the practice of showing the way to returning ghosts. Doré (1918: vol. I, xvi) describes the custom of "floating little lamps on streams to guide wandering ghosts" on the fifteenth day of the seventh month. [20] Of course, one's own ancestral ghosts are more likely to be welcome than the homeless wanderers.

Although the Hungry Ghost Festival is the most important, it is not the only traditional ceremony for seeing to the needs of the spirits. One of the worst things that can happen is for the person to die away from home under circumstances that prevent the body from being returned for proper disposal and worship. Hsu (1967: 164, 165) discusses the "calling home" ritual used by priests to draw the spirit home with rhythmic beats of drums and cymbals. Several of my informants told me that it had been the practice in China to beat the drum to make the actual corpse hop back in rhythm. A whole troop of these zombies on one occasion could allegedly be heard marching, or rather hopping, through one village at about 1 a.m. No one actually saw them, I am told, because people had been warned to stay indoors when they were scheduled to pass through.

---

20   There is a parallel contrast in old Halloween customs, between disguising one's house and gate to hide from the spirits, and setting out lights and bonfires to attract them. Feeding the spirits to keep them from doing mischief is also an obvious parallel to the original meaning of "trick-or-treat"!

Decorations for the Hungry Ghost Festival in a public park

Fruits, incense, and altar cloth with long-life symbolism
for the Hungry Ghost Festival

After having touched base properly at home, spirits still have a difficult journey to the spirit world. Doré (1918: vol. I, 151-154) describes "ceremonies for rescuing departed souls" on their way over the bridge to heaven or through purgatory.

For other difficulties that may arise, one can always consult a spirit medium. Anthropologist Diana Martin refers to this as "preventive medicine," which may even be taken literally when one recalls that illness in the family is thought to be one consequence of not taking care of the ancestors.

Perhaps the spirit medium will pass along the spirit's desire to have certain paper effigies burned for use in the other world. She may even discover the need for a ghost marriage. As mentioned earlier, women should really be married in order to be worshiped through their husbands' families. Male spirits may need to get married if the family believes that older brothers should be married before younger ones. All of this unfinished kinship business can be taken care of by a wedding ceremony arranged by the living members of the two families involved.

Another problem that families have with ghosts, the vulnerability of children to evil spirits, has various ritual solutions. One is to give the children unattractive nicknames, making ghosts less interested in stealing their souls. On particularly dangerous days, like the fifth day of the fifth lunar month, little children can have a protective word written on their foreheads, or, better yet, stay home that day (Christie, 1968: 117).

If these precautions fail and the child dies, more serious antidotes may be required. Especially if more than one child in the family has died, as Hsu reports (1967: 206), "the face of the second child who dies will be slapped by shoes, and its body will be thrown into the lake instead of being buried in the ground," on the theory that it is possessed by a persistent soul-stealing ghost. The ghost will not be able to come back easily after "drowning," remember, not until it finds a substitute drowning victim.

Finally, there are some other ways of dealing with ghost trouble that can be applied by individuals. For one thing, ghosts are not supposed to be able to turn corners. Therefore, a screen set outside directly in front

[Above and below] Hell bank notes, burning incense sticks, and paper articles on sidewalk for relatives in the underworld

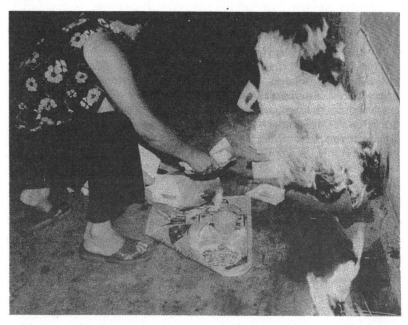

of a doorway will block any evil spirits from entering (Christie, 1968: 117).

When walking down the street, especially at night, stay out in the open and away from walls and corners, one Buddhist monk told me. Since ghosts move along walls, [21] if you run into one there, it won't be able to get around you, and you may end up possessed.

Not only Buddhist monks and Taoist priests have been considered experts on how to deal with ghosts. In Chinese lore, Confucian scholars were supposedly able "to avert evil and to command erring spirits" (Willoughby-Meade, 1926: 17). More recently, Chinese Communists have put out "papers on techniques for combatting ghosts" (Kingston, 1976: 88). The involvement of Confucians and Communists in ghost control is surely an ironic emphasis on the importance of ghosts in Chinese culture, since Confucians and Communists aren't even supposed to believe in them!

2017: Given the central purpose of this book, to examine reports of Chinese ghosts, this still serves as a good introduction to traditional Chinese ghost culture. Later on in chapter 13 (New Materials), however, some additional sources relevant to this chapter will be considered.

---

21 This belief is not to be confused with a type of ghost called the "wall ghost," which boxes in its victims on all sides. The trick here is to sit down and concentrate, staring ahead, dissolving the ghost.

4

Who Believes in Ghosts?

They say the Chinese take it for granted that everybody should believe in ghosts. The only question is whether you're afraid of them! This is somewhat of an exaggeration, but it is true that the Hong Kong Chinese in my study showed a much higher level of belief than Americans did who were surveyed in a 1978 Gallup poll (Emmons and Sobal, 1981b), 50% vs. 12%. [22]

In fact, Table 1 (page 325) shows that ghosts rank highest of fourteen paranormal beliefs among the Hong Kong Chinese. Moreover, ghost belief is unique (among nine beliefs for which there is a comparison available) in being so much stronger among the Chinese than it is among the Americans.

One problem in determining the real amount of ghost belief among the Chinese is that the fear of ghosts may make people reluctant to admit the belief that is supposedly "taken for granted." Many Chinese believe that seeing or even talking about ghosts can be very unlucky. Case G002 (Chapter 1), "Harvest Homecoming," illustrated the idea that the first person to see a ghost may die. Especially older people are thought to be

---

22   The two studies are not exactly comparable, mainly because the Hong Kong telephone survey included respondents under eighteen years of age, 56% of whom believe in ghosts, whereas the Gallup poll sampled only those eighteen or over. However, if the under-eighteen group is eliminated from the Hong Kong study, still 49% of the rest claim to believe in ghosts.

vulnerable to death by apparition. According to one Chinese saying,"If you see a ghost, death will come within three days."

"You're not trying to scare me, are you?"

When asked whether she believed in ghosts, one telephone respondent said in an apparently serious tone, "Don't scare me," and continued to answer the questions. Two others, however, terminated the interview at that point. The one, a man, said, "You're not trying to scare me, are you? Are you a ghost? Are you a ghost?" "No, I'm not a ghost," my wife Chee, the interviewer, replied. Stuttering hysterically, he then said very politely, "Excuse me, I have to hang up now!" [23]

The other person to hang up on this question, a woman, said "*Daai-lo* ["big brother," extremely polite, especially when directed to a woman!], please I beg of you don't talk about such a subject!" "Why not?" Chee asked. "You just don't talk about such a subject," the woman replied. Too unlucky, in other words. "I have to hang up now; we're busy."

Another reluctant woman asked, "Do I have to answer this question?" but proceeded to say that she did *not* believe in ghosts. One woman said, "I don't dare to say whether ther they exist or not," but then said that she believed a little bit. Five others commented that they were afraid to say, but answered the question. Altogether, twenty-three people expressed some kind of fear of ghosts (without any mention of fear in the survey question), and only five volunteered to say that they were not afraid, some of whom may have been "whistling in the dark." Seven of the twenty-three ghost fearers, however, then claimed not to believe in ghosts, and three more refused to answer the question! Illogical? This seems to indicate that many Chinese who believe in ghosts are unwilling to admit it because the topic is unlucky or frightening.

Some comments also reflect the nature and conditions of this fear. One woman pointed out half-seriously, "I live alone; I better not believe

---

23 Although no one in the study ever reported experiencing any "phone calls from the dead" (cf. Rogo and Bayless, 1979), this respondent acted as if he were receiving one at the time!

in ghosts!" Another woman said. "My husband is never home, but I'm never afraid." Three other women, when asked if they believed in ghosts, stated specifically that they were afraid of the dark.

What is there to fear from ghosts? Three people mentioned their ugly, horrible faces. One little girl of twelve related the following: "I was told that you shouldn't turn the water on after midnight, because a ghost will come out and will follow you and give you bad luck and illness." Perhaps this bogeyman is a supernatural sanction used by parents who want to save on the water bill.

Some of those who claim not to fear ghosts nevertheless as much as admit that there is something to be feared, at least conditionally, when they say that only the weak, the unlucky, and the sinful need to believe in or to fear ghosts. In short, only deviates and immoral people need to be afraid; this supports the supernatural-sanction concept: otherworldly forces punish the weak and the wicked.

If you behave appropriately, you have nothing to fear. Both a forty-two-year-old woman on the telephone survey and a high-school senior from another group said that if you don't harm ghosts they won't harm you. Four other people said that they didn't have to be afraid of ghosts because they had never done anything wrong.

As one woman put it, ghosts "only do harm to evil people; if you're righteous, ghosts won't bother you." Sometimes, righteousness can be borrowed. One respondent claimed that she was not bothered by ghosts in a Taiwan hotel, unlike the other members of her tour, because she had a Bible in her room, although she is a Buddhist. Just what is the relationship between religion and the belief in ghosts?

"If there's a God above, there must be ghosts"

The thirty-year-old man who made this statement scored high on ghost belief, but, ironically, he said that he had no religion! On the other hand, the only four others on the telephone survey to comment on the matter were Christians who claimed just the opposite: three Protestants who said they believed in God or Christ and therefore not in ghosts and someone who said he didn't believe in ghosts because he was a Catholic. The irony of this view that ghosts are a superstition unworthy of Christians is that some sixteenth- and seventeenth-century Christian scholars in Europe gathered apparition reports as evidence for spirituality. [24]

Before examining the survey results to see whether Chinese Christians are actually more or less likely than other Chinese to believe in ghosts, we should notice that there is some difficulty with the concept of "ghost" in Chinese, especially for Christians. The word "guai" means not only "ghost" but also "devil" or sometimes specifically an "evil spirit." It remains to be seen whether Chinese Christians will equate their concept of "soul" or "spirit" (*ling wun* in the Cantonese language used in Hong Kong) with "guai;" the word for ghost used on the questionnaire.

In fact, only three respondents on the telephone survey emphasized that guai were devils or evil spirits only, including one Catholic who said, "I just believe in souls [ling wun]. Ghosts [guai] are evil and strange." There were thirty-seven by contrast who commented that guai were the same as ling wun, and all but four of these people said they believed in guai (ghosts). Of the thirty-seven, twenty five were Christians, which is more than three times the percentage that Christians are of the entire sample. This shows that Christians are the ones most in need of interpreting what ghosts are in their religious world view. When people were asked for ghost experiences on the survey, however. their reports, including the reports from Christians, show that the meaning of "ghost" must have been reasonably clear and standard to them. They almost invariably described apparitions of human beings.

Now, what are the relevant religious categories to be compared in terms of their belief in ghosts? I know of no reliable estimates of the religious preference of residents of Hong Kong Island before this study. According

---

24   For example, Joseph Glanvill (1689: viii), an Anglican clergyman, quoted his mentor, Henry More, as saying, "No spirit, no God." The sixteenth-century French Capuchin monk Father Noel Taillepied (1933: xix) wrote that spirits were "either Good Angels or bad, or the Souls of the Departed." Both men thought that devils could impersonate other souls, but they clearly accepted ghosts as real, for good or ill.

to the random telephone survey, there are 62% who claim no religion, 16% Buddhists, 11% Protestants, 10% Roman Catholics, and only traces of other religions. The largest groups of Protestants are Anglicans (58%), Baptists (19%), and Methodists (7%). Ancestor worship, which complicates the situation, is not considered a religion by the Chinese but will be discussed later.

It turns out that the Christians are split on ghost belief. The Catholics and Buddhists are the big ghost believers, 58% each; Catholics actually have 24% with *high* levels of belief, compared with 18% of Buddhists. Of Protestants, 46% believe in ghosts; of those with no religion, 47%.

Compared with the situation in the United States, the Catholic-Protestant difference is not surprising. Catholics, whose church has long been more receptive to claims of modern miracles and mysticism than Protestant churches have been, show higher rates of ghost belief in the U.S. as well, 16% vs. 9% for Protestants (Emmons and Sobal, 1981b). However, in the U.S., those with *no* religion are the most likely to believe in ghosts, 23%, which illustrates the tendency for belief in paranormal phenomena like ghosts and ESP to be a replacement, or "functional alternative" for religion among the "nonreligious" in America (Emmons and Sobal, 1981b). Not only in regard to ghost belief, but generally throughout the list of paranormal beliefs in this study, the "no religion" group in Hong Kong actually has significantly *lower* belief than average. They show no tendency to make up for their lack of religious identity with a belief in the paranormal.

Sociologists have learned to be wary of simple survey findings. Is it possible that there are other factors distorting the results just mentioned? For example, if younger people believed heavily in ghosts, and if Catholics in Hong Kong turned out to be very young for some reason, then the percentage of Hong Kong Catholics who believe in ghosts would be deceptively high. In other words, Catholics would be big believers, but only because they were so young, not because of their Catholicism per se. Then, my claim that Catholicism is correlated with ghost belief would be a distortion, or "spurious correlation."

But there are statistical procedures that can eliminate or "hold constant" the effects of other variables, letting us see a truer correlation between the variables we are looking at, for example, Catholicism and ghost belief. Table 2 (page 326) shows the "zero-order" correlations (nothing controlled) and the "partial" correlations (controlling for other variables) between the religions and ghost belief. After controlling for age, sex, education, Westernization, [25] and ancestor worship, there is still a strong positive correlation between Catholicism and ghost belief, and a somewhat weaker one between Buddhism and ghost belief. Having no religion is strongly *negatively* related (that is, they are *less* likely to believe), and Protestantism shows no significant relationship one way or the other.

There is one more surprise, however, in regard to Protestants. Dividing them by denomination shows that Baptists are just as likely to believe in ghosts as are Catholics or Buddhists, 58%! Only 41% of Anglicans in Hong Kong say they believe. [26]

This lack of belief only on the part of Anglicans among the Protestants seems hard to explain. It may be that the Anglican Church, the most prestigious Christian church in Hong Kong, is more effective in changing traditional Chinese patterns of belief and practice than the Baptists are. Some ministers told me that no self-respecting Christian would practice ancestor worship, for example. In fact, 36% of Baptists and 24% of Anglicans reported at least some ancestor worship, compared with 72% of all respondents in the survey.

"I don't believe in just any ghost, but I believe in Grandma"

If there is any special aspect of Chinese culture that leads people to believe in ghosts, surely it ought to be ancestor worship. As pointed out in Chapter

---

25   "Westernization" was determined by a question asking respondents whether they considered themselves "very Westernized," "mainly Westernized," "about half Westernized and half Chinese," "mainly Chinese," or "very Chinese."

26   As this is the only statistically significant difference between Anglicans and Baptists on any of the beliefs, Protestants are considered as one group in Table 2.

3, ancestor worshipers do not merely "remember" their ancestors. They put offerings of food for them on the altar, burn paper effigies to send articles to them in the other world, contact them sometimes through spirit mediums, and even expect them to return on special days. Doesn't all of this indicate that spirits are considered to survive death and to appear as ghosts in the land of the living?

According to the telephone survey, 53% of those who practice ancestor worship believe in ghosts, compared with 43% of those who are not ancestor worshipers. Table 3 indicates that the relationship between ancestor worship and ghost belief holds up even when the religious and other social variables are controlled.

Nevertheless, one might expect a still higher percentage of ancestor worshipers to believe. How can the other 47% *not* believe in ghosts? Why don't they all agree with one fifty-year-old Buddhist woman, with an average score on the ancestor worship scale, [27] who said that she believed in ghosts because, after all, "I burn incense to worship them"?

The comment of a sixty-five-year-old woman with the same ancestor-worship score but who claimed no religion may give a clue: she said that she did not believe in ghosts; "We only worship our *own* ancestors." Precisely. "I don't believe in just any ghost, but I believe in Grandma," said a thirteen-year-old Buddhist girl with an above-average ancestor-worship score. She said she "believed a little" in ghosts; she had seen her grandmother's apparition! Not everyone who practices ancestor worship as a family-centered activity necessarily shares an abstract belief in ghosts. As anthropologists know, belief and practice (ritual) are not perfectly congruent.

I pointed out earlier that Chinese do not consider ancestor worship to be a religion, and yet both religion and ancestor worship affect people's

---

27   Four is average on the eight-point maximum ancestor-worship scale, which gives one point for celebrating the Hungry Ghost Festival, one for burning incense on Chung Yeung (September 9), one for burning incense on the Spring Festival, one for burning on any other holiday, two for burning on the first and fifteenth of each lunar month, four for every day, one for the birth and/or death day, and one each for a miscellany of other activities.

ideas about spirits and ghosts. How do the two belief systems interrelate? First of all, ancestor worship is practiced by 33% of Protestants and 33% of Catholics, by 94% of Buddhists, and even by 73% of those with "no religion."

Except in the case of Buddhists, where there are too few non-ancestor worshipers to make a valid comparison, the ancestor worshipers in each religious category are more likely to believe in ghosts than the non-ancestor worshipers are. The only ones who really have no religion at all in the broad anthropological sense are the ones with neither ancestor worship nor a religious preference; only 39% of this group believe in ghosts. Again, the Chinese nonreligious are least likely to believe in ghosts, just the opposite of the American nonligious, who believe in ghosts and other paranormal phenomena as a functional alternative to standard religion (Emmons and Sobal, 1981b).

Could this low belief among the Chinese nonreligious be a clue that ghost belief in Hong Kong will decline further as traditional and religious influences are continually replaced by modern and secular ones?

"In the scientific world, could there still be ghosts?"

This quote from a nonbelieving twenty-seven-year-old man with no religion and a low ancestor-worship score resonates with the modernism of two other nonbelievers who said: "In the twentieth century, there's no such thing," and "This is the twentieth century. I don't believe in ghosts any more." Even a thirteen-year-old Buddhist girl with a high ancestor-worship score (a combination of characteristics that make her highly likely to believe) said that she didn't believe in ghosts, "not in Hong Kong." In other words, people know that pre-Communist China had lots of occult things, but they don't particularly expect modern, Westernized Hong Kong to have ghosts and spirit mediums.

Six nonbelievers in ghosts emphasized that only superstitious people believe in them. Ironically, however, four of these "nonsuperstitious" individuals admitted to believing in from one to three of the following:

two each believed in fortune telling, reincarnation, ESP, and UFOs; one believed in *feng shui* (geomancy).

"I'm very civilized. I don't believe in such things," said a seventy-year-old woman with no religion and no ancestor worship. She consistently claimed not to believe in *any* of the fourteen paranormal phenomena. On the other hand, a forty-three-year-old Buddhist man with a low ancestor-worship score who made a similar statement – that he didn't believe in ghosts because "I'm a learned person" – went on to confess a number of other paranormal beliefs, as did the four "nonsuperstitious" persons mentioned above. This man believed in *feng shui*, water monsters, witches, and even spirit mediums. Moreover, he said he had seen a Buddhist monk possessed by his grandmother's spirit.

What, in fact, is the relationship between "learning" and ghost belief among Hong Kong Chinese? The telephone survey shows with a high degree of statistical significance that education is *positively* related to ghost belief, although it is not a very important factor compared with, say, religion. More specifically, the biggest differences are among the lower leveis of education: 39% of those with no education believe in ghosts, 43% of those with one to four years of education, 48% of those with five or six years, and 56% of those with seven or eight years. Above eight years of education, ghost belief declines slightly again and levels out at about the 50% average. Checking Table 3 (page 327), we see that the small positive correlation between education and ghost belief is not reduced when controlling for other variabies. In the United States, there is virtually no relationship between education and ghost belief (Emmons and Sobal, 1981a), although people with some college but no degree are more likely to believe than others.

In contrast to the comments about ghosts and superstition, a few people argued for the rationality of ghost belief. One woman said that she had read about the case of the Rating and Evaluation Building (cf. Chapter 14, case SP009) in the newspapers. Even the Westerners believed it was haunted and had it exorcised; therefore she believed, too. Another woman said, "I have seen too many movies not to believe a little bit."

One wonders how convincing *that* argument is (cf. Chapter 8, "Ghost Lore and Popular Culture").

Others used vaguer rationales for their belief. As one man put it, "The world is so huge; anything could exist." In other words, there are more things in heaven and earth.... Twenty-five people invoked the Chinese saying, "If you believe, it exists!" You could consider that either a copout or an astute equivalent of the sociological principle of "the self-fulfilling prophecy": "If men define situations as real, they are real in their consequences" (Thomas, 1928). If enough people believe in ghosts, they will be important in the society.

Remarkably, only two of the twenty-five who used the "if you believe" expression claimed not to believe in ghosts, yet *all* of the believers said they only believed a little. In the entire survey, 50% said they did not believe, 35% believed a little, and 15% scored high on belief. Perhaps, "if you believe, it exists" is an excuse for believing used by those who timidly admit to believing a little, when they know that some people may accuse them of being superstitious. That as many as 50% on the survey admitted they believe, and that nonbelievers are concentrated more in *low* rather than high educational levels, would seem to argue that ghost belief is both normal and respectable in Hong Kong. However, if enough people think the opposite, this will be another clue, along with the problem of ghost fear, that 50% is a low estimate for ghost belief among Hong Kong Chinese, because some people are reluctant to admit their belief.

"I'm too young to believe in anything"

By now it should not be a surprise that "common sense" does not always reflect social reality very precisely. The seventeen-year-old girl who made the above comment was relating the common belief that "young people don't believe" in ghosts, as a thirty-five-year-old man said. Although only these two mentioned the point on the telephone survey, I have heard several people in Hong Kong say that traditional Chinese beliefs in things like ghosts, spirit mediums, and feng shui magic are dying out among the young.

But *not true* for ghost belief. The young are more likely to believe than the old are. Age groups from eight to twenty-nine have a rather constant level of belief at about 57%. [28] Then, between thirty and fifty-nine there is up-and-down fluctuation around an average of 46%. Finally, only 28% of the people aged sixty and over say they believe in ghosts.

Since higher ages have lower percentages of believers, it is appropriate to say that age and ghost belief are *negatively* related. The relationship is slightly stronger than that between education and ghost belief and is not reduced by controlling for other variables (cf. Table 3). Religion is still the strongest factor.

In the United States, age is also negatively related to ghost belief, but even more strongly (Emmons and Sobal, 1981a). Perhaps this reflects the recent worldwide spread of interest in paranormal phenomena. It seems likely that older people would be less influenced by such trends in popular culture.

"Ask some women; men don't believe in such things"

Sometimes, common sense reflects social reality but exaggerates or distorts it. That the above quotation is stereotypic can be illustrated by the ironical fact that it came from a man who also said that he believed in ghosts a little bit! Although 53% of women in the telephone survey believe in ghosts, men are not far behind, with 47%. After controlling for other factors, sex is still about as important as age in explaining ghost belief (cf. "male" in Table 3).

If sex is *not* related to ghost belief in the U.S. (Emmons and Sobal, 1981a), we seem to have hit upon a cultural difference. In Chinese culture, it is part of the female role to consult spirit mediums when necessary and to tend to routine aspects of ancestor worship. With the relationship between ancestor worship and ghost belief, it is not surprising that such activities should wear off on women in terms of higher rates of belief.

---

28   I think it is interesting that only 56% of the 8-17-year-old group believe, which is about the same as the 18-29-year-olds. This argues against the very youngest having any special childlike gullibility.

"Ask them to come and look for me"

So said a twenty-three-year-old man who believed in ghosts but had never experienced any. Another man, thirty years old, said he did not believe and had never seen one, but "I'd like to see a ghost myself." Considering the ghost fear discussed earlier, these two statements are unusual, although the first one sounds like sarcastic humor and only the second one sounds serious. The next two are more to be expected; both are from young women believers, who may be under less obligation to sound brave: "Luckily I haven't met one" and "I hope I'll never see one."

Apart from these attitudes about the desirability of seeing an apparition, what ideas do people have about the relationship between experiences and belief? An eighteen-year-old woman with no religion and an average score on ancestor worship said, "If I see one, I'll believe"; but she already said she believed a little. One thirty-year-old man with no religion and no ancestor worship took a more skeptical attitude. He said he didn't know whether he believed or not because he had never seen one.

But as one respondent said, "It is very difficult to see ghosts. People who are psychic can see ghosts." or people who have *yum-yeung* (yin-yang) eyes (cf. Chapter 12, "Gifted Subjects and Yin-Yang Eyes"). In the next chapter, we begin to explore ghost experiences in theory and in example.

> *2017: There is one major update to this chapter. Since 1982 there has been a big increase in reported belief in ghosts in the United States. Unfortunately no one has collected comparable data for Hong Kong, but my sense of things is that ghost belief is still strong among young people in Hong Kong. As you can see below, in Hong Kong younger people and more highly educated people had higher levels of belief in 1980; so we would not expect ghost belief to decline anytime soon.*
>
> *Belief in ghosts in the U.S. has increased from 12% in 1978 to 25% in 1990, 28% in 1991, 33% in 1999, 38% in 2001 (Newport, 1999; Newport and Strausberg, 2001; Emmons, 2003),*

32% in 2005 (Lyons, 2005), 48% in 2009 (Alfano, 2009), and 45% in 2012 (Spiegel, 2013). Although the upward trend is clear, some of the unevenness of the increase is probably due to different phrasings in different polls and the high percentage of "uncertain" in some polls. I think that the increase in belief in the U.S. is related to popular media treatments of the paranormal and to an upsurge in New Age or spiritual (vs. religious) interest (Emmons, 2003).

In this chapter I made the statement that sex (use the word "gender" now) was not related to ghost belief in the U.S., based on Gallup Poll data from 1978. By now, however, there seems to be a big difference: 38% of men believing in ghosts compared to 56% of women (Alfano, 2009), which might reflect the greater interest in New Age spirituality on the part of women.

At any rate, it is interesting to see that the level of ghost belief admitted on surveys in the U.S. is almost up to the 50% for Hong Kong in 1980. Remember, however, that I thought that 50% was a low figure for Hong Kong, because many people were afraid to talk about it on the survey. And of course, probably a lot of those who say they believe in ghosts in the U.S. have a very superficial, pop culture type of belief compared to a more serious belief in Hong Kong.

5

GHOST EXPERIENCES: THEORY AND REPORTS

2017: This chapter reports surveys in the West in the 1890s showing 9.9% and 12% of people claiming to have had a ghost experience. A CBS poll in 2009 finds 22% of Americans claiming to have experienced a ghost (14% of men and 29% of women, the same kind of gender difference as with belief in ghosts) (Alfano, 2009). Probably the higher percentage claiming experience now is related to the higher percentage of belief. In other words, people may be more likely to frame their anomalous experiences as ghosts if they believe they are possible.

This still doesn't solve the curious issue of why I found such a low percentage of people having experiences in Hong Kong in 1980 (4.1% experiencing compared to 50% believing). I can only guess that ghost experiences are considered so unlucky in Hong Kong that people don't want to talk about them. However, they also don't like talking about belief either, but maybe not so strongly. The most important thing to me, however, remains the fact that I did not get a very high percentage claiming experiences, because then I would have worried that people were making things up or exaggerating borderline experiences that might just as well have been something "normal".

For an updated theoretical discussion of parapsychological theories of apparitions (ghosts), see especially pp. 102-112 in Science and Spirit: Exploring the Limits of Consciousness *(Emmons and*

Emmons, 2012). And for a wider discussion of survival (life after death), see the entire book. I still would not disagree with any of the theoretical discussion in the 1980 edition of this book, reproduced here.

If case G008 (in chapter 1), "Boy Scout Picnic" is my favorite collective apparition in Hong Kong, there is another favorite case that I collected in Gettysburg later in the 1980s. I studied one allegedly haunted house in Gettysburg over several years, comparing notes from interviews with students who had not known previous students who had had similar experiences there. I consider it highly evidential because of all the similar independent reports. For example, multiple witnesses over the years noticed a strange perfume smell from time to time in the same bedroom.

The most interesting part of my investigation involved several women who rented the house one year. They were talking among themselves one day when they all heard a tremendous crash coming from the adjacent dining room. They thought that an intruder had knocked over a China cabinet. Without checking the dining room first, they ran out to get help from some male students next door. Armed with a baseball bat, they entered the dining room to find nothing amiss, to their great surprise. Nothing knocked over, nothing broken. However, as they walked through the room, they heard the tinkling sound of broken glass, as if they were walking through it. However, there was no broken glass to be seen. This illustrates both the principle of a collective apparition and that there was actually no physical effect, merely an apparitional sound that would have been consistent with an apparitional breaking of glass.

In chapter 13 I will present some further experiences collected since 1980.

Up to now, parapsychologists have based their theories of apparitions almost exclusively on ghost reports from Europe and America. It is exciting to anticipate a comparison between these Western ghosts and ones from China. But what about the Chinese people who report having the ghost experiences? We know from Chapter 4 that social factors like age and religion have an effect on ghost belief. Are people in certain social categories more likely to claim ghost experiences as well?

Who experiences ghosts?

Although 50% of those interviewed in the random telephone survey of Hong Kong Island said they believed in ghosts, only 4.1% had experienced any. By contrast, 9.9% in the English Census of Hallucinations in 1890, with a sample of 17,000 people, said that they had (Tyrrell, 1963: 19). A combined sample collected at the same time from France, Germany, and the United States found 12% claiming apparition experiences (Tyrrell, 1963: 25, 26). How could ghosts be so much more common in the West than among the Chinese, when only 12% of Americans in 1978 said they even *believed* in ghosts (cf. Table 1)?

One possibility is that ghost belief was much higher in Europe and America ninety years ago, although the fact that younger Americans today are more likely to believe than older ones suggests the opposite trend at least in recent decades. A stronger possibility is that the 9.9% and 12% figures were inflated because the interviewers in the 1890 studies seem to have selected some respondents with known experiences instead of drawing a completely random sample (Tyrrell, 1963: 24, 26).

As far as the 4.1% figure from the telephone survey in Hong Kong is concerned, it is probably an underestimate because of the problem of ghost fear discussed in Chapter 4. Although such a low percentage is a disadvantage in the sense that large numbers of people must be interviewed to get significant numbers of ghost experiences, it is also a very good sign that there is no widespread tendency for Hong Kong Chinese to make up or to imagine ghost stories just because they believe in them.

However, I shall also include ghost reports from sources other than the telephone survey, especially from the questionnaires filled out by 1,989 secondary-school students. Did the students give me lots of phony reports either as a prank or because they were highly impressionable youths? Actually, there was very little sign of pranksterism, [29] and in spite of a very high belief rate, 83%, [30] only 3.8% claimed to have had a ghost experience, even less than the 4.1% in the telephone survey. [31]

The striking thing about the reports from young people is that they contain very little that sounds fantastic compared with the other reports. If anything, they seem to have more borderline cases that might have been just natural phenomena: funny noises from the hallway or noises in the night on a camping trip, a squeaky bench, a hand outside the window. In other words, teenagers seem readier to label as paranormal the things, especially noises, that older people are more likely to ignore: the "Nervous Nellie Syndrome"! This was my impression in 23% of the school cases. I am not suggesting that their reports are generally less reliable or valid. [32]

---

29   In three or four cases, I detected possibly frivolous replies. One student started to write, "I saw three green ghosts," but crossed it out, apparently thinking better of it.

30   The age group of under-eighteen-year-olds in the telephone survey had 56% ghost believers, compared with 83% in the school sample whose ages clustered around thirteen and sixteen.

31   The 3.8% looks even lower when compared with the figure for just the under-eighteen-year-olds in the telephone survey: 6.2%. Although the student questionnaire especially encouraged details on ghost experiences, and the take-home form gave more time to recall experiences, many students probably neglected to write them down because they didn't want to take the time to do so.

32   Validity is certainly a reasonable concern for all of the reports. As I indicated in Chapter 2, my general impression is that very few of the firsthand reports in this study were fabricated. Parapsychologists would certainly like to do more detective work on such reports, but my emphasis is on looking for patterns in a luge number of cases, being suspicious of the few odd cases that get no statistical support from others. Secondhand, hearsay reports are much more suspect, however (cf. Chapters 8 and 9 on ghost lore). All of the reports in Chapter 5 are firsthand. Any cases in other chapters that are not firsthand are so identified.

Louisa E. Rhine (1956: 240, 241) makes the interesting argument that early parapsychological researchers, such as those working in Britain in the late nineteenth century, had too "strict standards of authentication" regarding apparition reports. By eliminating all but the best cases, they may have established a selection process that created a bias of types, distorting the statistical profile of

Next, we must look again at the random telephone survey to consider the possibility that the social factors that influence ghost belief also influence ghost experiences. The significant factors in Chapter 4 on belief were religious preference, ancestor worship, education, age, and sex. Religious preference is related to experience, and the relationship is statistically significant, [33] but Protestants come out highest, 5.6% with an experience, instead of being lowest, as they were in the case of ghost belief. The other groups are in the right order (based on the belief data): 4.9% of Catholics, 4.2% of Buddhists, and 3.5% of those with no religion claimed to have one or more ghost experiences.

Ancestor worship relates to experience in the predicted direction, but not strongly enough to be statistically significant: 4.3% of ancestor worshipers and 3.5% of nonworshipers report an experience. Age is significantly related, [34] but experience is highest among people under twenty-five years old, is much lower after that, and rises again after age forty-five. [35] Remember that age related strongly to belief (Chapter 4), but belief declined rather consistently with age and was especially low among the oldest. However, it is logical that older people should report more experiences, since they have accumulated more years in which to

---

the characteristics of apparitions. Rhine, on the other hand, bases her analysis on all of the cases in her file. As her cases are not a random sample (unlike my Chinese cases, which are close to a random sample on the telephone survey; cf. Preface), they may be statistically non-representative as well. More serious, however, is her inclusion of some secondhand reports, for which Hart (1957) criticizes her. Rhine's (1957c) defense is that her analysis is presented not as proof but in order to suggest hypotheses, which she believes is all that one can hope for with research on spontaneous cases, as opposed to research with controlled experiments.

33   Chi-square significance is p<.02.

34   The percent of experiencers by age group is as follows: 6.2% for ages 8-17, 7.2% for 18-24, 3.8% for 25-29, 2.9% for 30-34, 0.0% for 35-39, 1.4% for 40-44, 4.0% for 45-49, 5.2% for 50-59, 3.5% for 60-80.

35   I know of one man in Gettysburg who took a rather unusual tack in ridiculing his son's ghost fear. After the boy had complained several times about the noises in the night, the father supposedly said, "Quit making such a fuss; it's only the ghost!"

have them. On the other hand, Green (1973: 22) found that very young children in England were highly susceptible to apparitions, but they were "socialized" out of it by their parents. Age may bring experience, but it can also bring skepticism about the paranormal.

Education relates the same way to experience as it does to belief, with the highest percentages of ghost experiences in the middle levels of education, but the relationship is not statistically significant this time. Sex is not significantly related either: 4.7% of women and 3.4% of men claiming a ghost experience.

All in all, these findings show mixed results. Social factors generally relate the same way to experience as they do to belief, but not very strongly. One reason for the lack of statistical significance is that the analysis is based on so few experiences; chance factors operate more strongly in small samples, and the statistics are designed to allow for this. As belief is more common, more certain statistic conclusions can be made about it.

Even if we conclude that the social factors are related to the tendency to experience ghosts, at least weakly related, it would be dangerous to assume cause and effect. Of course, it is logical that believers would be more likely to define a strange experience as paranormal than nonbelievers would. However, this could be seen as an openness to experiences that nonbelievers might shut out and not necessarily as a bias that creates false ghosts in the form of hallucinations. The questionnaire, moreover, was designed to ask only believers if they had experienced a ghost, on the theory that anybody who felt he or she had encountered a ghost would at least end up believing in them "a little" after the experience if not before. This may have resulted in an exaggerated correlation between experience and the social factors affecting belief, although even nonbelievers had a chance to mention any miscellaneous experiences later in the questionnaire. [36]

---

36   In fact, no nonbelievers in ghosts listed any ghost experiences under the miscellaneous experience question.

Telepathy, survival, and the "phantom within"

Before comparing the Chinese ghost cases with a checklist of apparition characteristics found to be typical of western cases, let us establish the basic theoretical foundation of what ghosts are supposed to be according to Western parapsychologists. Certainly, the dominant theory is that apparitions are caused by ESP, more specifically by mental telepathy.

Since the late nineteenth century, British parapsychologists have given various telepathic explanations for ghosts, but Tyrrell's explanation, first presented in 1942, now stands as the classic in the field. In his book *Apparitions* (1963), Tyrrell argues convincingly that the spark of an apparition is caused by a telepathic message from a sender ("agent")to a receiver ("percipient"), whose mind turns the spark of an idea into a projected drama that seems to be taking place physically in the receiver's surroundings. Sometimes, there are bystanders in the area of the receiver who fail to perceive the apparition,which shows that it is not really there in a physical sense. Sometimes, however, the bystanders do perceive it which shows that the apparition is a shared telepathic experience rather than merely a subjective hallucination.

Tyrrell (1963: 35-45) recognizes four classes of apparitions: (1) experimental cases, in which a living sender deliberately tries to make him- or herself seen by a particular receiver; (2) crisis cases, in which the apparition occurs close to the time when the sender is experiencing a crisis, such as an accident or death; (3) post-mortem cases, in which the apparition of a recognized person occurs more than twelve hours after the death of the sender, and (4) hauntings (or "ghosts" in the narrow sense), in which apparitions of the sender occur in a place previously important to him or her.

Problems arise especially in explaining how telepathic messages can be sent in post-mortem cases and in hauntings. Now, we are faced with the possibility that the surviving spirit of the dead person is communicating telepathically with the living receiver. In order to avoid the "survival" or "continuity hypothesis," which requires us to believe not only in ESP but in life after death, we must find another source for the ESP message that sparks the apparition.

One possibility is that a third party is doing the sending, someone who knew about the person who appears now as a ghost. The drawback to this theory is that finding someone like this is a tenuous exercise in many cases; and, although the sending might be subconscious, some parapsychologists argue that the sending of apparitions requires more emotional motivation than third parties typically have.

Another way to preserve the ESP explanation without the need for a surviving spirit is to claim that the receiver's ESP is looking back into the past (retrocognition), reliving scenes in which the ghost took part. What triggers the apparition is the motivation of the receiver in post-mortem cases, which are nearly all ghosts of relatives and friends who were close to the receiver in life. What triggers the apparition in hauntings is the haunted place itself, which somehow helps to focus psychic communication, just as in other cases of "psychometry," the use of objects to channel ESP about their owners.

Ghosts, in short, are linked either to persons who knew them or to places to which they were emotionally attached. [37] According to the "super-ESP" hypothesis, ESP can communicate without limitation by time [38] or space, as long as it is focused by a strong emotional tie. If so, there would be no need for either a living sender or a surviving spirit to cause the apparition. The receiver simply could be seeing the past through retrocognition.

One counterargument to using the retrocognition explanation for all apparitions of the dead is that some of these ghosts appear to know what's going on in the present and react to it. For example, one man

---

37   One claim of a rare exception to this is the case of Harry Price, the famous "ghost hunter," who allegedly appeared several times after his death in a place he had never been to a man in Sweden he had not known in his life (Björkhem, 1973: 150-160).

38   For an illustration of a haunting going back 2,000 years, see the case of the apparitions of Roman soldiers in York, England, observed in the 1950s (Hallam, 1976: 101).

in England, who had tended his lawn with loving care in life, appeared after death shaking his head disapprovingly over an unsuccessful attempt by new tenants to plant bulbs in one part of the lawn. The tenant who saw the apparition out on the lawn and was able to describe the man accurately had never seen him before (Alexander, 1975: 160, 161). In other words, this is an "evidential case," since it contains information the receiver should not have known; moreover, the most logical motivation for creating the apparition seems to come from the dead person reacting to a current situation of importance to him.

Tyrrell (1963: 39-41) discusses another case in which a husband and wife both saw an apparition of the husband's father, who appeared to be upset with his son. In fact, the husband was in financial trouble at the time and became very ill shortly thereafter. Although this is also an evidential case in the sense that there were two witnesses, providing evidence that it was not just an individual hallucination, we cannot be sure that the motivation for the apparition came from the surviving spirit of the father. It could also be that the troubled husband was motivated to see his father and that he created the apparition by shared telepathic communication with his wife.

One of the most famous reports used to support the survival theory is the Chaffin will case (Rogo, 1974:219-222). In 1925, the ghost of James L. Chaffin, a North Carolina farmer, directed one of his sons to a previously undiscovered will, which reversed an earlier will that had left the son disinherited. Although this complicated affair has many possible explanations, including ESP without survival, some parapsychologists argue that the simplest explanation is survival of the father's spirit.

The same is true of some classic communications through spirit mediums (cf. Chapter 15), which could be explained by super-ESP but only by postulating a combination of ESP steps, such as combining a telepathic reading of one person's knowledge with a clairvoyant reading of a code from another source. The simpler explanation is communication from a surviving spirit. In another sense, however, the theory that uses ESP alone is simpler, because it requires us to believe in only one paranormal phenomenon, instead of ESP *plus* survival. The current consensus seems to be that the debate between the super-ESP theory and the survival hypothesis is in "a position of virtual stalemate" (Wolman, 1977: 615).

One intriguing version of the survival theory of apparitions comes from D. Scott Rogo, who argues that we all have a "phantom within" us that can leave the body and create apparitions of the same type both before and after the body itself dies. In "out-of-body experiences" (OBEs or OOBs), people perceive themselves actually leaving the body and floating around, seeing their surroundings from a new perspective outside the physical body, and not just as if they were having an ESP view of another place. Sometimes, people in the out-of-body state are seen as apparitions by others (Rogo, 1974: 130, 131).

Rogo thinks that such apparitions are not caused by ESP alone, but that a "psychic body" is actually present in the location of the apparition. In some cases, physical objects have been moved by OBE ghosts, he says (Rogo, 1974: 131-136). Although he admits that there may be various types of ghosts, Rogo thinks that Tyrrell's telepathic theory is insufficient to explain them all. How could an apparition be reflected in a mirror, for example, if it were not really there in a physical sense (Rogo, 1974: 199)?

Tyrrell's answer would be that when a ghost's reflection shows in a mirror (as it may according to the evidence and contrary to popular lore about ghosts and vampires!) the reflection itself is merely part of the apparitional drama. The reflection is no more real than the ghost it reflects. Tyrrell's theory in a nutshell is that apparitions are *imitations* of real scenes. They approach, however imperfectly, realistic dramas, but careful analysis reveals that they exist only in the minds of one or more receivers.

In spite of such partial challenges to the ESP theory as Rogo's "psychic body" notion, Tyrrell's framework has remained essentially the dominant one since he first presented it in the early 1940s. Since the early 1950s, however Louisa E. Rhine has made by far the most extensive contribution to the serious parapsychological literature on apparitions. Rhine clearly supports Tyrrell's theory in general, but with certain modifications. For a good overall integration of her work with many newly published examples, see *The Invisible Picture* (Rhine, Louisa E., 1981). I shall refer to the journal articles on which the book is largely based, since they are generally more complete in term of analysis of data.

Like Tyrrell, Louisa E. Rhine (1953a) considers apparitions to be ESP-generated. She puts them in a typology of ESP expression, which also includes three others: intuitive ESP, unrealistic dreaming, and realistic dreaming. Her reference to apparitions as "hallucinations" emphasizes their nonphysical character and is reminiscent of the "Census of Hallucinations" in 1889, 1890. The term is unfortunate in that it fails to distinguish them from "mere hallucinations" generated in other than paranormal ways. Among the four types of spontaneous ESP, Rhine (1962:93) has found hallucinations to be the rarest, only about 10%.

Rhine (1962: 89, 90; 1978: 24) basically accepts Tyrrell's (1946-49) theory that there are two stages in paranormal cognition. First, there is the parapsychological stage in which contact is made with a target or source of information. Second, psychological processes bring this information into some kind of recognition in the conscious mind in one of the four ways mentioned above, including apparitions. Although the details of the process at each stage remain a mystery, Rhine (1953b: 201) has shown that conditions of strong emotion and crisis commonly trigger spontaneous cases of ESP.

One notable difference between Tyrrell and Louisa E. Rhine centers on their interpretation of how apparitions are initiated. As stated above, Tyrrell (1963) prefers to think that the ESP involved is telepathic, a message from agent (sender) to percipient (receiver). He is uncomfortable with the idea of clairvoyance, which is ESP knowledge of a situation on the part of the percipient without any help from an agent (Tyrrell,1963: 135·139). Rhine (1956: 241), however, argues that there is no need to assume that apparitions are agent-initiated, now that clairvoyance is a generally accepted phenomenon in parapsychology.

In the analysis of her own collection of cases, Rhine (1957a: 42) failed to find any living agents who had "the intention of appearing to the percipient." However, she presents one case in which an egg lady appears to a customer on the steps of the customer's residence before actually arriving. Later, the egg lady says that she had been thinking about the customer at the time and wondering if she wanted some eggs. In this case, as in others, Rhine (1957a: 22) states that "the agent had no intention of actually appearing to the percipient and was quite unaware that the percipient had so seen [her]." Surely, this under emphasizes the point that the agent was focusing her thoughts not only on the percipient but on the very activity in which she was perceived in the apparition. One wonders how often this occurred in reports not quoted in Rhine's article.

In another fascinating report, a man, while away from home, was dreaming about being back in a field on his farm. At the same time, his mother saw his apparition in that field. Rhine's (1957a: 23) emphasis is on the fact that the percipient, the mother, did not figure in the man's dream. Far from convincing me that the percipient initiated her own apparition, this case makes me think in terms of such phenomena as "traveling clairvoyance" (Tyrrell, 1963: 131, 135) and the out-of-body experience, in which an individual has the sensation of appearing in another place. Whether intending to be seen or not, the "psychic traveler" may have sparked the apparition seen by his mother.

Another line of argument Rhine (1957a) uses for her conclusion that the percipient initiates the apparition is that the apparition tends to be seen in ways that fit the expectations and visual perspective of the percipient, especially when the "agent" is close to the place where the apparition occurs. However, this seems to me to confuse the initiation of the ESP message with the way it is dramatized in the actual apparition.

This is surprising, since Rhine accepts Tyrrell's two-stage theory. Applied to apparitions (Tyrrell, 1963: 110-121), the theory implies that the first stage can be sparked by the agent, but the second stage is influenced by the percipient. It is only to be expected that the percipient will flesh out the apparitional image and drama in a way that fits the surroundings of the percipient. When the image is unrealistic, like a flash of light, Rhine (1957a: 27) argues that it seems "almost necessarily to have been... created and fashioned by the percipient...." Again, this confuses the initiation of the experience with the realism of its portrayal.

Hart (1958) objects to Rhine's insistence on percipient initiation of apparitions, stating that she ignores the possibility of subconscious motivation on the part of the agent. Although Rhine found none in her collection, Hart (1957) refers to "experimental cases" documented elsewhere, in which living agents (senders) have deliberately tried to make themselves seen by particular percipients (receivers). As mentioned above, such cases are one of Tyrrell's four classes of apparitions.

Why all the furor over the issue of agent-initiation of apparitions? Rhine and other parapsychologists know that survival cannot yet be proven or disproven. However, if it can be shown that percipients can create their own apparitions, as Rhine argues, then there is no need to invoke the survival of dead agents to explain apparitions of the dead.

The next section considers the firsthand Chinese ghost reports in terms of several features of apparitions according to Tyrrell, and with some comparisons to the Census of Hallucinations and to the spontaneous cases of Louisa E. Rhine.

A Ghostly Profile

1. Four classes: experimental, crisis, post-mortem, haunting

Although Tyrrell (1963: 38) states that he has uncovered sixteen experimental cases in which the living sender consciously wills him-herself to be seen as an apparition by someone else, apparently this type is rare. None of the 176 Chinese firsthand experiences in my study for which I have a report is experimental, as far as I can tell. Four cases, 2.3% of the total, are crisis cases, occurring on the day of death. [39] Post-

---

39 Tyrrell (1963: 19-23) discusses the argument that the telepathic explanation is supported by the fact that death-crisis apparitions occur much more often than

mortem cases are 21.6%, calculated from the thirty-eight apparitions whose identity was known or assumed but who had died prior to the day of the apparition. This leaves 76.1% (134), which are either hauntings, linked to the place in which they appeared, or apparitions in one of the other classes that could not be identified as such.

A fifty-nine-year-old man gave the following reports, first a death-crisis case (G010), then a postmortem case (G011) that happened a week later.

G010. Crisis at a Distance

People who are psychic can see ghosts. I have seen them twice. When I was about ten years old, and my mother had gone to visit friends about one hundred miles away, I got a high temperature. Then I saw my mother. They told me it was a dream, but I don't think it was. She looked very sad to me and then disappeared. I found out later that my mother died at that exact time.

G011. Return Visit

Seven days later, I saw my mother again. She was not crying this time, and she looked happier. I told people about it and described the house exactly that I could see in the background this time. They told me that I had described the very place where she had been visiting.

---

would be expected by chance. Only one in 19,000 apparitions of recognized living persons should have occurred on the day of death, given death rates in England and Wales from 1881 to 1890, whereas 2.3% of the recognized apparitions in the Census of Hallucinations were death-coincidences, 438 times the expected rate. Although only 23.9% (forty-two of 176) of the Chinese cases involved recognized persons (which seems to be less than half the percentage recognized in Tyrrell's cases), the percentage of recognized apparitions that are death-coincidences is 9.5% (four of forty-two). This is certainly a high figure though based on a small number of cases and not a reliable estimate. However, I am not especially impressed by this argument (neither is Tyrrell), except when the cases are "evidential." Three of the four Chinese cases are evidential.

The next report is another crisis case. It comes from the thirteen-year-old girl I referred to in Chapter 4 who said that she believed in ghosts a little bit, not in "just any ghost, but I believe in Grandma."

G012. "I Believe in Grandma"

When I was about ten, my grandmother died. She died suddenly in the morning, and I didn't get to see her. I wasn't there. I was my grandmother's favorite granddaughter. That night, I was very sad and cried. Then I saw my grandmother sitting at the side of the bed, smiling at me. I was very scared and covered my head up with a blanket. When I looked again, she was gone. My dad and mom said they had seen her in the house that night, too.

Because this apparition occurred on the day of death, it is considered a crisis case, but it clearly happened *after* the death, just like a post-mortem case. Therefore, the distinction between the two classes is arbitrary in such situations. Any apparition that happens after death raises the survival issue, unless we agree with Gurney (Tyrrell, 1933: 36), who thought that apparitions up to twelve hours after death were sent telepathically by the death victim while still alive but emerged as ghosts some hours later.

The following cases, from a twenty-one-year-old Mormon woman (G013) and from a thirty-year-old Catholic woman (G014), are both apparitions of close relatives, very similar to the previous ones, but both are post-mortem instead of crisis cases.

G013. The Figure in the Hallway

When I was ten years old, I was sitting in a room reading and saw a dark figure go quickly by in the hallway. Although I couldn't see the face, I recognized from the shape that it was my grandmother, who had died recently and had lived in the house.

G014. Dad, the Joking Ghost

The week my father died, he appeared to me twice, wearing the same clothes both times. At the first moment, I forgot that he had died. He talked to me jokingly, kidding me. He seemed entirely normal but then faded out slowly. I was told I probably missed him too much and imagined things. But I know I saw him.

In the last case, the receiver of the apparition was told that she must be "seeing things," but the twelve-year-old girl in the next post-mortem report received encouragement (about which she was somewhat puzzled). Not surprisingly, she had a high ancestor-worship score on the interview.

G015. Grandma by the Window

One week after my mom's mother died, every night around 3 a.m., I would get up uncontrollably and stare at the window. I saw my grandma standing by the window. She was like when she was alive. She wore black clothing, didn't move, didn't say anything, just stared at me. But I wasn't scared. I saw her three nights in a row, but I didn't tell anybody. Then my mom said that she had seen the same thing, and I told Mom about it then. Later on and up to now, my mom has burned some paper [ancestor worship] and it hasn't happened again. What I didn't understand was this: my mom also got up at 3 a.m. How come she didn't see me, and I didn't see her?

If the boundary between crisis and post-mortem cases is not always clear, the same can be said about the dividing line between post-mortem cases and hauntings. Although I classified G016 as a haunting, because the ghost seems to be linked to her old classroom after dying a violent death, it might also be a post-mortem appearance to the fifteen-year-old girl who reported it and to the other student present.

G016. The Haunted Classroom

This year before school was out, a girlfriend and I were walking around in the hallway after a concert at school one night. We both heard laughter and crying coming from a locked classroom. There was no light on in there. It sounded like a student who had burned to death at home about a month before. It was her classroom.

If hauntings are ghosts linked to places and the other three classes are ghosts linked to people, the next case is a mystery, because it neither stays in one place nor is recognized by the people it appears to. That alone makes me suspicious of the case, and my suspicions are fed even more by the atypical way the ghost's head is hanging and by the hysterical condition of the friend, which may have spread to the fifteen-year-old girl who made the report. I do not suspect any fraud in the report but think that it might be an example of "mass hysteria" (or "collective delusion"), which can distort one's perception.

G017. The Follower Ghost

It happened in July 1980. During class, one student started to cry without any reason. We asked her why. She didn't answer, just started at us. Her eyes looked horrible. Then she fell asleep for a few minutes. When she woke up, she was sweating all over and was very scared. She said she saw a ghost sitting on the air conditioner outside the window. She told me she didn't want to sit at her place any more, and she asked the teacher to change her seat. The teacher didn't believe what she said but saw how pitiful she looked and asked me to change seats with her. At that time, I didn't believe in ghosts, but she was still looking at us with her horrible eyes.

When classes were out, we were supposed to go home, but she felt somebody following her. She didn't dare to go home. I saw how frightened she was, so I accompanied her home. There were only very few people in her house, just her parents and her very old grandma. Her father worked nights and returned in the daytime. Her mother always played mah-jongg all day until midnight. Only her old grandma and she were left at home.

Before midnight, she and I went to sleep. A little while later, I got up first and looked out the window and saw opposite us a very bright and long white cloth. Then it disappeared. I was very scared. Then my friend got up. She said she also saw a long white cloth [on a woman's body] and a head hanging next to the body. She yelled and started to cry. At that time I didn't know what to do.

[Later] I woke her up and turned on the light and radio. We sat until dawn. That night it also rained until 4 or 5 in the morning. My friend couldn't take it and fell asleep again. But I couldn't sleep so I sat up. After I sat for awhile I saw nothing so I went back to lie down in bed. Then I saw a head hanging by a long white cloth, which appeared outside the window. Then it disappeared.

So I think I've really seen a ghost. I do believe in ghosts. Even when the sun came up I was still frightened. Then my friend woke up. After a few days it was all over. Nothing more happened.

2. Senses: visual, auditory, tactile, olfactory

Every sense but taste is involved in the 176 Chinese cases: 70% (123) are visual, 27% (forty-seven) auditory, 13% (twenty-two) tactile, 1% (two) olfactory, and none gustatory. [40] These total more than 100% because some involve more than one sense. There is a tendency for the different senses to correlate negatively with each other – that is, not to overlap.

---

40   This is not to say that apparitions can never involve taste. Rogo (1975: 126) discusses a case collected by Louisa Rhine in which a woman woke up as if hit in the mouth and tasted blood (that wasn't there) at the same time that her husband was actually injured in the mouth in a sailing accident.

For example, 27% of *all* reports are auditory, but only 10% of the visual reports involve hearing. Although 13% of all reports are tactile, only 9.8% of visual ones and 9% of auditory ones involve touch.

There seems to be no easy explanation for the lack of overlap. One possibility is that some of the reports ares misperceptions of things that are neither human nor apparitions, like "funny noises in the hall." All seventeen of the "Nervous Nellie" cases that I mentioned earlier turn out to be either visual only or auditory only. Eliminating all of these cases from the analysis doesn't change much. For example, it makes 25% of all cases auditory and 11% of visual cases auditory, compared with 27% and 10% before the exclusion of the Nervous Nellies. Another explanation could be that the paranormal imitation of a sensory image is rare enough, and it is not not that easy for the other sense to be dragged along. [41] Of course, in a few cases the visual apparition may be too far away to hear, or the ghost just might not feel like making any noise!

Louisa E. Rhine (1962: 102, 103) also records a lack of overlap between the senses in her collection of apparition reports. Using one set of her statistics that provides a comparison of sensory modalities, I calculate that 58% of all cases were auditory, but only 22% of visual cases were auditory. Likewise, 29% of all cases were visual, but only 11% of auditory cases were visual. She observes that both the lack of multiple-sensory apparitions and the relative rarity of apparitions as a type of ESP experience (about 10% of all spontaneous ESP cases, as noted earlier) seem to indicate that "few personalities are so constructed that the sensory pathway is easily or effectively activated" (Rhine, 1962: 109).

---

41   Another reason is purely statistical. It is hard for visual and auditory apparitions to be highly correlated because very few of the apparitions are neither visual nor auditory, only 10%. This distorts the table on which the percentage comparison is based. However, even when the rarer senses are compared, auditory (27%) and tactile (13%), which don't have the same statistical constraint, only 18% of tactile are auditory and 9% of auditory are tactile instead of 27% and 13% as expected. Worse yet, if eleven of the tactile cases that seem not really to involve a touch from the apparition (cf. Chapter 11)are excluded, none of the remaining eleven tactile cases are auditory.

A full comparison with the Census of Hallucinations in England is not possible because Tyrrell (1963: 24) does not give all the relevant statistics, but he does indicate that there were 1,087 visual and 493 auditory cases, a ratio of 2.2 visual for each auditory. The ratio is very close to that in the Chinese cases, 2.6. Although sight is evidently of prime importance in apparitions, followed by hearing in both cultures, it might be easier for people to explain away strange sounds and smells, if not touch, thereby resulting in a failure to label many strange nonvisual experiences as apparitions.

In fact, Louisa E. Rhine has found more auditory cases than visual ones. In a larger, more inclusive set of cases than the one of hers just mentioned above, 53% were auditory and 28% visual; moreover, a relatively sizable 4% were olfactory (Rhine, 1957a: 17). She blames the "very strict standards of authentication" (Rhine, 1956: 240) of earlier researchers for a possibly biased selection process (see note 25, this chapter), resulting in too high a percentage of the more impressive visual cases. The Chinese survey was not "selective," and it had even a slightly higher ratio of visual to auditory cases than the Census of Hallucinations did. Although the Rhine data set has the distinct drawback of not being a random sample, it nevertheless has the advantage of *not* resulting from a specific survey question about ghosts. It is a subcategory of a collection of spontaneous ESP experiences of all kinds. Although we asked people in the Chinese survey if they had ever "experienced" ghosts, rather than "seen" any, the popular conception of what a ghost experience is probably centers more on the visual, in both cultures.

It seems hardly necessary to give examples of visual apparitions, but let us look at one case from a fourteen-year-old boy that is unusual because it involves an apparent mirror reflection, one of the characteristics Rogo feels does not fit the telepathic (nonphysical) theory. Tyrrell (1963: 69), who found three cases of mirror reflections, considers them part of the sensory deception of the apparition, as I do.

G018. Reflections on a Green Ghost

One night a few months ago, after going to the bathroom, I passed through the living room on the way back to my bedroom. In the living room, I saw a mirror. When I looked in the mirror I saw a person-like figure next to me. It was green in color. In a second it disappeared.

Among the auditory apparitions, 43% involved a human voice. In only one of these twenty cases did the respondent claim to engage the ghost in a lengthy conversation. This fits Tyrrell's (1963: 86) statement: "The apparition might speak to us, and possibly might go as far as to answer a question; but we should not be able to engage it in any long conversation." A thirty-year-old woman reported the following apparition of two types of sound, including a conversationless voice.

G019. Laughter in the Bathroom

When I was in the theater once, I went to the bathroom in the middle of the movie. Nobody else was in there. One stall was locked; it had the "occupied" sign on. There were no feet showing underneath, but I heard urinating and a woman's voice giggling with a horrible laugh. I left the theater.

In the next, from a fourteen-year-old girl, we get a voice with words associated with a visual apparition that disappears before a real conversation can get under way. Because of the fever, however, we must consider the possibility that she is having a "normal" hallucination.

G020. The Friendly Ghosts

This happened when I was in Primary 6. One Sunday morning, the sky was still dark and I was still asleep with a high fever. When I opened my eyes I saw a few blurry men and women by my bed, kindly asking how I was. I was just about to answer when they all disappeared. Then I really woke up. I think they

were no different than normal people. They were very friendly
and very concerned.

Sometimes, an apparitional voice is close enough that one certainly
expects to see the speaker, but none appears. The experience of the
eighteen-year-old girl in G021 is striking to me, because it is so similar
to an apparitional ear-whispering episode that a professor claims to have
had in my own house in Gettysburg, Pennsylvania. [42]

G021. Haunted Ears

Several times in the last few months, I have heard a person making
noises next to my left and right ears. Sometimes, it sounded like
sighing, sometimes like a sharp scream. It was very clear, like a
person talking right next to me. But when I looked around, I
couldn't see anybody. It sounded like a middle-aged woman's or
a young man's voice.

Although Tyrrell doesn't state what percentage of the apparitions in the
1890 study in England involved touch, it is evidently a fairly unusual

---

42   While on sabbatical leave in Hong Kong and China in 1980-81, we
rented the upstairs of our house to my replacement for the year in the Sociology
Department at Gettysburg College. Earlier, my wife, Chee, thought she had
heard a man whisper "Wait!" to her from down the hall on the second floor, but
we never attached much significance to it. The new tenant, who knew nothing
about that incident, told me when we returned, that one night after some friends
had left the flat, he heard a young woman's voice whisper by his left ear, "Your
friends want back in; your friends want back in!" Although a nonbeliever in the
paranormal, he was quite startled. His friends did not ask to be let in again, by
the way. On two other occasions, the water went on by itself in the bathtub as
he was getting in. And once, when another person was present, they both heard
a loud rattling of the main door to the top floor, but apparently no one could
have been there. Although he has experienced nothing else for several months,
I intend to investigate this haunting of the seldom-used second floor after he
moves out!

phenomenon, [43] because he says that he has encountered a grand total of fifty-six in his work (Tyrrell, 1963: 63). Moreover, "in nearly all cases it is the apparition which [actively] touches the percipient, and not [vice versa]" (Tyrrell, 1963: 64). This is true of all but one of the Chinese cases as well. Case G022 is a tactile case from a seventeen-year-old girl.

G022. A Ghostly Feeling

Last year, during the Ghost Festival, I purposely went to bed early. I don't know what time it was, but I felt somebody feeling my face. At that moment, I was very scared. I was determined though to open my eyes to see who it was. I discovered the light was on, but there was nobody by my bed. To this day, I still cannot explain what happened.

If tactile apparitions are unusual, olfactory ones are positively rare. Excepting those in the Rhine collection, I have heard or read about only a few, involving perfume, smoke, and cooking smells. Here is one of the two in the Chinese reports, this one from a forty-nine-year-old man.

G023. The Lucky Opium Smoker

Twenty years ago, my mother used to have a small house in Hong Kong at #18 _____ Street. My bedroom was very small, like an alleyway. I came home very late one night. (I was always very careful about locking the door.) When I went into the house, I smelled a very strong odor of opium, but there was no smoke or anything visible. Then I saw a person in white sitting there sideways on my bed. It was pretty dark, so I couldn't tell much about the figure (even whether it was male or female), and it disappeared after a couple of seconds. After that, I have been

---

43   I found twenty-one (12%), but as I indicated in footnote 41, Chapter 11 will show that only eleven (6%) really seem to involve something tactile from the apparition itself.

very lucky, winning at mah-jongg all the time, tens of thousands of dollars!

Very impressive, even in Hong Kong dollars, which equal twenty U.S. cents each! At least, we discover that not everyone in Hong Kong considers it unlucky to see, or smell, a ghost.

3. The feeling of a "presence"

The previous section emphasizes the different sensory modalities that apparitions stimulate, or rather "simulate" according to the ESP theory. Sometime, however, people "just know" there's a ghost there and perhaps never experience anything sensory. It's as if the ESP message were received and waiting in the wings but had not yet popped out onto the sensory stage. People have told me that they know the sex and emotional attitude of the ghost (e.g., "a foreboding male presence"), and once even what it was wearing ("a woman in a black dress"), all without a sense experience. To take an example from Tyrrell (1963: 81-83), "I ... *felt* a short, dark woman was coming towards my bed." Case G024, reported by a twenty-two-year-old woman, is one of the five (3%) cases of a "presence" in the Chinese study. Notice that some of the girls did have a vague visual impression as well.

G024. Set an Extra Place

Two years ago, six or seven of us girls went to the New Territories for a picnic. We all felt that there was an extra person with us. I felt that the person, a female, was very friendly. We weren't afraid of her. Some of my friends saw a shadowy figure, very tall and thin, just a shape. When we went into a restaurant we gave her an extra place setting. At the table we couldn't see her, but when we were outside some could. Nobody knew who it might have been. It left when we came back to Hong Kong Island.

4. "Bag and baggage"

Perhaps apparitions with nothing apparently sensory about them are less of a problem for people to comprehend than ghosts with lots of paraphernalia attached: not only clothing but even equipment or their own background scenery. At least as early as the first century A. D. in China, this was a point of debate brought up by the naturalist philosopher Wang Ch'ung (Chan, 1963: 301): "If the earthly spirit [ghost] is really the spirit of a dead man, then [it ought to be] nude... because garments have no spirit. "

To be sure, this is a brilliant comment, but, as Tyrrell (1963: 73) would say, "it arises from a false conception of what an apparition is." By the ESP theory, even if there is a surviving spirit behind a ghost, what we perceive is not something physical but merely a projected drama of the mind, and some dramas need props or scenery.

In the Chinese cases, fifty-one (29%) specifically mentioned seeing clothing, and twelve (7%) mentioned some other equipment. Of course, some of the visual apparitions must have been too indistinct to reveal clothing, and in others the respondent probably just neglected to mention the clothing. Nobody claimed to have seen a naked ghost, a point that I hardly think would have gone unmentioned!

In the following post-mortem case, from a thirteen-year-old girl, Grandpa is not only wearing clothes (presumably), but takes more from the closet. If the ESP theory is correct, the doors open only as part of the scenery in the apparitional drama and not in reality.

G025. Grandpa's Winter Clothes

When I was little, my grandpa died. I don't remember how many days after his death it was, but one winter night I vaguely saw my grandpa open the door of the room. Then he slowly opened the closet door and took a few winter clothes out, closed the door, and left.

Next, a forty-five-year-old woman relates her experience of another post-mortem case, this time an apparition carrying a prop other than clothing.

G026. Boy with a Lantern

I lived in Shanghai when I was in my teens. One night, I was sitting in the courtyard with ten to twenty friends from the neighborhood when I saw a boy with a lantern walking in a circle and then disappear. Everybody saw the ghost and saw him disappear. He only appeared for a few seconds and was about twenty feet away. He was a boy who lived in the neighborhood and had just passed away seven days before.

Finally, a sixteen-year-old girl describes an odd apparition with a piece of equipment. The scene sounds as if it could be a near-drowning observed out of context.

G027. The Ghost and the Life Preserver

One night before the Hungry Ghost Festival, I saw a person at the end of the hallway hanging on top of a life preserver. It was about 8 or 9 at night. My brother and sister and I all saw it. We ran home quickly. He (or she) could have been a ghost. He had long flying hair.

5. Collective apparitions

One of the most crucial proofs for the ESP theory of ghosts is that some apparitions are seen by only one person when there are multiple potential witnesses present, and others are seen by the other people present as well. When more than one person sees the same thing, it rules out individual hallucination (although we must watch out for collective delusion, in which people imagine things suggested to them by others).When only one person sees it, this argues against the apparition being physically there. The only third possibility is ESP, not merely hallucinatory because it is triggered from an external source and not physical because it is *extra*sensory (not really perceived normally).

In one and only one case did I find a situation in which more than one, but not all of those present perceived an apparition; unless we also count case G024 above, in which some only felt the ghost's presence and failed to see it. The ideal case I refer to is G008, "Boy Scout Picnic" (cf. Chapter 1). Five or six boys saw the glowing couple, but roughly a dozen more did not! This single case provides evidence both against hallucination and against there being a physical reality. Tyrrell does not discuss partially collective cases, nor do I recall coming across any others anywhere. At any rate, they seem to be rare. Why they should be uncommon escapes me, but it strikes me as possibly an important clue. After all, if it is common for one person and not others present to see a ghost, and common for all of those present to see one, why should it be rare for *two* or more to see one when others present do not? It suggests that once the spark of ESP goes beyond one receiver present, it has an overwhelming tendency to swamp the whole group. [44]

In the Census of Hallucinations in England, 9% of all visual apparitions were collective, and 7% of all auditory ones; if only cases with other potential witnesses present are included, 34% of such visual ones were collective, and 36% of such auditory ones (Tyrrell, 1963: 24, 25). These figures are surprisingly lower than in the Chinese study. After excluding Chinese reports that did not provide information about other witnesses, I found 23% of all visual apparitions (25/111) and 32% of all auditory apparitions (14/44) to be collective. Based on only cases with multiple

---

44   The idea that there should be two separate ESP stages seems reasonable: one originating from a telepathic sender or other ESP source in another place and even in another time perhaps, plus a second one (definitely telepathic this time) originating in the recipient of the first message and spreading to others present. This is consistent with Tyrrell's (1963: 121-127) ideas about how bystanders get drawn into perceiving an apparition "intended for" someone else. What makes my theory unlikely is the fact that in most types of ESP some people make much better receivers than others. I cannot say why this second ESP wave should sweep either all the bystanders or none at all in nearly every case.

potential witnesses, 71% of visual (25/35) and 93% of auditory (14/15) apparitions were collective. [45]

Interestingly, Tyrrell (1963: 76, 77) quotes Gurney as saying that "the cases where the experience has been shared by a second person appear to be more numerous than those where a second person has been present, awake and rightly situated, and has not shared the experience." Certainly, my 71% of visual and 93% of auditory figures would support this claim. In one other small study (Hart, 1956: 204), 57% (26/46) of cases in which another person present might have seen the apparition were collective. Perhaps, there is something peculiar about the gathering or processing of the English "Census" data.

In the Chinese study, the largest number [46] of people to see an apparition at one time is the "twenty or thirty" in G002, "Harvest Homecoming" (cf. Chapter 1) who watched their neighbor's ghost cross the patio. In nearly every other case, there were a half-dozen witnesses or fewer. Although we have seen several collective cases already, let us take one more for illustration, one that made quite an impression on the fourteen-year-old respondent and her mother.

G028. Eviction Notice
Last year we were living in an old house built before World War II. My mother and I came home very late one night and saw a woman with long hair and white clothing sitting on the bed in the bedroom. Her face and whole figure were blurry and shadowy. She talked to us in Chinese and told us to move out of her house.

---

45   None of the twenty-two tactile and neither of the olfactory apparitions were collective. In fact, in only one of the tactile and in neither of the olfactory cases was there more than one potential witness. However, the unusual sleep-related nature of many of the tactile cases makes the presence of more than one awake person unlikely (cf. Chapter 11).

46   Hallam (1976: 37, 121, 122) refers to two cases that may have involved larger numbers of people, although it is not entirely clear whether everyone saw the apparition all at once in the first case (twenty-six witnesses of a phantom army), or how many witnesses there were or what they saw in the second case (a white something at a window seen from the marketplace).

We both heard it. It disappeared all of a sudden. We have no idea who it was. We did move out. The ghost sat motionless; we could tell it was a woman from the voice, a horrible voice.

On the other hand, imagine the feeling of someone like the thirteen-year-old girl in G029, who sees something peculiar when others present do not, a noncollective apparition.

G029. The Disappearing, Floating Man

Two years ago, after a picnic, some friends and I were walking home on the street in the evening. I saw a man walking very funny as if he were walking in water. He looked just like anybody on the street. solid though floating. He was facing us, coming our way. Then he disappeared in an instant. I asked my friends, but none of them saw him.

6. Evidential cases

As I have mentioned, evidential cases are ones that give "evidence" that they are not merely hallucinations produced in a natural way by the mind, assuming the report is accurate. In the Chinese study, fifty-one cases (29%) are evidential, forty-six because they are collective, as illustrated above, and five because they provided information that should not have been known otherwise. The precognitive apparition in Chapter 1 (G009) and the crisis and postmortem cases G010 and G011 in this chapter belong in the latter category. One more report that involves paranormal knowing is the following from a fifty-nine-year-old woman who described someone she had never seen in life.

G030. Visit from a Former Tenant

Thirty years ago, right after World War II, we were staying in an old house in Hong Kong. Early one morning, I was home by myself lying in bed when I saw a man in his thirties with a conservative, straight, Western haircut, and in a Chinese tunic, walking past my door. I'm not sure, but I think he had no legs. I saw just the top half. I saw him for the few seconds it took him to walk by. He looked normal except for his half body.

He was walking into the kitchen when I said, "Who is it?" There was no answer, and he didn't look at me. I got up and ran out but saw no one there. I checked the kitchen and the bathroom. When my son came back, he checked with the landlord, and found that a guy answering the description had lived there right before us and had killed himself.

7. Participation by animals

Tyrrell (1963: 84, 85) notes that animals are sometimes involved in apparitions, either as ghosts themselves or as receivers of apparitions. The ghostly screams of slaughtered pigs were heard in G006, "Animal Spirits?" (Chapter 1). And two dogs bark, growl, and wag their tails at a human ghost in G127 (Chapter 14). A forty-nine-year-old man, however, remarks at the *lack* of response from his dog to an apparitional cat in the next case.

G031. The Ghost of the Big Black Cat

In the house I'm in now, I was asleep late at night on a little balcony [loft] with a ladder going up to it, when I heard footsteps very clearly coming up the ladder. I looked and saw nothing. After a while, I saw a big black cat in the corner of the loft, and then it disappeared. The most amazing thing is that our huge dog, which barks at everything, was making no noise.

8. Nonphysical vs. physical

According to the ESP theory, apparitions imitate a realistic drama but often give themselves away by some feature or other that shows that they are not physically real. Rogo (1974: 110-112, 130-133), however, claims that physical effects have actually been produced by some visual apparitions. I found only two Chinese cases (1%) in which this appeared to occur, although it takes a careful look at the cases to eliminate several others that appear to be physical at first glance.

Some apparitions give themselves away easily, by leaving no physical evidence afterward when there should definitely be some. Such is the case in G032, told reluctantly by a twenty-three-year-old woman who didn't want to think or talk about it again at first.

G032. The Phantom Bookworm

[It happened] in Hong Kong when I was very young, thirteen or fourteen, around midnight, when I was alone in my bedroom. I heard books falling out on the floor, pouring out. I saw nothing, but I felt a presence. I heard the ghost climbing on my bed, walking around, and making noises, but it said nothing. The next day everything was O.K., in order [no books on the floor]. I think an evil spirit was trying to disturb me.

The next report is not part of the Chinese-case statistics, because the respondent was a British woman, but it happened in Hong Kong a few years ago, and the ghost was Chinese. The case illustrates how a haunting ghost can perform somewhat normally but then give itself away by appearing to walk *through* a door instead of opening it first.

G033. Through the Loo Door

I saw a very tall Chinese man in a tall top hat and a black smock (not really a traditional Chinese one, I don't think) that came down to his feet. He was wearing rope-soled shoes, and tippy-toed along, making no sound. He came right *through* the closed door of the loo [bathroom], looked around, and then looked straight at me. He had an evil look. He kept looking at me until he walked back straight through the loo door again. I'm not sure if there was always a loo in that room or not.

At least, the Chinese gentleman walked through the doorway, even if he neglected to open the door first. Some ghosts go right through the wall, as in the following case from a sixteen-year-old boy.

G034. Side Exit

About three years ago, I went to the 12:30 p.m. show at a theater with a friend. It wasn't crowded. My friend went to the bathroom. Then I thought I saw my friend walking back. It was a person walking very strangely, uniformly, wearing white maybe. I looked up and saw this person walk into the side wall. The hair was long and black maybe, but it seemed to be a man from the way it walked. It was dark and hard to see.

The next brief report, from a fourteen-year-old boy, is intriguing because it violates a physical barrier just like the previous cases in spite of the indefinite character of the apparition.

G035. In and out of the Wall

A few years ago at home, I saw a white transparent shadow going in and out of the wall, making no noise.

In G036, could we have an actual physical effect, with the hand pulling up the blanket? Careful reading shows that the sixteen-year-old girl (twenty when she reported it) was pulling up her own blanket, and the ghostly hand only appeared to be "helping."

G036. The Helping Hand

Four years ago in Hong Kong, I woke up half asleep about midnight and saw a white shadowy figure next to the wall. There's a Chinese saying, *Guai bai kau cheung*, "Ghosts stay near the wall" [cf. Chapter 3]. It had a long white robe, no hands or feet, and the back was facing me. It had long hair and was blurry. I couldn't see the face. I got real scared and pulled the blanket over me. I also saw a hand helping me pull the blanket up. I saw the hand only. It's as if there were two different ghosts, but I couldn't see them both at the same time. Then I closed my eyes, not wanting to see anything.

Two or three minutes later, I opened my eyes again and saw the same ghost. It didn't move or change position [the one by the wall]. The hand helped me again as I pulled up the blanket. When I opened my eyes a third time, I saw the apparition again. I pulled the blanket up again, but there was no hand that time. I went to sleep, and saw nothing in the morning. It was a very old house. I have no idea who the apparition was.

Although the next case, reported by a twenty-three-year-old man, seems to be a little borderline, it is one of the two cases I classified as an apparition performing a physical effect. The push was probably real rather than subjective, but could the "white figure" have been a real person rather than a ghost?

G037. The Phantom Push

One night three to five years ago, I was going into the elevator when a figure wearing white followed me in and ran right into me. I felt a force and almost fell. I looked again and there was nothing there. I couldn't see the face; 1 saw this out of the corner of my eye. Then the door closed.

Finally, an eighteen-year-old boy gives us an account that surely must be either a physical effect linked directly to an apparition, an unusual delusion, or a fraud. I have no evidence or even suspicions of fraud based on his school questionnaire, which seems to have been filled out conscientiously.

G038. Incident at the Railway Station

When I was in grade school, I went to a wedding feast in the New Territories. I drank one glass of beer. That evening my family and I walked to Ma Liu Shui Railway Station [the University stop]. As we walked to the ticket window on the platform, there were a bunch of dark-clothed persons opposite walking toward us. I wanted to see their faces, but I couldn't. They were like people and shadows both. They looked like dark shadows and like a picture drawn by charcoal pencil. When these "people" got near me, they pushed me down on the railway tracks. I was very upset and climbed back up on the platform. My family asked if I was drunk. They said ordinarily I could drink four or five glasses of wine and not get drunk. I explained to them that it was the work of those people, and they right away said that I was drunk because nobody had even passed by there. I looked around and saw nobody.

This case reminds me of one related by Glanvill (1689: 421-423) in the seventeenth century. A Dutch naval lieutenant, who had been taken prisoner from a sinking ship, claimed to the British in Woodbridge, Suffolk, that he could see ghosts. One day as he walked down the street with a Mr. Broom, he said that he saw a ghost coming, swinging a gloved hand and arm. When the skeptical Mr. Broom refused to let him get out of the way of the approaching ghost, the lieutenant was knocked down into the street and broke his knee. This physical case is also an evidential one, because it was later discovered that a man answering the description died just at that time (crisis case of the death-coincidence type).

Although there may indeed be a few such rare cases of visual apparitions causing physical effects, the nonphysical assumption of the ESP theory of ghosts seems to be generally valid. And when a certain set of reports emphasizes physical effects, there is reason to be suspicious. Ghost cases associated with Chinese ancestor worship are one such set of reports. Therefore, they deserve special attention in Chapter 6.

6

ANCESTOR-WORSHIP CASES

2017: This chapter is interesting in terms of experiential-source theory vs. cultural-source theory, as I pointed out at the beginning of chapter 2. There are certainly cultural effects in these cases, because they entail ancestor worship. However, in spite of there being physical effects, these effects do not occur directly as part of the apparition, but as separate "haunting" effects. This separation of apparitional and physical haunting effects fits the dominant parapsychological theory that has been applied to cases in the West. Therefore, ghost experiences are basically the same in Chinese and in Western culture, supporting the experiential-source theory. At the same time, I recognize that culture has an impact on how people interpret their personal experiences.

Altogether twenty-five (14%) of the Chinese reports are connected to ancestor worship, even if only in the sense that the spirits are expected to return after death, typically seven days after death. This prescribed time for ghosts to appear does not necessarily violate parapsychological theory. In fact, if there is survival of the spirit, spirits might be motivated to communicate according to the cultural expectations of their close relatives.

However, in view of the great importance of ancestor worship in Chinese culture (cf. "Ancestors: ghost relatives" in Chapter 3), perhaps such great expectations distort the perceptions of the living. This was evidently the opinion of the young man, a college student, who reported the following to me in a personal interview.

G039. Hearing Things

Specialists can calculate and tell you the very hour a spirit should come back. We waited for my grandmother to come back, and the family all heard noises. I would have been surprised if we *hadn't* heard something. We expected it.

Under conditions of heightened suggestibility, likeminded people can easily fall prey to emotional contagion (the spread of an attitude or perception from others). I asked several people if parents might not fake some of the noises and physical effects of returning relatives for the benefit of the young children, something like eating the milk and cookies set out for Santa Claus in the United States. Apparently, that was going a bit too far. No, they replied, because the parents also believe in the ancestors, although they might not believe in their having returned in particular situations. The parents of the thirteen-year-old girl who reported the next case actually made light of her experience, although they practiced the night vigil.

G040. The Clattering Chopsticks

It happened on the night my grandmother's soul was supposed to return to the house. That night, my family and I crowded into one room to sleep. I was very frightened when I fell asleep in the middle of the night. I kicked my blanket on the floor. When I woke up, I jumped down to pick up my blanket. At that time, everybody else was sound asleep. I went back to bed, quietly looking out the window by the bed to the living room. I couldn't see anything. Before I could fall asleep again, I heard the noise of a pair of chopsticks falling on the table. I looked out the window to the living room and still couldn't see anything. I passed the night in fear. The next morning, I told my parents about it. They didn't believe me and thought I was silly. But I haven't been able to forget this incident up to now. It made a very deep impression on me.

Another flaw in the Santa Claus analogy becomes apparent as we see not joyous expectation but Chinese ghost fear again, described this time by a seventeen-year-old boy.

G041. Chains and Chairs

I remember clearly it was about 3:14 a.m. the night my grandfather's soul returned to the house. I heard noises like a person walking with chains on and like a person pushing a chair. I didn't dare to get out of bed, so I lay in bed continually keeping track of the noise. After it disappeared, I fell asleep. I didn't get out of bed to look because I didn't have the guts.

In the three previous cases, the noises heard were attributed to spirits of particular relatives who were expected to return on particular nights shortly after death, although the noises themselves were not said to be characteristic of those individuals. G042, by contrast, from a twenty-seven-year-old man, actually identifies the visual apparition of someone who was neither a relative nor expected to return on a particular day. What makes it an ancestor worship case is the fact that the family kept her commemorative tablet on the altar.

G042. The Floating Tenant

It was about ten years ago in Canton. I was living in a very old house. That night, a woman tenant who had lived there appeared right around the altar where we kept this woman's tablet. She floated by the altar. Her face was green and horrible. Otherwise, she looked normal. She didn't look at anybody and disappeared

instantly after a couple of seconds. She had been dead for a
month.

The next case, related by a thirty-two-year-old woman, is even farther
removed from the anxious expectations of a returning relative. The
"antidote" to the haunting, however, is definitely prescribed by the culture
of ancestor worship.

G043. White Figure in the Bedroom

About ten years ago, I was studying for an exam at night in the
living room. I felt a cold chill and looked up. I saw a body in a
white robe, white and lumpy, self-luminous; but I couldn't tell
the sex. It floated into the bedroom from the living room, facing
that direction. I went into the bedroom but couldn't see it. This
happened twice the same way that week. I don't know who it
could have been, because we bought the house new ten years
before, and no one died in it.

My mother and sister both insist they each saw it once. My
married sister had come home with her children for a visit, and
she was taking a nap in that same bedroom. She was half-asleep,
couldn't move, and saw this white figure; but she couldn't see the
face because it was too dark. The figure talked to her (it was a
woman's voice, maybe in her forties or fifties) and said that she
was very poor with no clothes and no food. She asked if we would
burn her some incense and money, etc. Then she disappeared.
My sister got very scared and told Mother about it. My mother
had seen the ghost float into that room too. She burned the paper
right away then, and we haven't seen the ghost since.

To clarify, the respondent reported that her mother had seen it first, then
the respondent, and her sister third. However, since they did not see it at

the same time, I do not consider this a collective apparition. Moreover, the second paragraph is not a firsthand ghost report. [47]

Like the last case, G044 involves ancestor worship of a nonrelative, but this time the woman is told that her ghost is a special, lucky one.

G044. To Exorcise or Not to Exorcise

Eighteen years ago, I lived in a house that was about twenty years old; many other people had lived there. Within a few days, I saw a ghost three times. It was a woman, seemed like in her thirties, with half a body, the top. She looked realistic and wore traditional Chinese clothing with a yellow-flower pattern on a black background. She was not transparent. Once I saw her in the alleyway just outside the bedroom, twice in the bedroom. She looked at me for a few seconds and then disappeared; she didn't move. Once, I was afraid and pulled the blanket over myself. Two years later, I went to a fortune-teller, who told me I had a genie following me around and not to exorcise it. I burn incense to her every year at the Hungry Ghost Festival.

From cases involving auditory or visual apparitions only, let us move to cases in which the food set out for the spirits is physically affected. G045 is actually a continuation from G004 (Chapter 1), in which a woman reported that when she was fifteen back in 1949, she and her father apparently saw the ghost of her sister, who had died from cholera earlier that day. Now, we see how the situation develops into a full-blown problem that must be solved by ghost marriage.

---

47   As will become clearer in Chapter 8, secondhand or hearsay reports should be categorized as folklore, even when no conscious distortion or fraud is suspected. Notice, for example, the atypical feature in this one that the ghost requests the burning of incense and paper articles. It is easier to remember one's own experience accurately than someone else's report.

G045. Paranormal Peanuts, and a Ghost Marriage

My sister later appeared to everybody else in the family, as a shadow, floating in the air. We could see her features. She often appeared in our dreams, too. Because she suffered and died a violent death, she was fierce as a ghost. Even dogs and cats were afraid. The seventh day after her death, she came back according to the custom to get her belongings. We put them all outside the gate, along with peanuts (my sister's favorite food) and other food. The next day, the peanuts were gone from inside the shells, which were still intact; I saw them myself. When her soul returned, my father knew, because his heart burned like fire.

All my relatives used to get pain all over their bodies if we forgot to burn incense and pray to my sister. They would call my mother up and say, "Did you forget to burn incense for her?" "Oh yes," she would say, and burn it in the middle of the night.

This is no longer a problem since my sister got married. My sister was seven or eight when she died, and her husband [husband-to-be; the marriage had not yet been arranged] was eight or nine years older. They knew each other; they played together as next-door neighbors. During the war, he walked up to Canton, and on the way was confronted by robbers, who killed him. His body was never found, only his clothes. Eventually, they buried the clothes next to my sister in Diamond Hill Cemetery.

After they both had died, my mother had a dream that my sister wanted to marry the guy next door. The next day the mother of the boy came over and asked to have him marry my sister. They were married exactly as if they were still alive: dowry, celebration, and everything. I saw the matchmaker coming down the stairs with her ancestor-worship tablet. It's unlucky to see it before she gets married, but it was O.K. because I was close to my sister. It's the boy's family's duty to worship her now.

My aunt had a dream after that in which she saw my sister and asked her about the marriage. My sister said it was fine, except that the bridegroom was ugly. My aunt asked my mother if he was ugly, and my mother said no, but maybe the robbers had chopped him in the face. His clothes had been all chopped up too.

In another report of ancestral food offering, G046, from a thirteen-year-old girl, a noise, but no visual apparition, accompanies the episode of physical effects.

G046. Grandpa's Food

My grandpa came back on the seventh night after his death. His room window made a lot of strange noise. It was very horrible. The next day, all the food, water, and candy had been eaten or moved around.

An eighteen-year-old boy tells of another food case with a more elaborate noise.

G047. Bucket and Buns

The day my grandmother's soul was supposed to return, I was not yet ten years old. That day, my family prepared the altar, including food and fruit. We went to bed. I remember it was only about 12 noon to 1p.m. After it passed 3 in the afternoon, I heard an aluminum bucket making noise in the bathroom. After that, it seemed like a chain was dragged from the bathroom to the area next to the altar, making noise continuously (there's a long hallway from the bathroom to the altar). At that time, I felt that it was very strange. My whole family was asleep.

And then at night, my whole family got up. We went to the altar. We found that the fish there was gone, and the strangest thing is that one of the longlife buns had a handprint on it, very clear and black. This is a riddle. My family cannot explain it. We just have to believe that it was my grandmother's soul leaving the best evidence to us.

In the next report, from a thirteen-year-old girl, we find more evidence of someone touching the food.

G048. Fingerprints in the Rice

During Chinese New Year, 1977, a neighbor who was living in our house went out for a walk. He didn't know how, but he fell down. He was sent to the hospital and died. His family put an altar in our house. One night, they put some wine and food on the table for him to come back and eat. That night, my whole family went to stay in another person's house. The next day, there was some food missing because he ate it. In a bowl of rice there were a few fingerprints.

I have secondhand accounts of physical effects on food as well. One said that some food for an ancestor "was left with three black fingerprints," reminiscent of the last two cases. Another claimed that food offerings "dropped down from the altar to the floor." In one final food report, G049, an eighteen-year-old girl describes an unusual physical effect of sand appearing in the room. [48]

G049. The Mysterious Sand

My father died about four or five years ago. That night, all the members of the family were eager to know whether my father would come back. In fact, it is a Chinese belief that the soul of a dead person comes back. At first, we were very patient to wait.

---

48   The sand seems to be a type of psychokinetic effect (PK) called an "apport." Apports, physical objects appearing or disappearing in thin air, have often been natural objects like stones or pools or water, but I do not recall any involving sand in particular. One Chinese cultural expectation that may be related is the idea of putting down sand to see if the ancestors come back and checking for footprints the next day.

But later we all fell asleep. The next day, we found lots of sand on the floor. We didn't know where the sand came from. Maybe the wind blew it in. But there wasn't any window in the dining room. Besides, we found the wine and the food that we put on the table had been drunk and eaten up a bit. May I ask, what's that prove?

Another unusual physical effect is claimed by a twenty-three-year-old woman. If the report is accurate, the tactile effect was physical and not merely apparitional.

G050. Bruised by a Ghost?

Two years ago, I went up to the roof at 11 p.m. to burn incense. There was nobody around. I was hit on the leg and bruised.

At the end of Chapter 5, I stated that ancestor worship cases should be examined carefully because they contain so many examples of physical effects. What can be concluded from this examination?

Remember that apparitions should not cause physical effects, according to the ESP theory. However, in spite of all the physical effects contained in the ancestor reports (food eaten or touched, sand on the floor, even a bruised leg), not a single one of the reports linked a physical effect directly to a visual apparition. To be sure, there were ghosts seen and noises heard (either physical or apparitional noises, we can't be sure), but not a single ghost was seen handling the food, for example. Moreover, neither one of the two cases in the entire study that involved an apparition performing a physical effect was an ancestor-worship case.

Considering the strong expectations in Chinese ancestor-worship culture that ghosts should perform physical acts like eating food, it is quite remarkable that not a single person reported seeing a ghost do so. Not only does this finding give support to the ESP theory, it also argues strongly for the honesty and accuracy of the reports. If any of the reports are distorted by cultural expectations, it should be the ancestor ones.

One problem remains. Even if the nonphysical nature of the apparitions themselves has been confirmed, where did the alleged physical effects in these cases come from? This question must wait for the further treatment of physical effects in Chapter 10, "Hauntings and Poltergeists."

7

Abnormal Features of Perception

2017: Since 1982 I have come across many cases like this in the U.S. and UK that fit into the treatment in this chapter. For example, in Gettysburg there is one report of a "woman in white" appearing at night on the battlefield. Two women (collective apparition) saw her from their car one night. It makes sense to assume that if the figure were not self-lit she would not have been visible to the witnesses in the dark.

In one interesting case in the UK, Roman soldiers were seen walking through the cellar of an old building. They were visible only upwards from their knees, which were at floor level. Once they got to a spot in the cellar that had been excavated down to the Roman road underneath the floor, their lower legs were visible as they walked across it. In other words, their lower legs were missing only because the apparition was consistent with the level of the site as it had been during the Roman occupation of Britain. In other cases in this chapter, lower extremities seem to be missing because they are less important information.

It has already been observed that the matter of physical effects poses a major potential problem, since they are strongly anticipated in Chinese ghost culture but are not supposed to exist according to the ESP theory of apparitions. Chapter 6, however, shows that visual apparitions themselves rarely cause physical effects in the Chinese firsthand reports, in spite of the expectations of ancestor worshipers.

As we were gathering these reports, a second major problem occurred to me. I began to notice that many of them contained weird details, like half-bodies and pale faces, or that the ghost glowed in the dark or floated instead of walked. I suspected that we were getting a lot of fictionalized reports, influenced by stereotypes of horrible ghosts from Chinese folklore.

After all, Tyrrell (1963: 65-72) emphasizes that apparitions imitate normal perception. Ghosts, I thought, should look just like regular living people in most cases, not like the fantastic floating sheets of American ghost lore or like the horrible monsters of Chinese ghost lore.

Most of the excellent cases of apparitions emphasized in parapsychological studies are surprisingly realistic. For example, "Her skin was so lifelike that I could see the glow of moisture on its surface, and on the whole, there was no change in her appearance, otherwise than when alive" (Bennett, 1939: 146).

Then, it occurred to me that the less remarkable cases might contain more of the "weird" features we were getting. Although I have never seen any analysis or statistics on what percentage of cases might have them, I combed the dozens of cases in Bennett's (1939) *Apparitions and Haunted Houses*, collected from letters in response to a British radio broadcast in 1934, and double-checked cases from Tyrrell (1963). To my amazement, all of the weird features in the Chinese reports had their almost exact parallels in the British cases.

At that point, my thinking turned to the hypothesis that the ghosts themselves are not weird, but rather that the perception of the ghosts is incomplete or abnormal. After all, ESP is not a completely realistic and reliable imitation of normal sense perception. It is logical to expect that apparitions that are based on ESP should contain "abnormal features of perception" as well. The startling fact is that both Western and Chinese apparitions have the same abnormal features, which suggests a universal ghost phenomenon in spite of differences in the culture of the receiver (percipient) of the apparition. The eight features I have detected are listed below with examples.

1. Disappearing or fading out

Disappearing per se is not at all unusual for apparitions, nor does it make the ghost look "abnormal" while it lasts. In the Chinese cases, 32% of the visual ones (thirty-nine of 123) were reported to have disappeared (instantaneously), [49] as in G051 from a twenty-year-old man.

G051. The Phantom of the Record Shop

One morning last winter, I went to a record shop. I was looking at record albums when I felt a cold chill. I looked around and saw a pair of legs and feet with slacks and shoes on. There was no upper part of the body. After a second it disappeared. Nobody else saw it evidently. I ran out of the store and left.

Stranger than disappearing instantaneously, and rarer (3%), is the "slow fade." I found this feature in Bennett (1939: 125, 136) as well: "The apparition slowly faded," and "With her eyes still meeting mine, she faded from my sight – not suddenly but quite gradually." A fourteen-year-old boy relates the following example in Hong Kong:

G052. The Illusive Figure

One time we were out camping, my classmate and I. We went out looking for adventure. Passing by a wooded area, we saw a half-transparent figure. Strangely, we weren't afraid. It had no legs, but it had a pair of eyes staring at us. We wanted to reach out and touch it, but it disintegrated like dew. We saw it for about three minutes.

---

49   Other apparitions may have disappeared as well, but the respondents may have neglected to mention the fact. In many cases, the ghost had no chance to disappear, as it turned the corner or otherwise left the scene.

The disintegration is not only a type of "fading" but it also illustrates another interesting parallel with the British cases. Tyrrell (1963: 64, 65) points out that people who try to touch ghosts are usually foiled in the attempt, because the apparition either moves away or vanishes. [50] Apparently, the ghosts in the next case, reported by a twenty-five-year-old man, faded in a similar manner as they approached.

G053. A Pale Pair of Persons

Two different times, I saw two ghosts at night on the street in Hong Kong. They wore long white robes and had pale white [bloodless] faces. Otherwise, they looked like normal persons. They walked toward me with their heads down and suddenly turned into lump-like clouds and disappeared when they got close. They had two different faces.

Sometimes, it is impossible to tell whether the apparition disappeared all at once or gradually, because the observer closed his or her eyes for a moment. In 11% of the visual cases, the ghost was gone before a second look, which is what happened to the sixteen-year-old girl in G054.

G054. Blur on the Hillside

I was in Hong Kong, less than ten years old. I went out to pour some dirty water on the street, when I saw a white, blurry figure by the hillside. I thought it was a woman, but I couldn't see the ghost's face because it was blurry. You can't see ghosts' faces, you know. They won't let you. It was at night, too.

   I couldn't move until somebody yelled at me. I looked back to see who it was. When I looked at the hillside again, the figure

---

50   Tyrrell (1963: 65) thinks that the logic of the apparition requires this, because apparitions strive for consistency. Because they are nonphysical, the receiver would observe a contradiction if he or she managed to grab the ghost: the receiver's hands would sink through the apparition, as there is nothing there physically, while an imitation of touch would make it feel as if the hands were stopped at the surface.

was no longer there. It was about ten feet away. Nobody else was there to see it. It didn't move or anything.

Usually, the ghost is not still there after the receiver closes his or her eyes for a while and opens them again, although G036 in Chapter 5 is such a case. In G055, a thirty-two-year-old woman reports the same thing.

G055. Image in a Cantonese Inn

When I was very young, my mother took me to Canton during summer vacation. We stopped at a very old inn. We stayed in a room with two single beds. Just at midnight, I woke up and saw a man in Chinese-style clothing ("Tang Dynasty clothing," but people still wore it then). He was looking in my direction, but not really staring at me. I was real scared, closed my eyes, and opened them again three times. He was still there. I was so scared I didn't want to look again; I closed my eyes and fell asleep. He had nothing below the waist, but otherwise was normal in appearance He was normal height, standing at the door, not moving. It made such a strong impression on me that I can still remember what he looked like.

2. Insubstantial image

If the ESP image of a ghost sometimes fades away or breaks up on its way out, it is not surprising that it should often be somewhat lacking in substance throughout the entire viewing. Such is the case in 28% of the visual reports in the Chinese study. Insubstantial images are described by such words as "transparent," "blurry," "shadowy," "lumpy," "cloudy-like," and "smokey."

The transparent type is described as follows in some of Bennett's (1939: 178, 180) British cases: "I could clearly see through his body... I could see the bricks through my uncle's form"; and in another, "To our amazement, we could see through him, he was dressed in his usual black clothes." G056, from a fourteen-year-old boy, is a transparent case from Hong Kong.

G056. The Transparent Gods

When I was in the second grade, I accidentally looked at the southeast side of the sky. I saw a bunch of people walking around. Their bodies were all transparent. At that time, I asked my family to look at it right away, but they couldn't see anything. My mom said that they were the gods at the south door to the sky.

"Shadowy" is another typical description, as in this report sent to Bennett (1939: 61): "I saw a figure pass across the end of the room, and disappear through the door... . The figure glided, rather than walked; it was dark and shadowy, but I could see plainly it was no shadow." As we have already seen in several earlier Chinese reports, the next, related by a sixty-three-year-old man, is shadowy and blurry.

G057. The Speedy Shadow

I think I might have seen one [a ghost] on the street one night. I saw a shadow-like figure moving very quickly. The only impression I got was that the figure was very blurry. I'm not sure if it was a ghost or not. I didn't think a living person could move that fast.

Another British report (Bennett, 1939: 268) states that two figures "looked dark and mist-like." Although such things are probably difficult to visualize, this reminds me of the "thin, grayish light, very smokey but not changing in shape" in case G001 (Chapter 1). Recall also the "lump-like clouds" of G053, and the figure that "disintegrated like dew" in G052 in this chapter. [51]

---

51   As a footnote to this section, I might point out that I checked to see if insubstantial visual apparitions were less likely to be collective than the solid visual apparitions were. My hypothesis was that insubstantial apparitions represent incomplete ESP and that they might be harder to share with others as

3. Glowing (self-luminescence)

At first, I thought that glowing or self-lit apparitions might be the bright extreme in contrast with shadowy, insubstantial ones at the dark extreme. However, 40% of the glowing ones are insubstantial, whereas only 28% of all visual apparitions are insubstantial. Although the numbers are small (only ten, or 8%, of all visual ones, are glowing), it appears that insubstantiality and glowing are two different features. They may be somewhat positively correlated, and at least they are evidently not opposites of the same feature.

One of the English cases was "clothed with brightness," and Bennett (1939: 2, 155) noted that ghosts appear "sometimes at night with a luminosity of their own." The first Chinese case below, from a fourteen-year-old boy, shows that shadowiness and luminosity can go together.

G058. The Glowing "Underground" Ghost

I don't remember what day it was. At midnight, I woke up and saw a shadowy figure, luminous. I couldn't see the lower half of the body, as if he had climbed up from underground. I saw the side of its face. At that time, there was thunder and lightning. I have heard that if there is thunder and lightning, ghosts will climb up from under the ground. I was very scared. I covered my head up with a blanket. I didn't even go out to pee. The next day when I got up, I had even sweated all over. I believe that it was the guy in this building who jumped out of his flat and killed himself.

In the next report, a thirteen-year-old girl describes a curious partial-body apparition that seems to be self-lit, based on the "bright" designation.

---

well. However, the difference is small and statistically insignificant. When other potential observers were present, 67% of insubstantial visual apparitions were collective (six of nine) compared with 73% of solid ones (nineteen of twenty-six).

G059. Chrome Dome

I saw it when I was in Primary 3 or 4. I remember it was early in the morning. The sky was still dark. I got out of bed and sat in a chair by the window looking out on the street. Suddenly, I saw a human head appear in front of a garage. It was shaking.

It looked like a human's face and also wore a pair of glasses. The head was very big and bald and not fierce. I'm not sure whether it was human or not. If it was human, how come it was so bright and big? Also, why didn't it do anything but shake? I saw it in Tai Hang [district of Hong Kong Island], on _____ Street outside the door of a certain garage.

Although G060, reported by a sixteen--year-old girl, does not specifically emphasize the glowing aspect, it is clear that it must have been self-luminous. Notice also that the apparition had started into a lumpy fadeout when the receiver closed her eyes. [52]

G060. The Disintegrating Mannequin

When I was very little, I witnessed a very strange thing. Even now I still wonder whether it was real or false. In the house that I lived in before, there was a bunk bed. My mom and I slept on the lower bunk. One night, I was sleeping soundly; so was my mother and the whole house. After a while, I thought I was dreaming. It was still dark as I woke up from my dream. I felt that I was surrounded by a big ball-like thing. When I opened my eyes, I saw a fashion-model mannequin standing next to my bed. When I was still doubting whether it existed or not, I saw that it was turning into small lumps, lumps of white cloud-like

---

52   There are other fascinating aspects to this report that make it one of the most interesting cases in the entire study. Why did she "feel" as if she were surrounded by a big ball? Perhaps she had a "feeling of a presence," which represented a whole scene. Why did she think she saw a mannequin? Perhaps it was the lack of movement so often found in apparitions or a lack of color, which made her think that the woman (presumably) was not real.

stuff floating in the air. Unfortunately, when I blinked my eyes, they disappeared. At that point I held my mom and was scared, but I didn't think of waking my mom up. I just closed my eyes tightly and fell asleep. But I know I was not seeing things. That room was very dark and made the white smoke-like thing stand out even more. It wouldn't move, wouldn't even blink its eyes. It was very quiet. I saw it just divide into lumps of smoke. Very horrible!

This last, and the next report (G061, from an eighteen-year-old woman) help lead us to an answer to the question, "Why should apparitions glow?" Although the self-luminescence of an image of a person is an "abnormal feature of perception," based on the nature of normal persons, it is essential for an apparition seen in the dark to be self-lit if it is to be seen at all! The apparitional drama will be more realistic if it seems to be reflecting the light in its environment, but since many apparitions are associated with near-sleep and therefore seen at night, they cannot always be both realistic and observable. [53]

G061. The Glowing White Figure

This year in Hong Kong, the street was very dark and I was walking home by myself when I saw a white figure. Maybe it was sort of glowing in the dark; that's why I could see it. It was about a block away. It was moving very quickly, like lightning, into an alleyway. It looked like a person, but it was all white.

Finally, Bennett (1939: 66, 67) refers to a case in which the figure in a haunting becomes brighter over time in several sightings, almost to

---

53   There is also a set of other paranormal phenomena that have been associated with glowing: mystical experiences, out-of-body experiences, religious visions, "beyond-and-back" or near-death experiences, etc. For a discussion of how some of these might be related to glowing apparitions, cf. Rogo (1974: 96-114).

the point that he could be seen at night without a candle. [54] Some are obviously brighter than that.

4. White and dark clothing

Tyrrell (1963: 70) and Bennett (1939: 178, 180) give examples of white, grayish-white, and black clothing in the British apparitions, but they do not give statistics on the percentage that are in black-and-white as opposed to color. Among the forty-two Chinese visual cases that give the color of clothing, 71% are white, 7% dark, 7% black and white together, and only 14% in other colors. This suggests that most apparitions are not normally colored. The high percentage of white also suggests that white, like the glowing feature, helps make apparitions visible. However, glowing and whiteness are apparently not strongly related features: only three of the ten glowing apparitions were reported to have any particular color of clothing (about the same percentage of all visuals that state the color of clothing), although all three were white. Cases G062 and G063, from a middle-aged woman and a teenaged girl respectively, illustrate the common feature of white clothing.

G062. The Haunted Sitting-Room

Some years ago, I arrived at a large house of the courtyard type owned by my extended family in a village near Canton. I was to live in one of the unoccupied rooms. When I looked into one of the unoccupied sitting-rooms, I saw a man walk by inside. I saw only the top half. He was wearing a white, modern Chinese-style top and had a short, modern hair style. He did not look at me. His arms were going back and forth in a normal walking motion. I thought perhaps I didn't see some dark trousers because it was not bright enough in the room. I asked the servants why

---

54 In other haunting cases that have stretched over a period of time, apparitions have become more difficult to see, or less substantial. An example of the latter is the famous "Morton" case (Bennett, 1939: 185-209; Tyrrell, 1963: 60, 61, 155-158).

somebody was in there, since I thought it was unoccupied. They said nothing. Later, one servant told me that it was the ghost of a young man who had died of cancer at age nineteen. When they wanted to clean the room they sent in the man who had been his servant when alive.

G063. Instant Audience

Once when I was real little, in the sixth grade, only my sister and I were home. She is three years older than I am. Around 2 p.m. we were playing ping pong on the floor. I saw a person appear behind her. I yelled, "Ghost!" Then he disappeared. It happened so fast, I couldn't see his head or feet, but I couldn't say for sure he had no head and feet. He wore faded-white, old traditional clothing.

5. Sickly, horrible look

Bennett (1939: 30, 123) includes descriptions of British ghosts that have a "ghastly waxen pallor" or that have a sickly, horrible look for various other reasons. Only nine (7%) of the Chinese visual apparitions have this particular abnormal feature: six because of a sickly complexion, and three for other reasons (one bloody, one cut up and bloody, and another that looked like a skull in only a fleeting glance). I thought that the sickly-complexion ones might be perceived that way only because the whole apparition was white or black-and-white. Case G053 in this chapter seems to fit, because the two ghosts were dressed in white robes and had "bloodless" (*mo-huet sic*, "no-blood-colored") faces. However, this is the only one of the six sickly-complexion cases that has the color of clothing mentioned in the report.

If it is not the lack of color per se that makes some ghosts look sickly or horrible, why *should* they look that way? Going by the survival-based hypothesis that haunting ghosts are emotionally trapped in a place, often because of a violent death, perhaps haunting ghosts should be more likely to look horrible than other kinds. Out of the seventeen visual cases that could be identified as hauntings, four (24%) had "sickly, horrible" ghosts, whereas only five (5%) of the 106 other visual cases were sickly or horrible. This result is statistically quite significant and supports the hypothesis. [55]

In G064, a twelve-year-old girl reports a pale, white type of sickly-looking ghost. In G065, a fifteen-year-old girl describes the one that was "cut up and bloody. "

G064. Blank Face in the Bathroom

Last year, when I was in the bathroom one time, I saw just a head in the corner of the bathroom. It had no facial features, just a white, blank face. I'm the only one who saw it. I asked my friends, who should have seen it too, if they had seen it, and they said no. I saw it for only a second, but the bathroom was not dark. I was horrified. It had long hair, and it was a clear image. It disappeared instantly.

G065. Picnic Phantom

Last year, I went on a picnic to the outskirts with my friends, three or four of them. In the evening, we all saw a person in dark clothing with long hair approaching us. The image was not completely solid, and it disappeared all of a sudden. The face was cut up and bloody. We saw it for just a minute.

6. Partial body

In 24% (thirty of 123) of visual apparitions, a partial body was reported. This is only one way for an image to be incomplete; as we have already seen, other ways, for example, are being insubstantial or lacking full color. However, should we expect certain parts of the body to be missing more

---

55   The chi-square value for the 2x2 table is 8.1, $p<.01$. Generally speaking, parapsychologists have noticed that haunting cases act less "normal" than others, not only looking strange but acting self-preoccupied rather than acting concerned about the living people present (Tyrrell, 1963: 42).

often than others? As was noted in the famous Morton case (Bennett, 1939: 200), "The upper part of the figure always left a more distinct impression than the lower, but this may be partly due to the fact that one naturally looks at people's faces before their feet."

The idea that more important parts of the body should appear more often certainly fits the Chinese cases. Nine of the thirty partial-body reports involve the top half of the body only, but only two are bottom half only. G055 in this chapter illustrates the top-half type. Although the head might be left out because it is an attachment to the torso, it is certainly an important attachment. Indeed, seven are heads only, compared with four that are headless. G066 and G067 are both head-only examples, the first from a twenty-five-year-old woman and the second from a fifteen-year-old girl. By contrast, a fifty-seven-year-old man describes a headless ghost in G068.

G066. The Head at Stanley Beach

Seven or eight years ago, my husband and I were at Stanley Beach in Hong Kong at about 5 in the afternoon. We were about ten or fifteen feet away from some trees. Looking into the trees, we saw a head close to a tree, about eye level. It was a Chinese woman with short hair. It looked alive but had little expression. We both saw it and ran. It clearly had no body below it. It was looking our direction but took no notice of us.

G067. The Floating Head

Last year, at 12 midnight outside our apartment in the resettlement housing, I saw a head passing by the window with no neck and no body. It had long hair, and I couldn't see her face. It was going down the hallway, floating.

G068. The Headless Floater

I was eleven years old. As I passed by the entrance of a reservoir construction site [Shing Moon Reservoir] around 8 p.m., I saw a body with no head in a long white robe. I'm not sure about any hands or feet. It was floating by, going the same direction parallel to me, across the street. I turned around, very frightened, to yell for help. Several people came by, but they couldn't find anything.

As heads are more important than feet, there ought to be more footless ghosts than headless ones; this is barely so, five to four. But at least there are none with feet alone, in contrast to seven with heads only. Of course, the eight bottomless and two topless ghosts mentioned above are also footless and headless respectively. Case G069, which a woman called in to me on a radio program in Hong Kong, is a footless example.

G069. Footless Soldiers

One night, I was awakened by my dog, whose hair was standing on end. When I looked out the window. I saw a whole group of soldiers, but I couldn't see their feet. It was cloudy around their feet. They wore khaki uniforms and had long guns. I saw their backs, but I think they were English. I noticed a man walking by, and I asked him later about the soldiers, but he hadn't seen them!

Another extremity, the hand, is the only part of the body present in four reports, and in three the hands in particular are missing. Hands that are idle would seem more likely not to be included, but hands can also be centers of focus when active. The next case, reported by a fourteen-year-old girl, involves a hand by itself.

G070. The Hand from the Streetcar

I always take a tram with my friend to Central District. One day, when the tram was someplace in Central District, I saw a hand projecting out from the end part of the tram, which was going the opposite direction. After that, the tram left.

If the location of the hand projecting from the streetcar seems bizarre, note the similarity to a British case in Bennett (1939: 115): a face was looking around a bookcase, " 'But it had an odd appearance as if the body were in the bookcase.' " Eventually, the body seemed to " 'rotate out of the end of the bookcase.' " If ghosts can walk in and out of walls, they can be seen partly jutting out as well.

For another strange hand effect, recall G036 in Chapter 5, in which a hand seems to help pull up the blanket, while a figure stands farther away, independent of the hand. A fourteen-year-old girl reports a similarly unconnected part of a hand in association with a human figure in G071.

G071. The Ghost with Five Fingers [56]

I was in the classroom studying when I heard and saw somebody knocking or tapping on the classroom door. It was five fingers without a hand. Then I saw the fingers and something like a white cloth or a woman in a long robe move away. I was the only one there. I screamed. I didn't leave the room, just waited until class.

It occurred to me that partial-body apparitions might represent a stage of half-disappearance, as in an intriguing British report from Bennett (1939: 316): " ' He slowly vanished until only his shoulders and face were left and then only the face and then the top of the head and then he was gone. ' " However, not one of the Chinese cases refers to part of the body disappearing before another part. Nor are the fading apparitions any more likely to involve partial bodies than are nonfading apparitions in this sample of cases. [57]

---

56 Apparitions of a single hand without a body remind me of the motif of the "hand monster" in popular culture, such as the film *The Beast with Five Fingers*, in which a horrified Peter Lorre keeps saying, "The hand, the hand!"

57 However, the number of fading apparitions in the sample is too small to draw any conclusions. One of four is a partial-body case, or 25%, compared with

7. Abnormal walking

In 13% of visual apparitions, the ghost engaged in "abnormal walking" –
that is, it floated, darted too fast, "glided rather than walked" (as Bennett,
1939: 61, described one British case), or (in G008 in Chapter 1) jumped
strangely. However, in another 35% of the visuals, the respondent
specifically stated that the apparition was not moving. Therefore,
abnormal walking is even more common than 13% among the moving
ones taken separately.

G072, reported by a twenty-four-year-old man, is the only case that
links abnormal walking to a lack of feet. [58]

G072. A Man upon the Stair

Around ten years ago, I was living in a very old building built
before the Second World War. It's been torn down now. I was
going down the public stairwell at 4 o'clock one morning, but it
was not that dark. I could vividly see the back of a ghost. It was
a man with medium-length hair, wearing a checker-like shirt and
gray pants. He clearly had no feet. The figure glided down the
stairs. I didn't think about getting scared then. I saw it for a few
seconds, going down three or four steps, and then it disappeared
all of a sudden. I looked at his feet since he was gliding so funny;
he had hone. There was no one else around.

Next, an eighteen-year-old woman describes a floating ghost that might
not have had feet visible because of the long robe (which, by the way, is
unusually seen as red instead of white or black).

24% of nonfading ones (twenty-nine of 119). There is no relationship between
disappearing and partials either.

58   One might expect that partial-body ghosts would be more likely than
others to walk abnormally. However, of thirteen partials that had the upper torso
present but were missing at least the feet if not everything below the waist, only
one walked abnormally, although eight more were not moving.

G073. The Girl in Red

One night, we stayed at school for a barbecue. I had to go to the bathroom.... So a few (three or so) students went to the toilet. That night was very windy. We went to a covered playground. The big fan-like iron gate shut by itself. We didn't pay much attention and continued to go on. Near the wall of the playground there are a lot of long benches. We saw a young girl sitting on one of them. We thought she was a classmate; but she was wearing a long red robe, and she smiled at us and followed us. We were scared and ran off. She was floating and not walking. When we turned to look, she disappeared. She looked like a normal person but floated and didn't walk.

In G074, a sixteen-year-old girl describes the floating glide walk somewhat differently, although it may be the same as the others.

G074. "Flying" in the Typhoon

On one rainy and windy night when I was little, I couldn't sleep because the typhoon was attacking. Through the window I saw a person in white clothing and white hat. I thought it was very strange that somebody could stand in the parking lot in heavy wind and rain. He stood there for a while without moving at all. I continued to watch and didn't rest. But my eyes could only see his back. I was very scared. When he turned around to look, I didn't dare to look [stare] any more. But he could walk very fast. When he walked, it seemed like he didn't use his feet. It seemed like he was flying, and he disappeared quickly. I was very afraid.

For comparison, notice not a person floating along the ground but just a floating hand in the next report from a seventeen-year-old boy. If he had seen the entire body, perhaps the hand would have appeared to be in normal motion.

G075. The Floating Hand

A year ago, in my old house at night, I turned around and saw a hand. It was floating up from the floor to the wall and then disappeared. This took a couple of seconds. There was nobody else there. It was in my bedroom.

8. Abnormal sound

So far, all seven of the "abnormal features of perception" have been visual abnormalities. None of the Chinese cases involves taste, and neither of the two olfactory ones "smelled funny." Tactile ones are generally peculiar, as we have already seen, in that the receiver of the apparition is rarely able to touch the ghost normally (cf. the disintegration of the image in G052 earlier in this chapter). [59]

Now, however, let us focus on auditory abnormalities. One problem is that many visual apparitions are accompanied by either no sound or too faint a sound when normally they should be heard if their activity were physically real. In a British case (Bennett, 1939: 266), the ghost of one man "took great strides though perfectly noiseless." On the "Kirsty Hamilton Show," a radio program in Hong Kong, a woman called in to tell me that she was first alerted to the fact that a vicar walking by her was a ghost by the way his footsteps made no echo when they should have.

In other cases, a voice is "heard" in such a way that the receiver of the apparition suspects that it is not there in reality. One report to Bennett (1939: 76) described it this way, " 'The voice was not like ... any voice I have ever heard; it seemed to sing through my head.' "

Among the Chinese reports, 17% (eight of forty-seven) of the auditory cases involve abnormal sound. One is partly soundless, two are unclear, two "sound funny," one is too sustained for a human voice, and two are the unreal, ESP type just described. A thirteen-year-old girl reports what appears to be an ESP voice in case G076.

---

59   Also recall G001 in Chapter 1, in which the ghost abnormally "touched" the respondent, by floating up through his body.

G076. Balcony Leaper

We have a big house. To go to the study room from the bathroom, you have to pass the balcony. At night a few months ago, I was studying and went by the balcony to go to the bathroom. There on the balcony I saw a figure with long hair in a white robe, with its back to me, facing the street. I was very afraid and screamed. The ghost jumped downstairs from the balcony right after I yelled. My mother and I went and looked down and saw nothing there. It was very dark so I couldn't see any other details. The figure seemed to look normal. I think I may have heard a male voice say, "Don't be afraid," but I think I may have been thinking it to myself.

Sometimes, the apparition itself does not appear to have an ESP voice, but the receiver tries to communicate back telepathically, as did the woman in G077, who is well known in Hong Kong as a healer (partly through psychic means).

G077. Night Voices

One time I went to Manila to help heal a man in a Fukienese [regional language group in China] family I knew. The first night in my room, I heard a man say to me angrily in Cantonese, "What are you doing here?" I closed my eyes and kept them closed, and answered *in my heart*, "I'm here to help cure so-and-so. If you're a good man, you'll help give me the power. Thank you, I'm tired now. Good night." Something like that. The next night I heard three men discussing something in my room, the man from the previous night and two others. They were speaking in a language I didn't know, maybe Tagalog [the standard language of the Philippines]. I kept my eyes closed again, so I experienced only the sound of the talking both times. The neighbors told me that the house was haunted. The family had heard things too. [60]

In conclusion, we have looked at eight abnormal features of perception: disappearing or fading out, insubstantial image, glowing, white and dark clothing, sickly look, partial body, abnormal walking, and abnormal sound. None of these occurs in a majority of cases, but 87% of visual apparitions (1071 of 123) have at least one of the first seven. If ones that only disappear or are gone after the receiver opens his or her eyes again are eliminated, on the grounds that they are normal while they last, then 74% (ninety-one of 123) are still "abnormal." Therefore, the abnormal is normal for Chinese visual apparitions. I do not know what percentage of British or American apparitions are abnormal, but I have already shown that all of the eight features described here have been found in at least some Western reports. Moreover, these abnormalities are all congruent with the ESP theory of apparitions, as it is to be expected that ESP messages will not always be as realistic as regular, sensory ones.

Not only are apparitions often lacking in sensory realism, but they are typically incomplete in other ways as well. We have already noted in Chapter 5 that it is unusual for more than one sense (such as visual plus auditory) to be involved. Louisa E. Rhine (1962) has also discovered that apparitions tend to be even less "complete" than other forms of ESP experience – that is, to communicate less information content about the situations that generated them. When the causal situation could later be identified, such as the death of a relative, only 32% of "hallucinations" (apparitions) carried complete information, compared with 55% of intuitive ESP experiences, 72% of unrealistic ESP dreams, and 91% of realistic ESP dreams (Rhine, 1962: 93). Interestingly, visual apparitions

---

60   An American once told me that he tried to exorcise the spirit of a boy who had drowned when the family had lived in the house by just thinking in his mind what he wanted to say. When he felt the boy's presence, he told him telepathically that his family was no longer in the house and that he should go over "to the other side." The presence was not felt after that.

were least likely to be complete (17%), auditory ones better (33%), and apparitions with both of these senses a very high 84% (Rhine, 1962: 102, 103). On the other hand, it was common for the person to create a meaning through "secondary rationalization" in Rhine's cases; for example, seeing the ghost of a relative might be interpreted as a bad omen, later linked to the news that the relative had died at that moment.

Up to now, I have been careful to use only firsthand ghost reports in testing the ESP theory (although I have mentioned a few hearsay reports in passing). And, so far, I have found that these reports have the same characteristics as Western ghost reports, except for certain cultural differences, especially involving ancestor worship. Even the ancestor-worship cases turn out not to contradict the ESP theory. In Chapter 8, however, we shall depart from the firsthand reports in order to examine hearsay, folklore, and popular culture – and discover a different result.

8

Ghost Lore and Popular Culture

2017: This chapter is a side-light in the sense that it is off the main topic of what ghost experiences are actually like. Nevertheless folklore and popular culture are important in the sense that they represent cultural expectations. The fact that the first-hand ghost experiences do not conform to these expectations in their basic content (especially, they very seldom contain physical effects attached to the apparitions themselves) supports the experiential-source theory.

Also, there are good reasons for studying rumors, folklore, and media representations, if you want to understand the culture and social processes connected to ghosts. Most of the material I have been able to collect on Chinese ghosts since 1980 falls into these categories, as you will see in chapter 13.

When does a ghost report become a ghost story? By my standard, a ghost report must be directly reported by the person who had the experience to a competent researcher who records it. Once it passes through even one extra person before being recorded, it becomes folklore, even if no fraud or exaggeration is intended. Of course, ghost stories can also be fictional, written by authors who make then part of popular culture, standardizing them in print, film, or tape, whether the ideas come originally from their own minds or from an earlier folklore version.

Tyrrell (1963: 89, 90) is dissatisfied with hearsay ghost stories, because they so often have fictitious elements in them. The giveaway in many of the stories is that they contain physical effects to "prove" that the ghost was really there, in violation of the nonphysical, ESP pattern found in the reliable firsthand reports. For the purpose of testing the evidence, the distinction between firsthand accounts and everything else is sufficient. However, there are important things to be learned about the culture of ghosts by looking further.

Folklore involves cultural materials that are spread orally rather than in some standardized form like writing (Brunvand, 1968: 3-5). If a ghost story, for example, is spread by word of mouth, even among only a few people, it is folklore. Specifically, it will be a "legend" if it is told as if it were true, but a "folktale" if it is *meant* to be fictitious. Although folklore is often considered part of popular culture, there are also *written* ghost stories (or filmed ones, etc.) in popular culture. If the written popular culture of ghosts is clearly labeled fiction, then there is nothing unethical about the fact that it is "fictitious," although it may help to create an erroneous popular conception about the nature of the ghost experience.

Tyrrell explains the fictitious elements in ghost lore and popular culture as a way of making the story seem more realistic (for example, the ghost leaves a ring behind as evidence). Stories may also be distorted or created to be more exciting. Folklorists and students of popular culture, however, would also expect such stories to reflect certain "motifs," themes that are common in the culture.

Therefore, studying the stories should tell us something about the society that has molded them. And since we have already established (in Chapters 5-7) the existence of a common pattern for both Chinese and Western ghost reports, any marked differences between the reports and the stories will further underline the fact that culture has not been responsible for the peculiar nature and consistency of the reports.

Ghosts in Chinese and Western folklore

It is my general impression that ghosts have been more malevolent and horrible, although not necessarily more inclined to produce physical effects, in Chinese than in European and American folklore. As there are no random samples of Chinese and Western ghost lore to make a completely valid comparison, there can be no proof given for my impression. A comparison of folklore motifs (themes) about ghosts from the different cultures collected in Stith Thompson's (1966) *Motif-Index of Folk Literature* [61] shows remarkable similarity and universality of motifs, but it can not tell how frequently each motif is used in each culture.

Both Chinese and Western examples are given for malevolent and for friendly returns from the dead, loaded with physical effects all around (Thompson, 1966). Some malevolent returns are the fatal kiss from the dead and the slap of the cheating son's face (both Western) and the avenging ghost of an unjustly executed man and the ghost sucking people's breath (both Chinese). Two friendly ones are the dead mother returning to suckle her child, and a ghost returning from the dead to give counsel (both are Western *and* Chinese).

Although the Thompson index has insufficient Chinese examples to illustrate the point, surely the major cultural difference between Western and Chinese ghost lore revolves around the importance of ancestor worship in Chinese culture. In the context of ancestor-worship beliefs, visits from the dead are mainly unwelcome (cf. Chapter 3). Whereas the distinct minority of Westerners who believe in ghosts may be curious or even thrilled to contact the ghosts of their relatives, most Chinese are afraid that even their ancestors' ghosts will be upset about some failure on the part of the worshipers. And the really evil demons are to be avoided at all costs. The Hungry Ghost Festival, for example, has no serious counterpart in most modern Western societies, now that Halloween has become a juvenile junk-food celebration.

---

61   The main relevant motifs in the index are found listed under "ghosts" (E200-E599 in the index numbers) and "soul" (E700-E790).

This may make Chinese folklore ghosts more frequently malevolent, but in both cultures it is interesting to note the wide range of rewarding and punishing behaviors engaged in according to the motif index. It becomes apparent that folklore ghosts spend much of their time acting as supernatural agents of social control. [62] Having the capacity to perform physical effects makes them more convincing moral agents in the folklore. They punish deceitful sweethearts, spouses, and kin; accuse or kill their murderers; and guard buried treasures or prevent thefts. As grateful dead, they reward those who have buried them properly; they honor the brave; and they pay howdy calls to their deserving relatives. This is not to deny that many of the motifs are associated with random mischief or scary effects, but apparently the moral values of the culture have significant influence on the activities of folklore ghosts.

Ghosts in popular culture

Not all of the written forms of popular culture about ghosts stress social control, but a group of American ghost comics I collected in 1979 certainly does. [63] In a total of fourteen stories in six comic books, all fourteen involved moral justice in the outcome, all fourteen were malevolent or conflict-oriented (although in one the conflict was resolved at the end, and the ghost saved the life of his rival), and eight had the ghost performing some physical effect.

To illustrate, in "Music from the Grave" (Western Publishing, 1979, #53), a phony psychic composer writes a piece supposedly inspired by the

---

62   Cf. the section on "Unhappy and evil spirits" in Chapter 3.

63   I collected all of the comic books that had ghost stories in them and that were available at a local store over a six-month period. There were three issues of Grimm's Ghost Stories (Western Publishing, 1979) containing ten total ghost stories, two issues of Ghosts: New Tales of the Supernatural (DC Comics, 1979) with two relevant stories, and one issue of Ghost Manor (Charlton Publications, 1979) with two. Although all three comics were from different publishers, they were remarkably alike and apparently represented the same genre. Two other comics, the humorous type (to be discussed shortly in the text), were of a clearly different genre: Richie Rich and Casper the Friendly Ghost (Harvey Publications, 1979a) and Spooky (Harvey Publications, 1979b).

ghost of Beethoven. Beethoven himself returns at the opening concert and brings down the chandelier, which lands on the perpetrator of the fraud and kills him.

There is another comic-book ghost genre, of which Casper the Friendly Ghost is the best known. Casper (Harvey Publications, 1979a, #30) floats and flies and does minor physical effects; he can dive into the ground but gets grabbed by a wizard who confines him under "ghost-proof" glass. This magical, fantasy adventure is neither moralistic nor malevolent. It is, instead, humorous. Spooky (Harvey Publications, 1979b, #160) floats and flies like Casper but wears a normal hat. Like Casper, he also performs physical effects (such as blowing a whistle) and gets hit and stepped on. Although Spooky loves to scare people, he obviously fits the humorous genre as well.

Humorous, as opposed to malevolent and moralistic ghosts are also found in some children's books. The back cover of the *Arrow Book of Ghost Stories* (Kramer, 1960) says that they are "just scary enough," which is hardly at all. Even the story of "Spook's Bones" (Kramer, 1960: 78-95),in which the ghost tells two kids where his bones were buried after he was murdered, sounds grim in synopsis but is given very light treatment. Another book, *McBroom's Ghost* (Fleischman, 1971), is a humorous tall tale, in which the ghosts turn out to be frozen sounds (the winter was so cold that ...).

Ghosts in some of the popular literature in Hong Kong tend to be presented for shock value more than for morality or humor. Even in humorous comics, they look horrible, not cuddly like Casper. There is also a ghost genre of cheap pulps for adults, containing short stories in which the most common motif is sexual intercourse between a living male and a female ghost who appears real, even beautiful, at least on the night before the morning after.

In Hong Kong films of recent vintage, ghosts are given a farcical treatment, but as in the Chinese comics, they are made to look horrible. I have seen four of them in the past five years, all of them thoroughly delightful, in spite of the low prestige of most Cantonese films among the Chinese. They abound in physical effects: a cart pulled by an invisible ghost (in "Lantern Festival Adventure"); a ghost lifting the lid off his own coffin (in "Sensual Pleasures"); and a half-beautiful, half-ghastly ghost pulling a terrified man into the mirror with her long, rubbery arm (in "Close Encounters of the Spooky Kind"). [64]

On Hong Kong television in the fall of 1980, there was a weeknight soap opera called "Look for Something Precious," about a family possessed by four people who had died in the same apartment. In addition to speaking and acting strangely through the living persons, the invisible ghosts perform a few violent acts, like shoving people around and moving roller skates into their paths. The old father of the family prays and burns incense to the spirits, asking them to cool it. Although the ghosts are never seen, their acts are clearly malevolent. As in the Hong Kong films and comics, however, what sounds scary is actually treated humorously.

People in Hong Kong are also exposed to Western films about the occult, the ghosts in which have been neither benevolent nor humorous in recent years. Two examples are "The Amityville Horror" and "Full Circle." In the latter, a 1978 Anglo-Canadian film starring Mia Farrow, which played in Hong Kong in the fall of 1980, three apparently accidental deaths are in fact engineered by the spirit of a young girl. In the final scene, the apparition directly murders a woman by cutting her jugular vein with the cymbals on a clown doll. As far as the social control or moral justice theme is concerned, this film contains a bizarre sort of justice, in that the situation comes "full circle": the woman killed by the girl's ghost at the end had killed her own similar-looking daughter at the beginning of the film by cutting her windpipe in a vain attempt to save her from choking to death on a piece of apple.

---

64 This film, produced by David Chow and released in 1980, is a tour de force. The Chinese title, *Guai Da Guai*, means "Ghost Hits Ghost." It is a hilarious mixture of ghosts, zombies, Taoist magic and witchcraft, ESP, psychokinesis, and kung fu.

Hong Kong: rumors of ghosts

So far in this chapter, we have looked at ghosts in recent popular culture and in the accumulated folk tradition. Now we will focus on more recent folklore, legends of ghosts in Hong Kong. Even a rumor about ghosts that has traveled through just a few people would be classified as a "legend," if it is supposed to be true, as opposed to a "folktale," told as knowingly false. Probably some of these legends represent actual experiences, at least to a degree, but they cannot be assigned the same level of plausibility as the firsthand reports. It will become apparent that they are closer to the other folklore and to the popular culture, especially in their emphasis on malevolence and on physical effects.

1. Japanese-occupation ghosts

The cause to which more Hong Kong ghost stories are attributed than to any other is the occupation of the colony by the Japanese in World War II. Countless buildings are reputed to have been interrogation centers where hundreds of Chinese were allegedly executed by their Japanese captors. One unfortunate function of the ghost lore about these buildings is that it seems to support anti-Japanese prejudice even today. Of course, it is also plausible that many hauntings should arise from such violent deaths.

Some of the newspaper reporting about such cases appears to be quite responsible, but it is often difficult to separate firsthand reports from hearsay evidence. One major case is the alleged haunting of the officers' mess at Stanley Fort on the south side of Hong Kong Island. Although the Japanese occupied the fort only briefly during the war, one uniformed figure has been identified as possibly Japanese (*Hong Kong Star*, 1977b; Greeley, 1977; Sin, 1977). Several apparently reliable witnesses have seen this and perhaps a different apparition as well on the premises.

Except for a medicine bottle that fell on the floor close to one apparition (Sin, 1977), there is little on the face of it that makes the case suspicious. However, it does have two features common in so many of Hong Kong's ghost legends: the Japanese-occupation motif and the claim that they can't keep amahs (female servants) because the place is haunted (*Hong Kong Standard*, 1977).

2. Hospital ghosts

If Japanese-occupied buildings are the most popular location for ghosts in Hong Kong, then hospitals, also scenes of suffering and death, are probably in second place. One such hospital case hit the Chinese-language newspapers in 1980 (*Tin Tin Daily News*, 1980: 1). In translation, this is an excerpt:

Both incidents happened on the seventh floor E, sixth building private maternity ward across from the kitchen. That morning, after midnight, one female worker was in the kitchen doing dishes, and she heard a lot of noise in the hallway. She thought it was strange to have so many people talking at that time of the night. She went out into the hallway and saw nothing there. After returning to the kitchen she heard the noises again. She went out again, and again there was nothing. So she thought maybe there were ghosts, and she got very scared and wanted to run, but her feet were glued to the floor and she felt faint and couldn't move. She screamed and passed out. The nurse on duty heard her scream and woke her up, but after she learned what had happened, the nurse saw nobody in the hallway.

Ten days later, last Thursday night, the eleventh, another strange incident occurred. Another woman was washing dishes. When she went out to go to the bathroom, she saw a woman in white looking out the window. She thought it might be some patient who couldn't sleep, and she decided to talk her into going back to bed. Before she could open her mouth, however, this woman in white turned around. She saw a face with ... no eyeballs, and two very deep black holes. It was so horrible that she screamed and passed out.

Other workers claim to have seen ghosts all the time... .

The newspaper article also stated that the hospital tried to suppress the incidents on the grounds that they might have an effect on the patients. However, I received apparently good cooperation from the medical superintendent of the hospital when I called to verify the story. He told me that there was perhaps some distortion in the press. He had asked someone to interview one woman involved, who said that she had felt overworked and experienced a dizzy spell. She then told another amah, who told the story in an exaggerated form. There had been a long list of ghost stories, in fact, that had never been proved for lack of a proper account. He had not been able to discover who the other worker in the newspaper account was, but he offered to try to set up a telephone interview between my wife and the one worker. A few days later, he called back to say that the worker did not wish to be interviewed. After the newspaper article, she had been approached by many people, but now she was fed up with the whole affair. He could not tell whether she thought she had seen a ghost or not; she was now clamming up.

Twelve days after the newspaper story, one of the respondents on the telephone survey, a twenty-four-year-old woman, claimed to have had a ghost experience on the same floor of the same hospital! As it was so shortly after the publicity, we suspected that she might have been influenced by it.

G078. The Hospital Haunt

I went to Repulse Bay with two friends for a barbecue once when I was fourteen years old. One of my friends got her face burned by the fire. I had to take her to _____ Hospital. The two of us had to go up to the third floor, and we pressed the button, but the elevator went up to the seventh floor. It was 11 p.m., and the hallway was somewhat dark. It was light but not bright, and it was raining. At the end of the hallway, we saw a person sitting there, with the back facing us. The hair was straight and of medium length. I don't know whether it was male or female; I couldn't see the person very well. When we were about forty-five feet away, the person disappeared instantly. Just the chair was left. We both saw it and ran back downstairs.

3. Cinema lore

Another common type of ghost story in Hong Kong is the movie-theater-bathroom ghost. One reason for its popularity is probably the anxiety children in particular have over going to bathrooms in public places, sometimes with good reason because of the natural beings that may lurk there. On the other hand, there is one prominent theater haunting that may have had some kernel of truth in its legend.

In the Wanchai district of Hong Kong Island, there used to be a movie house, the East Town Cinema, on the site of what was previously the National Funeral Parlour. Now that the theater has been demolished, there are still reports of hauntings in the office building that has taken its place (*Hong Kong Star*, 1978).

Although the theater has not been there for many years, its ghost stories are still well known. Women had supposedly seen partial-body ghosts in the bathroom or would start screaming when thinking that they had been locked in, only to have others run and open the door easily (Greeley, 1977).

On Hong Kong television channel TVB, the popular evening variety show "Enjoy Yourself Tonight" [65] presented a portrayal of the East Town Cinema haunting, saying that the theater had closed because of the ghosts. A man with a gift certificate asks for a seat, but everywhere he sits, he turns to see that someone has appeared next to him. Unnerved, he keeps changing his seat. Certainly, this is a peculiar type of apparition!

Three days later, according to the show, two young hooligans introduce themselves to a pretty girl standing in line, then go sit with her. At one point, the girl asks one boy if he'd like to follow her to the bathroom. A couple working at the box office notice the pair going into the women's room but let them alone. Then we see that the boy has been locked in the

---

65   The program was aired on July 17, 1980, at 9 p.m.

bathroom, looking in horror at the girl, who is standing there with no facial features on her head and holding her hair in her hand.

At the end of the program, they give a disclaimer, claiming to have made it all up. I suppose that this was to avoid being held accountable for the accuracy of anything in particular, and they may have added their own dramatization to whatever stories they collected. Notice, however, that the theme of getting locked or apparently locked in the women's bathroom is found here as well as in the newspaper article I mentioned previously. About three months after the program, I received the following version of apparently the same legend from a high-school student.

> Several years ago, there was a cinema situated at Wanchai... Before demolition, people insisted on saying that cinema was haunted. Once a man sat behind a beautiful, charming lady. That lady left her seat, and the man followed and entered the ladies' [room]. Suddenly, men from outside heard some screams and yelling for help from the toilet. They rushed in and discovered a man [sitting] near the door. There was no one [there] except him. He trembled with fear. His face turned pale, and [he] became insane.... After that incident, no one dared to enter except those brave men.

4. Thespian lore

Live theater has its ghost lore as well. One actress reported getting a sore back after playing a ghost (*Tin Tin Daily News*, 1980a). The next time she played one, she pulled a leg muscle. Although they gave her a lucky-money envelope, they waited until *after* she had acted the part! Again malevolence and physical effects, although no apparition was involved.

In another newspaper story (*Ming Pao Weekly*, 1980), a movie star told the following about her mother, who had been an actress in Chinese opera. Once, she received an advance of money to perform. The next day, the real money had turned into hell bank notes. [66] They decided to perform anyway. As a precaution, however, they covered themselves up with a red cloth when putting on their makeup and costumes so that the ghosts wouldn't know how they had put them on and couldn't copy them. The next day after the performance, all the performers found themselves lying in a cemetery for unidentified bodies.

Certainly, nothing like this was reported in the firsthand accounts. However, a similar incident supposedly occurred in the late eighteenth century to the Pao Ho Pan, the premier theatrical troupe of Peking (Willoughby-Meade, 1926: 20, 21), which suggests the existence of a folklore motif, which might have originated from the legend of the Pao Ho Pan. The troupe, so the story goes, was asked to perform at a house outside Peking. When they arrived, they were asked to perform romantic pieces only, not to impersonate good spirits and not to make too much noise. Although they acted and sang from midnight until dawn, they were given no intermission or refreshments. Moreover, the audience behaved peculiarly, speaking only in hushed, unintelligible whispers. In anger, the actors brought out an imitation of a popular god making quite a racket. "Immediately the place went dark and the audience vanished. The players found themselves in a thicket before a tomb..." (Willoughby-Meade, 1926: 21).

5. Water ghosts

Sometimes, when people were asked about "water monsters" (sea monsters) on the telephone survey, they thought for a moment that the question was about "water ghosts," as the words for monster and ghost sound similar in Cantonese. Here is a case of the latter reported in the press (*China Mail*, 1965). On March 6, 1965, four persons were drowned when their junk sank near the village of Ngau Sze Fu. During the recovery attempt, the bodies were found supposedly glued to the rocks, making it

---

66   Hell bank notes are the ritual paper currency that is burned for the spirits during the Hungry Ghost Festival.

impossible to bring them in until ritual burning of incense and paper got the bodies to float to the surface.

After that, the evil spirits even came ashore to wander about the village and to knock loudly on people's doors. Perhaps, the real water ghosts causing the difficulty were thought to be people who had been killed by the Japanese in that area during the attack in December 1941, because other boats before 1965 were allegedly wrecked on the rocks in mysterious ways. At any rate, the event in 1965 caused seven fishing families to evacuate their homes in fear. Again, we have dangerous physical effects, this time fatal, attributed to ghosts, although without any apparitions caught in the act.

6. Rumor and extortion

In this case, the ghost legend turned out to be a rumor artificially caused and manipulated for profit (*Hong Kong Star*, 1980: 4). Within one year, a new planned-community resettlement area in the New Territories part of Hong Kong had experienced three suicide incidents; a man hanging himself; a man jumping out of a building; a pregnant woman killing her young son and daughter with a chopper, then killing herself. Residents then reported seeing a woman in red floating around, her horrifying face covered with blood. After midnight, people were afraid to walk by the building where the apparition had been sighted. Residents of the building even heard terrible screams in the middle of the night. Some of the older people were supposed to have spread the rumors most actively.

Before long, some young men began soliciting donations to exorcise the spirit, complaining if residents gave small amounts. Even with an average donation of one or two dollars (U.S.), there were so many households that a sizable sum of money was collected.

A few days later, a crowd gathered to watch an exorcism club exorcising spirits in the lobby. Afterward, however, noises were still heard in the building. One rainy night, two policemen making the rounds heard horrifying screams and saw some shadows in the first-floor hallway. They closed in, one with a flashlight, the other with a gun. There they found two young men in T-shirts and jeans with a small tape recorder playing scream noises. Under interrogation, the two young men admitted responsibility for the ghost noises, which they had staged in order to be able to collect money for exorcisms.

After that, nobody heard any more screaming ghosts, according to the newspaper. However, in this case as in several of the others, there might have been a genuine haunting that provided the original spark.

7. "Thrown on the bed and choked"

Although the last example involved actual fraud, I do not mean to suggest that there is always or even usually any conscious distortion in the telling of ghost stories. It is, nevertheless, easy for a ghost report to turn into a ghost story as it is filtered through the teller's subconscious motivations and shared cultural expectations. I had a rare opportunity to see an example of this process in an individual who is a dear friend of mine. She would certainly not intentionally distort the accounts she gave me, nor do they seem unusual as ghost reports go, except in one crucial detail, as you will see.

In the first account, my friend, a British woman living in Hong Kong, told me that she had known a doctor friend who had a house on Broadwood Road in Hong Kong. The servants and family said that they had seen the ghost of a Chinese man in a long white robe with a scraggly white beard looking into the house. They had also seen him under a banana tree on the property. The doctor scoffed at these claims until one day when he answered the doorbell and there was no one there, but a cold wind rushed past him. Later, in his room, something threw him on the bed and choked him.

At that point, he decided to sell the house, and they moved out. My friend was in her teens when this happened. Some years later, she moved into a house around the corner, which was also close to a graveyard. One day, her son said, "Mommy, see that man sitting on the lowest branch of that tree?" She said no. Only her son saw him. "He's Chinese and has a white robe and a scraggly white beard. I don't like him. He beckons

to me with his finger." She told her son not to go to him. "I won't," the
son replied, "because I don't like him." He saw him at other times, too.
Neighbors in that area still say that the neighborhood is haunted and give
the same description of the ghost.

Then my friend told me another account about two nurses who saw an
advertisement for a job at an attractive salary looking after an old man on
his estate. As they were friends, they flipped a coin to decide who would
apply. The winner got the position, but after two days on the job wrote
the loser to say that she could have the job if she wanted it. Their trains
crossed, and the two never saw each other. The woman of the house told
the second nurse that she was happy she had come, because it was so
lonely there that they couldn't keep anyone. [67]

One night, in the nurse's room, it kept getting colder and colder,
although there was a blazing fire going. Then she saw a shadowy hooded
figure in the corner of the room. It came closer and closer, then "threw
her on the bed and choked her." At this point, my friend stopped and
said that this was just like what a man on the radio had called in to tell me
when I had appeared on the "Kirsty Hamilton Show" to talk about my
ghost research: that he had been "thrown on the bed [and choked]."

In fact, the man on the call-in program, which I had taped, did *not*
say that he had been thrown, but only that he had felt pressure on top
of him while he was lying in bed. Although this may also sound like a
physical effect, or at least a tactile apparition, we shall see differently in
Chapter 11. The important point here is that I had witnessed the folklore
process in action. Without intention to distort, my friend had changed
the feeling of pressure into being "thrown on the bed." May we not also
suspect that "thrown on the bed and choked" was added to the other two
accounts she told me as well? This is crucial, as we already know, because
of the way physical effects linked to apparitions are hard to reconcile with
the ESP theory of ghosts.

---

67   Here is the common folklore and popular-culture motif of not being able
to keep servants in a haunted house, which could also be true in some instances,
of course.

8. The phantom soft-drink salesperson

Following the idea that it does not take very many steps to turn a report into a story, notice the earmarks of the folklore ghost with physical effects and malevolence that appear in this secondhand story I collected from a high-school student.

> Once, two of my friends went camping. Their destination was Cheung Shan ... in Sai Kung.... At about 12 o'clock, they came to the [foot] of the hill, but their campsite was just behind the hill, so they had to go [up] the "sky-ladder." When they were walking, they saw some weak yellow light near the top of the hill. Although they [felt something strange was going on, they continued on] their way. Soon, they went near... the top and saw an old woman sitting alongside of the yellow light... At the same time, they felt thirsty, and the water they brought along with them had already [been] used up. Then the old woman asked them whether they wanted to buy some soft drink or not.... Each of them [bought] one. After drinking, they intended to buy some more for reserve, but when they turned around, the old woman [had] disappeared. Both of them felt a little bit afraid and quickly left the place. When they went near the campsite, they felt uncomfortable, and their friends discovered that their faces were pale in color. After a while, the two boys vomited some watery fluid that [was] like the color of mud.

I have several reports of apparitions while camping out. Camping may be seen either as a common way of getting outside to be in the right place to see ghosts, or as a culturally defined situation in which "Nervous Nellies" imagine a lot of ghosts. At any rate, a case of two boys getting sick on contaminated soft drinks might turn into a ghost story as we get the impression that the old woman disappeared paranormally (which is not clear) and that the vomiting was of some strange fluid (which is not certain either).

9. Getting pushed in front of cars

Such hearsay cases, or "short-distance" legends, in Hong Kong ghost lore seem to emphasize unhealthy and dangerous effects. One type that I heard more than once has to do with ghosts pushing people in front of cars. It is important to remember that not a single person reported any such dangerous physical effect to his or her *own* person. Remember that the most serious "injury" claimed in the reports was merely a bruise on the leg that seemed to come from being hit there (case G050 in Chapter 6), and even then there was no visual apparition involved. The only two visual apparitions directly linked to a physical effect were the push onto the railroad tracks (G038 in Chapter 5) and the perhaps dubious push into the elevator (G037 in Chapter 5), neither of which resulted in injury.

Among the hearsay reports, however, one woman told me that her friend was mysteriously hit by a car while supposedly standing in a protected indentation at the side of the street. Although he was not badly hurt, he could not remember or explain what had happened. The driver said that he had run out from another house, but that did not seem likely. Therefore, they think that maybe he was pushed by a ghost. There is little clear evidence for what really happened in this case, but the significant point to me is that ghosts are a convenient cultural explanation for sickness and injury that can be drawn upon to account for such situations among the Chinese in Hong Kong.

In another incident, a second-grade child and her amah were knocked down by a car in front of a primary school, resulting in cuts to the face of the girl and a trip to the hospital for the amah. Another little girl witnessed the accident, which she attributed to ghosts, since it happened during the Hungry Ghost Festival (*Yu Lan Jit*). Becoming almost hysterical over the incident, she told my wife that things like this happen in the "*Yu Nan Jit*" (the "Run-into-Disaster Festival," her mistaken version of the phrase "Yu Lan Jit").

This seven-year-old girl had already been afraid of ghosts, especially of the ghosts her friends told her could be found lurking in the bathroom at school. [68] In the past year at school, she had gone to the bathroom only twice, waiting to get home before going. After the accident, she took to wearing a Christian cross as an amulet. I have heard of situations of mass hysteria in Hong Kong schools in which crosses cropped up all over as ghost fear spread throughout the student body. [69]

To conclude this chapter, we have seen how the folklore and popular culture of ghosts differ from the firsthand ghost reports. Although there are some cultural differences in such lore between China and the West, of course, there are also many general themes that are universal, especially in their emphasis on malevolence (more than in the reports), moral justice or social control, horror as well as humor, and physical effects.

In some cases (especially in sections 6 and 7 here), we have even seen how some ghost stories are created through either fraudulent or innocent changes in ghost reports. The next chapter relates the rare experience I had in tracking a popular ghost legend to its source, which was, paradoxically, neither fraudulent nor innocent.

---

68 Recall the section on cinema lore in this chapter, which shows the fear of bathroom ghosts.

69 I have also run across other cases of fear of the psychic or occult in my research, as individuals come to me as if I were not merely a researcher but a psychic "counselor." I have tried to calm people down about their alleged out-of-body experiences, hauntings, and ominous predictions by fortune tellers and even by an apparition once. One woman in Hong Kong was very upset over what she was seeing in a secret religious meditation session, which she was not allowed to describe to me in detail. Apparently, her "visions" were merely caused by a kind of hypnotic suggestion.

9

ANATOMY OF A LEGEND

2017: This is a very interesting case that helps illustrate the social processes involved in rumor, and sometimes eventually folklore. It would be wonderful to have a collection of such investigations over the years to see if they reflect, for example, anxieties in Hong Kong running up to 1997, when Hong Kong returned to the People's Republic of China, and to see if they reflect a different mood today.

I had been in Hong Kong only two weeks working on this research in June 1980, when I began to hear about ghosts at a certain institution of higher learning, which I shall simply refer to as "the college." [70] Although there were a few other minor miscellaneous ghosts mentioned, one kept cropping up: "Have you heard about the. . . ?" they would say helpfully. Most people I talked to at the college seemed to have heard of it.

The first version came from a female student attending the college. Supposedly, a Professor X had seen the ghost of a student right after the student had committed suicide due to the grade on his exam. I was immediately intrigued and thought about requesting an interview with the professor, whom she identified by name and department. However, I was also afraid that the subject might be rather sensitive, even painful, if the professor felt somehow responsible for the student's death.

---

70 I see nothing embarrassing or unfavorably controversial in this case either for the college or for the individuals involved, but I would rather avoid using proper names just to be on the safe side.

As the weeks and months went by, I kept hearing about it occasionally but was never convinced to investigate until I met another student at the college in October who told me a much fuller version. Professor X, he said, was waiting for the elevator at the bottom of the Z Building. A man and a woman were there together, too. When the three of them went into the elevator, Professor X pressed the button for his floor and asked the others what their floor was. They said 12, but there were only ten floors in the building. They also said that they wanted to pick up their diplomas and graduation certificates. They did not press a button. In the elevator, he saw their faces turn color. He got out alone at his floor, but then saw them again outside the elevator coming toward the elevator! He got scared and went quickly down to the parking lot. By his car, he saw them again. Later on, he went to the Administration Building to check the college records, and found the woman's picture. She had committed suicide after failing his course, but he couldn't find the young man's picture.

The student who told me this version said that Professor X shouldn't mind talking to me about it because he was interested in ghosts and had told his class about the apparition. He himself had heard it from someone in that class.

Two days later, I had an appointment to see Professor X. I was filled with curiosity. Would this turn out to be a sensational case of the real thing or would he say there was nothing to the rumors? The answer turned out to be neither.

Professor X was very helpful. First, yes, he had told the story! Second, he had just made it up! Students had asked him to tell them the story, which he did three or four times, but never in class. As the rumor spread, one significant detail was lost: he had never claimed that it was true!

Actually, it was not a total fabrication. Early in 1980, Professor X had heard talk about an elevator in the Z Building not stopping at the right floor. There were also rumors of a woman or of a man and a woman being seen as apparitions after the woman had failed in her college work and committed suicide. The people from whom he heard these things had not taken them seriously, nor did he. However, Professor X thought that it would be nice to create a longer and more exciting fictional account, unlike most ghost stories, which are short and not very interesting. When he unveiled his version, he emphasized to the listeners that he was telling it in the first person just for effect, and that it was fictional.

At first, Professor X was reluctant to tell me his story. "Does it matter?" he asked. "It takes ten or fifteen minutes." I assured him that I was interested. Then, with a twinkle in his eye, he began to tell me the following entirely from memory.

Professor X's Ghost Story

One evening last December, a Saturday, around 8 or 9 o'clock, I drove back to the college and parked on the ground floor [car park]. I had come back to the office to fetch some papers to take home to work on that Sunday. I went to one of the three lifts [elevators] at the back. Usually, when the lift comes it rings and a green light flashes on and off. But there was no ringing that night, and the light flashed white. I was surprised, and thought it could be due to some electrical disorder.

So I went into the lift and pressed 7. I noticed that it was a bit chilly inside. One of the two fluorescent lights in the lift was not lit. The other was lit but dim white, whiter and dimmer than usual. Then the lift started to climb, but it stopped at 2.

It shouldn't, because once it starts up it can't be stopped from the outside, and you can get in only on the way down. So I was very surprised.

I was even more surprised to see a young man standing there (outside the lift), about twenty-five years of age. He was a thin young man, average height, dressed in a white shirt and trousers. He asked me, "Sir, does the lift go up to the twelfth floor?" I told him, "This building has only ten floors. Have you gone to the wrong building?" He replied, "That could be the case. Thank you." He did not come in, and the lift closed.

It kept going up. The temperature was even lower in the lift now, and I was shivering. I decided to change my mind and go home as quickly as possible; so I pressed 4 immediately, since I had just passed 3 and it would be the quickest way out. I left the lift immediately on the fourth floor. Then I went around to the other set of lifts, the two in front, to change the environment.

I found that one of the lifts was already open and waiting. The conditions were about the same (one light off, one on dim and white, and the chill). I pressed "Ground," trying to get out as quickly as possible. But it did not stop at the ground floor; it went all the way to LG2 (past lower ground one). When the doors opened, I saw the young man again, together with a young lady, also dressed all in white: white blouse and skirt.

They both looked very serious and seemed to be arguing about something. I tried to get out, ignoring them, but they both went in side by side very quickly, blocking the way. The girl quickly pressed 10, and the doors closed before I could get out. So with some disappointment, I pressed G again.

The two people started to argue. The girl said, "I never mentioned the twelfth floor. I only said the building has practically twelve floors, including the car parks." The young man replied, "O.K., O.K., don't complain. You see, I just came back from Vancouver an hour ago, after a car accident. I haven't completely collected myself yet. Could you please not complain any more?"

Then I noticed that the lift had passed G without stopping, so I uttered some meaningless words to show my surprise, like, "Ah, ah, why...?" The girl then said to me, "It's no use, Dr. X; the lift is not under your control tonight. I know you wish to go to the seventh floor, so let me press it for you." She did.

I was very surprised to find that she knew my name. Then I searched deep in my brain. Suddenly, in a flash I remembered that I had interviewed her at a Discontinuation Committee meeting, together with other members. When a student is asked to withdraw, this committee is the highest authority, a last chance for appeal, with the decision final.

I remembered that she was called Betty, but I couldn't remember her last name. I also remembered that her appeal had not been successful because of her poor performance in the interview.

So I said to her, "What have you been doing?" She said, "I stay in the hostel." I asked in surprise, "How could you manage to stay in a college hostel?" She said, "It's simple. In the past I lived in the corridor, but now, since the warden has been replaced by a single lady, I have moved to her quarters. I stay in her bedroom in the daytime, studying a little, which I'm fond of. At night I sleep in the sitting room. Sometimes I still come back to attend some lectures. I like to sit at the back in a vacant seat."

Then I further asked, "Are you trying to do something here tonight?" She said, "Yes, I'm going up to the tenth floor with my friend to fetch my personal file from the Students' Section." The Department for Student Records is on the tenth floor.

Then the lift stopped on the seventh floor, and I quickly moved out. I rushed into my office, panicking, trying to rest for a minute. In a moment, I fetched my papers and tried to leave. Then the telephone rang, unusual for that time. Reluctantly, I answered the call.

It was a woman's voice. She said hurriedly, " Hi, Dr. X. This is Betty. Could you come up to the tenth floor right away to help me open the door of the Students' Section?" I answered, trembling, "Well, I don't have the key. I don't think I could be of any help. Perhaps you had better try some other way." She said, "It's all right. Any key to the Z building will do. Please come up quickly."

I dared not answer her any more. I put the phone down, turned off the light, went out, and locked the door. I tried to get home, but this time I didn't dare take any lifts. So I took the staircase to go down. I walked step by step. My feet were really going down, but my mind felt that I was going up. When I estimated that it should be the fourth floor, I suddenly discovered that it was the tenth floor.

There I met the young man and the woman. From the layout, I could tell that it was the tenth floor. The fourth and tenth have similar layouts, but I was familiar with the building. The woman said, "Oh good. Please give me the key, Dr. X." When I gave her the key, it seemed that I was not under my own control. I followed them to turn the corner and stopped in front of the Students' Section. She used my office key to open the door without difficulty. Then she returned the bunch of keys to me, and they went into the room. I noticed that the keys were very cold, as cold as a can of beer just out of the refrigerator. This made my brain clearer. My senses seemed to come back to me. Then I found that I was really on the fourth floor. I was very surprised, but there was no time to think any further.

Then I didn't dare to take either the lift or the regular staircase, so I went to the emergency exit stairs at the back of the building. The stairs were much wider, and there was light coming in from the windows. I felt a bit fresher and walked down two floors to the second floor, which has a passage leading to the lily pond outside the building.

When I got to the lily pond, I sat on a rock to rest. I watched the stars in the sky, feeling that everything was back to normal. The air was fresh. Then I noticed that the couple had also come out along the path [from the car park under the building], which led to the hostel. They were talking lightly, happily. They were very close together, the woman with a file under her arm. Apparently, they were concentrating on their own conversation and didn't notice me. They went along the path in the direction of the hostel. When they disappeared in the distance, I quickly left the place, turning the corner of the building and going down to the ground floor from the outside.

I drove away in my car. While I drove, I felt that my feet were very cold, making the car go very slowly as well. I had to cross the harbor via the tunnel. At the tunnel entrance, I saw the young man and the lady again, standing by the side of the road and waving at me to stop. So I stopped.

The lady said, "Dr. X, could you take us to Kowloon [across the harbor]? We're hurrying for a flight to Canada." I replied, "You have been so able, I don't think you need to take my car." She said, "No, no. I have never been away from Hong Kong, unlike my friend. Besides, I'm afraid of the water. I must get through the water well protected."

I was determined not to obey them and drove on. But a moment later I found that they were already in the back seat of my car, talking about finding a place of residence in Canada. I did not disturb them, and they did not talk to me. When I got out of the tunnel, I found that they had disappeared. I paid the toll and drove back home peacefully. Although I live on the twenty-third floor, I didn't dare take the lift, and walked up exhausted.

During the summer, Professor X told me, a student from the college wrote an "inferior" version of the story for a Chinese-language daily newspaper in Hong Kong, attributing the account to a professor with another name (but there is no such professor by that name at the college). Perhaps, that newspaper article helped to standardize the form of the legend somewhat.

Most of the versions I heard were very short. One staff worker at the college told me that she had heard two students talking about it on the bus. Supposedly, a female student had come to the office of her instructor (unnamed) in the Z Building, asking for her grades. He discovered later that she had died a few years before. Another staff person had read the newspaper version but could remember only a few details: a couple had come up to the seventh floor in the elevator, getting in when the elevator shouldn't stop on the way up; the professor had been working "overtime". Finally, another professor affiliated with the college told me that some professor had gone up in the elevator with ghosts in the Z Building, spoke to *him*, and found that the student had committed suicide.

This legend, which Professor X intended to be a folk tale (not told as true and oral rather than written down), can be understood both as folklore, and as a rumor. As folklore, it has earmarks of the "fictitious" apparition: physical effects and very long conversation (in contrast with firsthand reports). Notice the terror that builds throughout the story: not being able to get away, as in the cinema-lore case of the man who found a ghost next to him wherever he sat (cf. Chapter 8). Of course, Professor X's terror was low-key, and in the telling I got the impression that it was meant to be somewhat humorous, although not slapstick as in Cantonese horror / humor films (cf. Chapter 8). Also, the female ghost's fear of the water hints that she committed suicide in the water and that she has the Chinese folklore ghost's fear of being trapped at the place of drowning and / or suicide.

As a rumor, it shows all the classic changes (DeFleur, D'Antonio, and DeFleur, 1971: 360-362). It underwent "leveling" (became shorter, much shorter), and "sharpening" (essential details remaining, skipping all the trips up and down the stairs and elevators).

"Assimilation" is that aspect of the rumor process in which the message is modified to fit the attitudes and cultural expectations of those who pass the rumor on. Professor X himself did this in the sense that he took the rumors that he had heard earlier and incorporated certain important concerns in Hong Kong college-student culture: the pressure to succeed in college, college suicides due to failure, finding a marriage partner, and emigrating to North America. In later versions of the rumor, the ghost became Professor X's own student, asking about her (or his) grades, a more direct situation than the involved search for the student's file. Sometimes, the student was male, which might also be assimilation, if male students are considered to be more likely to have academic difficulties or to commit suicide in Hong Kong. [71]

Finally, "compounding" occurred, which means that one rumor led to another to explain the first. If students thought that Professor X's ghost story was true, even though he said it wasn't, it was a short leap to claiming that it had happened to him, since he was the one who told it in the first person. Of course, Professor X did most of the compounding, by inventing an elaborate story to account more precisely for the presence of the rumors he heard about the elevator and the unsuccessful student at the Z Building and to explain the presence of the second ghost.

---

71   I think they are. Indeed, tragically, a young man jumped from the "Z" Building itself one day when I was in it.

IO

HAUNTINGS AND POLTERGEISTS

2017: For a recent discussion of hauntings, see Emmons and Emmons (2012: 105-112). In this book the case of the "Haunted Townhouses" (G083 and G084) is one of the very few that I actually investigated in Hong Kong. The reason for this is that I had limited time and money, which I chose to spend gathering a large number of cases and looking for patterns instead of investigating a small number intensely.

One important thing about hauntings in Hong Kong is that they are seen as very unlucky. In chapter 13 I show that such matters are still taken very seriously in Hong Kong and have a big impact on the real estate market. Chinese in other parts of the world have similar ideas. For example, some of my Chinese friends in Gettysburg said that they ruled out living in one set of apartments in town because it was close to a cemetery.

In Chapters 8 and 9 we departed from a concentration on firsthand reports in order to see how folklore and popular culture tell a rather different ghost story. The story they tell gives insights into the culture but is not a reliable representation of the ghost experience itself. Now, we shall return to primarily firsthand reports in order to examine more closely an important type of apparition experience, the haunting, and the problem of physical effects that may or may not be a part of hauntings.

Of course, many of the folklore and popular-culture accounts were hauntings, too, such as the Japanese-occupation and hospital ghosts. The student ghost in Chapter 9 haunted the Z Building or could have been making a postmortem visit to Professor X (especially in the versions in which the student came to ask him about her or his grade).

Let's look at one more hearsay account, about a ghost who haunted his cemetery and hometown in China, as told by a man who lived there:

Green Snake

This happened in Yeung Chau in 1953 when the landlords were being criticized. [72] "Green Snake," a hooligan who was feared by the people before the Communists took over, was prosecuted in the farmers' market where everybody brought their produce to sell. Then he was taken to the outskirts of town and shot with his arms tied behind his back. He was the first one to be executed there. Afterward, they buried him in the cemetery close to where I lived, where they buried all the ones who had been executed. Even in the daytime, women were afraid to pass by there.

The town crier lived on the opposite side of the Cemetery from where I lived. He had been one of the judges before 1949, and for his punishment the Communists made him tell time at night with the gong. About 1 a.m. one night, he heard somebody calling him by name as he passed the cemetery.

He turned around and saw the guy who had just been executed. Supposedly, he couldn't get down to the underworld because he had been tied up when he was executed. The town crier asked, "Who is it?"

"Green Snake. Could you untie me?" The crier got scared and ran home. (Everybody knows about this.) The crier went to his own house, and his wife, who had been in the bathroom,

---

72   In the aftermath of the Communist victory in China in 1949, many of the landlords were tried as oppressors of the people, stripped of their possessions, and injured or even executed by the crowds.

answered the door. She hadn't even pulled her pants up yet. The wife saw somebody following him. It was Green Snake. She was so scared that she died.

From then on, ten more people were executed. And from then on they threw their shoes out into the lake or the sea to keep them from coming back. The spirits will follow their shoes, you know.

Although there may really have been a haunting that originally stimulated the legend of Green Snake, this account is more significant for its illustration of folk beliefs: how certain methods of execution can block reincarnation or entrance to the underworld (Comber, 1972: 22-29), the magical [73] connection between a person's shoes and spirit, and the trapping of drowned ghosts in the water. Some of the firsthand reports, like G079 here from a seventeen-year-old girl, sound very similar to the folklore ghosts, in this case like a cinema-bathroom ghost, but I take them more seriously as experiences because they have not gone through the rumor process.

G079. The Ghost on the Bathroom Floor

In the theater's bathroom, I saw a long-haired person in a white robe lying on the floor motionless. The hair was all over its face. I quickly went out and didn't tell anybody about it. It didn't look at me because I couldn't see its face. There was nobody else there.

One of the features commonly associated with hauntings is malevolence of some kind, often linked to the violent death of the person who becomes the ghost. Although the apparitional drama itself is much more likely to be malevolent or ominous in the hauntings of folklore and popular culture, we occasionally get a glimpse of something macabre in the firsthand

---

73   A form of "contagious" magic in fact: once the shoes are in "contact" with the owner, they are always in magical contact with him and can be used to harm him.

reports as well. I wonder if G080, reported by a sixteen-year-old boy, is a reenactment of foul play.

G080. Stabs in the Dark

One night, when I was sound asleep, I was suddenly awakened by a noise of some kind. I listened carefully. It was somebody wearing a pair of slippers walking back and forth. I also heard him turning pages in a newspaper. A few minutes later, it went away… [Then I saw] a shadow of a woman waving a sharp knife in the air.

A seventeen-year-old girl submitted the following intriguing case, which I speculate might be the ghost of a washroom attendant haunting her former place of employment!

G081. The Invisible Washroom Attendant

It happened one time when my classmate and I went to a bathroom on the fifth floor of our school. I went right into one of the stalls. My classmate wanted to choose one with a toilet that flushed. She went right into one closed stall and saw a lot of brooms and mops there. So she went back to the original one that she was going to go into, and a voice said, "This stall is out of order." At that time I was inside the next stall and heard the voice, too, but I didn't think it was very strange. When I came out, I forgot to flush the toilet, and I heard a voice say, "You must flush the toilet after using it." We were sure that nobody else was in the bathroom except the two of us. We still can't explain it.

The next case is not included in the Chinese ghost report statistics of earlier chapters, because the respondent is a British woman living in Hong Kong. However, it is an excellent example of a haunting in which the identity of the ghost is known. Although it qualifies as a post-mortem case, it also acts like a haunting in the way the presence seems to cling primarily to the house.

G082. Finally at Rest [74]

My father died on April 30, 1979. He was happy, smiling. But nine hours later, he went to the Chinese funeral home, where they bashed the body about. They had no refrigeration and did a bad job with dry ice, even smashed the face in. He was a very vain man, and would not have liked what they did to his face. We had to wait eight days for the cremation.

For those eight days, we felt a presence in the house most of the time. Occasionally, we thought, "He's not here just now," but when we went through the front door, we *felt* it, in all rooms equally throughout the house. I wasn't frightened. I knew he loved me; after all, I nursed him for two and a half years.

My girls [the two Philippine maids] heard him in the house at different times and knew he wasn't happy, although they knew he was happy when he died. Three times late at night, I smelled the gangrene (that he had in his foot), for about ten minutes each time, in my bedroom. It was very strong. At the same time the maids heard him downstairs. They heard him moaning, "Oh, my foot! My foot!" He coughed several times as he used to do also. The two of them know they heard the same thing. They heard him all odd times of day, in their room and in the living room where he died. It seemed as if he was moving about, but he was paralyzed and couldn't before he died. And they felt the presence.

---

74   In the Chinese-language reports, I usually make minor editorial changes in the English translation in cooperation with my wife, Chee, a native speaker of Cantonese. This involves word and word-order change, but requires no special mention as it is impossible to translate completely literally in any case. I should mention that this particular case, from the interview done in English, required departures from the actual order, but quotation marks are still appropriate as it is close to the respondent's wording.

They didn't hear any footsteps, but once they both independently heard him moving about in the kitchen.

He couldn't get there himself, but they used to wheel him in. I never heard anything, but my own hearing is not very good. I do have an acute sense of smell. The young maid is somewhat psychic; the older nurse is a strict Catholic. But they both shared the same experiences.

When we left the funeral home, there was some lightening of the pressure (of the oppressive mood we felt), then more improvement at the service in the cathedral. At a quarter to five, when we were buying an urn (for his ashes) in a shop in Wanchai [district of Hong Kong], all three of us knew, had a feeling that he was gone. It was probably right when the cremation began. When we returned home, the girls went from room to room and felt that he was gone. I could feel that the house was empty, no more presence.

I never believed in ghosts before, but I'm absolutely convinced now. I was not particularly or not strictly a Christian, but he was a believer.

The night before the anniversary of his death, I dreamed about him. The next day, one of the maids felt suddenly that he was with her. She hadn't realized that it was the day he died, but she experienced this about midday, the time he died. It was off our property, on the doggie path. It lasted for about ten minutes. He was not unhappy then.

So far, the hauntings presented in this chapter have contained no physical effects. However, hauntings have been found frequently to have physical effects in them (Rogo, 1975: 263). As I pointed out in Chapters 5 and 6, this does not necessarily contradict the ESP theory of apparitions, because visual apparitions have rarely been linked *directly* to physical effects. As psi (psychic energy) is thought to consist of both a sensory part, ESP, and a motor part, PK (psychokinesis), it is logical to think that they might both occur in the same psychic situation, even if not together precisely at the same moment. G083, like the last case, is from a British resident of Hong Kong; he is a college professor who struck me as a very down-to-earth but open-minded person. It begins the account of a haunting or series of hauntings that involves primarily apparitional but also some physical phenomena (in G084).

G083. The Haunted Townhouses

I was not told about anything paranormal when we moved into #7 Victoria Townhouses [pseudonym].

People considered that block to have bad *feng shui* [geomancy, magic]; the amahs didn't like it. It was near the cemetery, the Japanese had been there, and there were vague stories about prisoners having been in the houses. It is about sixty years old, and there are eight [townhouses] in one block, each with only one family in it. They are dark and gloomy, surrounded by trees and heavy foliage. The rooms are shadowy, and there is a staircase in the wall at the center going up to the mezzanine and then to the top floor. You can look down into the hall from the top. There are rooms for storage in the basement.

The children felt uncomfortable in certain parts of the house; there was a certain atmosphere on the staircase and in the front bedroom. Also, nobody liked the bathroom at the rear; the children hated it and refused to use it. They said they heard voices from there at night when they slept by it. Even when they were much older, they found it strange. My son was twelve and my daughter ten when we moved in.

In the first couple of years, I got almost daily impressions of seeing figures out of the corner of my eye, especially at night and in the front bedroom. Strong feelings sometimes. Once, I thought I saw someone moving from one room to another in the basement. I thought it was the amah, but she wasn't there in the house. It looked like a dark shadow, a sense of movement going by. I was looking down from the floor above. It was afternoon, but a bit dark in the house. I couldn't see the outline of a body or color or any other identifiable thing. I didn't hear anything either.

Sometimes, I thought I saw an older Chinese woman, since the figure would be somewhat bent, standing by the window or fireplace. There was also the impression of a young Chinese man. These two figures only.

Once in the middle of the day, when we had lunch guests, I passed the foot of the staircase and got the strong impression of someone descending the stairs. I heard the noise of a dress rustling. It was a strong *mental* impression only, that a woman in a long black dress was very close.

But I had a stronger visual impression in 1974: it was the Ides of March. We had turned an upper bedroom into a sitting room (using it as a TV room). My daughter had been to the bedroom on the same floor. The downstairs hall light was on too. I went to turn off the light in my daughter's bedroom, and then, walking back, looked over the bannister into the lit hall.

I saw a swirling black mass that came together into the figure of a man. It gradually came into focus, but there were no details or color. He was slinking around, moving suspiciously. He seemed Chinese by the shape. Then the figure went into the dining room (downstairs) in a matter of seconds.

I went back to the TV room, where my wife asked me what was the matter. I said I thought I had seen someone downstairs. My wife, thinking someone had broken in, had us go down and check, but we found no one. I heard nothing (when I saw the apparition). I can't remember my mental state, but I couldn't comprehend it and didn't worry. I could distinguish legs, and it walked normally although stealthily.

I noticed later that in fact the dining room doesn't appear that close up. I seemed to be able to see more of the dining room

and hall than you could normally. That is, it seemed closer up.
75

Another time, my wife and son and I [heard something] when the houses on both sides of us were vacant. My wife and I were asleep in the large bedroom and awoke two or three mornings at 3 to hear a man's and woman's voices. We couldn't distinguish the language. There was also the movement of objects, we couldn't tell where. Finally, we became alarmed and called the estates officer, fearing there was someone in the neighboring houses. They investigated and found no one. Then the sounds stopped and we never heard them again. This was very unusual since normally we couldn't hear people next door unless they shouted. Three of us heard this at the same time. They were talking in hushed, confidential tones; an emotionally level, ordinary conversation. The moving of objects came after the talking evidently.

No guests experienced things, but we very seldom had any house guests. I experienced more than the others, but my wife said that she often felt presences, especially in the kitchen, although she saw nothing.

My daughter saw something, though. It was after we had been in the house a short time. She was in the bedroom by the bathroom upstairs. It was about 8 or 9 in the morning, and she was lying in bed, maybe just having woken up. Through her bedroom door she saw a bright figure standing there (by the bathroom nobody liked). She couldn't tell whether it was a man or woman. There were no other details. The sun did not shine in there at that time.

We joked about it, saying that she must have been dreaming, etc., but she stuck to her story. The figure was just outside the

---

75   This is a fascinating detail. It has parallel in cases described by Tyrrell (1963: 67, 68, 72) in which distance and even direction of sight are paranormally distorted to allow the receivers to see more than they would normally be able to.

bathroom door. She used to lock the bathroom door but was not afraid of the bedroom itself.

When we had been in the house for a week or so, we left our daughter there in the daytime. When we returned, we found her sitting outside. She said she was frightened to be in there alone, but gave no reason for her fear.

At a party once, Mrs. Y told me, "We used to live there. Have you seen the ghost?!" She said that she had felt someone standing behind her when she was on the landings, just as I had had feelings about the landings and the staircase and hall. She didn't say that she had seen anything. I didn't tell her anything very specifically that had happened to me, because I was reluctant to talk about it. I was afraid she wouldn't believe me, but I was very impressed when she asked me about the ghost. [Since then] I have told Professor A, because he was seriously interested, but I never told the Bs, who live there now, because I didn't want to frighten the children.

Number 4 also has a bad reputation. It was exorcised by a Buddhist monk. We don't talk about this much. There is not a lot of folklore about Victoria Townhouses, although they are known for bad feng shui. People are skeptical.

The respondent, call him Professor C, told me this in late November, between two trips I took to the People's Republic of China. In a hurry to finish up the study in December after returning from China again, I managed to interview five of the eight current residents of Victoria Townhouses, including Professor C's old place, #7, and #4, which he said also had a psychic reputation.

Interestingly, none of the five had ever experienced anything strange there, nor had their families. Four of them had known about the alleged occupation of the place by the Japanese, three knew that amahs were supposedly reluctant to work there, and one had heard that an amah's child had died there sometime before the early 1970s at least. Three had heard about a ghost, including one who had heard it from Professor C himself and one who knew that it was either Professor C or the people next door.

No one seemed to be very impressed or knowledgeable about the subject, although they were all quite willing to talk to me about it. One man commented that the house was eerie and creaky. His wife had seen a possible burglar on the back steps, a local Chinese who was caught going into someone's flat. Another gentleman, from Scotland, said that there was "one wee laddie who peeps through the window!"

Later on, I told Professor C that I had been unable to find any confirmation of his report from other residents but thanked him again for his very interesting case. After returning to the U.S. in January, I began poring over all my notebooks and questionnaires. Then I realized (I could have kicked myself) that I had neglected to contact Mrs. Y. the woman at the party who had asked Professor C about "the ghost."

Doubting that I would ever get the information, I sent off a letter to what I thought was her address. Happily, Mrs. Y sent me the following thoughtful reply:

G084. The Haunted Townhouses, Revisited

We went to live in #4, Victoria Townhouses, in November 1959, taking my baby amah and cook amah and her daughter, eight years old, with us. The cook amah did not remain there very long, maybe three months – she left because of ghosts.

One day, when I was out shopping, the casing of a large thermos jug kept on the top shelf of the kitchen cracked with "a loud bang," she said – she was very upset about this. I tried to console her that it was probably the heat in the kitchen. (I was thinking it may have been her very naughty little girl responsible!) Anyway, she said it was due to ghosts in my house. I was most surprised, I can remember, for she was very modern (and youngish, in her thirties) for those times in the 1950s, and 1 wouldn't have thought that she would be so superstitious.

Shortly after, around Chinese New Year, the said thermos jug fell from the shelf with an almighty bang. I was there this time, and of course cook amah said she must go immediately. She said there were ghosts in the basement, and she did not want them to touch her little girl. I can't remember exactly what I felt then, but she left. My baby amah didn't seem to worry about ghosts, and she stayed on another year.

I was expecting another baby and tried to hire another cook. It was difficult to get anyone. I thought it was because this ... area was in those days quite inaccessible. My friend Mrs. D (who later lived at #6) informed me that her amah said I would never get an amah because all these houses were haunted, especially mine. The Japanese had killed people in these houses, and there were "bad things" (meaning ghosts, vibrations) in these houses.

This made me begin to think about ghosts! But I never got a funny feeling whilst I lived in this house [#4]. I can't say I liked the basement area [near the kitchen] (because of rats I suppose), but I tried to make it as nice as I could, so the baby amah would stay. Her cousin came as cook amah for a short while, but she left for better pay (with an American family!), she said. But the baby amah said her cousin said there was something not good about the basement – not healthy and bad feng shui. I didn't worry about ghosts or employing cook amahs after that – my baby amah became my sole help.

In 1958, at #5, my neighbors' eight-year-old son went to hospital with leukemia – and subsequently died. There was no talk of ghosts responsible at that time-but it came up at a later date.

Later in 1959, whilst we were in England "on leave" for eight months, the E family went to live in #4, and the F family went to live in #5. Mrs. F (a Canadian girl married to a Chinese) was my good friend. During this time, the E amah's child got sick (and I think died) and my friend Mrs. F's boy died of cancer of the stomach. He was only four years old. Then there was talk of ghosts! I heard the Es had #4 exorcised, or their servants did.

The amah at #3 also during my two years there at # 4 was always ill – and she left because of the "unhealthy" basement.

On returning [from leave and moving into] #7, I certainly had feelings in that house! I always felt someone was behind me on the landing at the top of the stairs. I kept a chest of drawers for the linen – bedsheets, etc. – and even during the day time if I went to put things away I would get the feeling. I had to get up several times during the night to see to the children sleeping in the large back bedroom and used to go through the main doorway of the front bedroom across the landing to their door and room.

I would always get this feeling someone was behind me, but it was not a frightening experience. It felt like a sad person behind me. I know that I thought that I must be a little tired and nervy. We had had a lot of traveling about on our "leave" in England, and also I had a fair amount of rheumaticky pain in my back and legs, which made me sort of half-awake in the nighttime.

The catches on the windows in the large back bedroom would come unhooked easily, and I seemed to have to get up and keep fixing them. I can remember thinking on one occasion, "Gosh, there must be a ghost around here. I'm forever doing up windows, and they seem quite firm to me. Why do they come open?!" I always used to think things like that happened because of vibrations from the road being higher at the back. I suppose in general – but odd things happened.

No one else in the house felt anything about the landing area or any other part of the house. My amah never said anything – she was not the original baby amah but a very traditional old cook amah, and she certainly would be the one who would think and would "feel" ghosts, so we never discussed ghosts at all.

As for an apparition, perhaps I did see one or could call it one. Coming from the master bedroom across the landing to go into the large back bedroom, I was looking ahead.... There is a little corridor leading to the second bathroom and a little back bedroom. Just before the second bathroom, there is a corner. It was as if I saw a filmy patch of light like a net curtain blowing – long enough to be a figure (no clue as to male or female) – and it just disappeared slickly round the bathroom door into the bathroom.

I remember thinking it must be a light from a car shining on the wall and then quickly disappearing. And I also remember thinking, "That's funny, the wall where I saw it is not opposite the bathroom window. It was in the corner, so how can it be reflected there? It must be a reflection from the room that is behind me." I know that I entered my bedroom again *not* via the landing but by the communicating door of the front bedroom and back bedroom after that!

And that's what I generally did afterward. I wasn't really scared, and I didn't want to think of ghosts. I put it all down to me being so tired I think. And some time afterward, when I moved to a house in the college grounds, I was reading a book about agoraphobia and other phobias including one about feeling something or someone behind you. I thought, "Ah, that's what I felt at #7, so I couldn't have been very well in that house."

As for discussing ghosts with anyone, ... after I returned from leave holiday in 1959 of course there was a little talk among neighbors as to the ghost of #4 and #5. But it was at a much later date, in 1976 or so, that I was talking with Mrs. G, who used to live also at #7, and I gather she had uneasy feelings at #7 also in the landing area.

Comparing G083 and G084, the most significant experiences occurred in #7 around the stairway and on the top floor and the bathroom and bedroom area at the back, which are raised up a half-flight from the top floor in split-level style. The bottom floor is a basement area, with a half-flight up to the kitchen in back. The second level, or "ground floor," contains the living room in front, dining room in back by the stairs, and a small bathroom and bedroom a half-flight up in the far back. The top floor is shown in the blueprint on page 170.

Following the key on the blueprint, [1] is the front bedroom where Mrs. Y and later Professor C had their master bedroom. Number [2] is the "large back bedroom" where Mrs. Y's children slept and that Professor C turned into a TV room. Mrs. Y felt that somebody was standing behind her on the landing marked [3]. Stairway [4] leads to the hall by the dining room downstairs, the area where the black figure appeared to Professor C. Professor C was standing on the higher landing at [5], close enough to the outside wall to look over the bannister and see between the up and down stairways into the hall below. Number [5] also locates the corner from which Mrs. Y saw a "filmy patch of light like a net curtain" move to [6] and into the bathroom [7]. Professor C's daughter may have been looking at the same ghost years later when she saw a "bright figure" at [6], right outside the door to the bathroom [7] that the Cs did not like, when she was lying in the bedroom [8].

From earlier chapters, it should be clear that this haunting has several common features of apparitions. Both Mrs. Y and the C family experienced the feeling of a presence, and even some details of emotion and dress without seeing anything. Most apparitions were visual only, but some were auditory only for the C family, including the collective one of the voices. All of the visual apparitions were insubstantial, but Professor C's were dark in contrast to the glowing ones seen near the bathroom by Mrs. Y and Professor C's daughter.

The possibility of collective delusion should be considered here, as there were rumors and as Professor C and Mrs. Y did compare notes. Both of them, however, seem to have experienced things independently and to have discussed the matter only afterward. Moreover, apparently neither of them knew that the other family had seen the light outside the

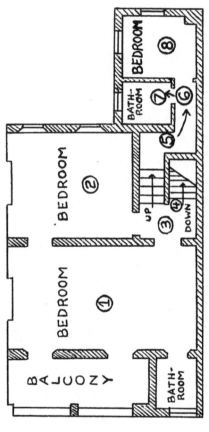

KEY

① FRONT BEDROOM (MASTER)
② "LARGE BACK BEDROOM"
③ LANDING (MRS. Y)
④ STAIRWAY TO DINING-ROOM HALL
⑤ "THE CORNER"
⑥ BY BATHROOM DOOR ("BRIGHT FIGURE")
⑤→⑥→⑦ PATH OF "PATCH OF LIGHT"
⑦ BATHROOM (DISLIKED BY C'S)
⑧ BEDROOM (OF C'S DAUGHTER)

TOP FLOOR AND UPPER TOP FLOOR PLAN

#7 VICTORIA TOWNHOUSES

same bathroom, a light that could not have been morning sun when the daughter saw it (because there are no east windows) and was evidently not headlights when Mrs. Y saw it. [76] Finally, except for the ghost scare involving the young children who died, there does not seem to have been much hysteria over ghosts among the residents of Victoria Townhouses.

Apart from the apparitions, we have the problem of the physical effects. If Mrs. Y's problem windows are a natural phenomenon, which she thinks they might be, then we are left with only the cracking, flying thermos in # 4, and nothing in #7 for either the Cs or the Ys. The thermos incidents are very typical PK (psychokinetic) activity, either mixed in as physical effects in a haunting or as evidence of a poltergeist, in which one living person, often a young female, is the "focus" of PK energy.

G085. "You Mean, Something Like a Black Sheep?"

People often ask me if my research makes me especially sensitive to psychic phenomena, or, simply, "Did you run into any ghosts in China?" Although many of the paranormal experiences reported in this book occurred in China, simply because most residents of Hong Kong were born there and emigrated, the entire study was conducted in Hong Kong. When I did go to China for a total of three weeks on two different trips, I was careful not to cause any breach of faith by doing any research on the sly. I asked one Chinese college student if he thought that I could get into his country again sometime for the purpose of studying ghosts. In a delightful bit of wit, jabbing both me and the bureaucracy, he replied, "I don't think there is a ghost committee, but if I am ever on the committee, I'll recommend you!"

---

76   Mrs. Y might have been seeing a reflection of a car headlight that shone through the front bathroom far behind her (at the lower left of the blueprint). However, such a light would probably have cast a shadow of Mrs. Y, moved through a very narrow angle, and certainly not have appeared to go past the corner to the bathroom door and enter the bathroom.

However, something interesting did happen to me in
Kunming, the capital of Yunnan Province, about 150 miles from
Vietnam. I present this more as an insight into how people react
to strange experiences than as a good example of a haunting (it
has low probability as a possibly paranormal occurrence). At 6:15
p.m., December 6, 1980, I was coming down the stairs from
the third floor in the Green Hotel, on my way to dinner. As
I approached the second-floor landing, I saw a woman to my
right and below me, coming around the post at the end of the
bannister and up toward me. In my peripheral vision I noticed
people walking straight ahead of me into the area of elevators on
the second floor. One man was turning to my right along what
was not another flight down but a level landing. This man was
Chinese, probably in his fifties, and wearing a gray cap and gray
"Mao suit."

He was headed along the hall from which the only exit was
a left turn leading to the lobby area. When I turned right at
the foot of the stairs, I was surprised not to see him in the hall,
because I thought that he was only ten or fifteen feet ahead of
me, and the hall was about twenty-five or thirty feet long, and I
am a fast walker. I was immediately curious and ran ahead to the
door on the left. There wasn't a single person in the lobby area.
Then I went back to the hall to see if there might be another way
out to the right. There wasn't.

My reaction at that point was to assume that I had not seen
what I thought I had seen. Maybe the man was going in toward
the second floor elevators instead of down the hall by the stairway
when I saw him. I went out to dinner and put it out of my mind.
Later that evening, I thought that this must be how most people
react to a strange experience: they deny it or give it a "normal"
interpretation, no matter how unlikely. It was absurd for me to
think that the man had gone the other direction; the only other
way to go was toward the elevators, and he had been headed *away*

from the other people going in that direction. I concluded that the only other possibility was that he had broken into a sprint, cleared the doorway into the lobby before I had gotten to the hall, and then ran into the dining room some thirty or forty feet off to the right inside the lobby area. I regretted not having gone in that entrance to the dining area to look for him. Either he had gone in there or he had disappeared.

Still not convinced that I had really seen a ghost, especially since the man had looked perfectly normal (the only clue being his apparent disappearance), I decided that it was at least a good opportunity to ask about ghosts. Therefore, I told the story that some night to our Chinese tour guide.

She was very kind and attentive, but had a puzzled look in her eye. I said, "Do you know what I mean by a 'ghost'?" She replied, "You mean, something like a black sheep?" She must have thought I was talking about a thief who disappeared! After I gave her the word for ghost in Chinese, she laughed merrily and understood it all of a sudden. I apologized, saying that I knew that believing in ghosts was not very acceptable in China anymore. But she said no, it was O.K. "Now that the Gang of Four is no longer in power?" I asked. "Yes," she laughed. No, she knew the hotel well, and people had not claimed to see any ghosts there.

That night before going to sleep, I told my roommate on the tour about it. We then got to talking about a peculiar watch I have, which I call my "psychic watch," because I seem to be able to make it lose time in ways that have no apparent explanation. He happened to have the same kind of watch, a Longines self-wind, which I stared at for a while to see if I could make it lose time, but I was unsuccessful.

However, at about 2:30 or 3 a.m. that night, a ceiling light in our room apparently turned on by itself. I wondered if it had done so by means of my PK that had been stirred up by the watch attempt. Or was it a physical aspect of a haunted hotel? It might also have been faulty wiring, although floor lamps are more susceptible to that. I also think that we had turned the toggle-switch off, and it had been working normally. When I got up and saw it on, I turned it off.

The whole business was very instructive to me. I would not have thought it very interesting as a report coming from someone else, but observing my own thought processes showed me how easy it is both to ignore strange evidence and to become overly sensitive to it. It was just as absurd to assume that the man was actually walking in the opposite direction as it was to think that the light that went on by itself was good evidence for a paranormal event.

In the next report, a hospital haunting related to me by a medical doctor working there (again, not Chinese and therefore not included in the statistics), there are no definitely apparitional aspects, although the knock and even the flashing lights might have been either apparitional or physical. Only the knocking belongs to the firsthand part of the report.

G086. Blankets and Midnight Oil

I have heard that, about thirty years ago, nurses on night duty used to go to sleep in the office when they had nothing to do. They said they felt blankets being taken off them at night. The blankets were found in the courtyard, which is across the corridor and down one floor.

[All events occurred in a small section of the hospital. The office referred to is close to the library.]

One evening about ten years ago, when I was studying in the library, I heard a knock. I said, "Come in!" When no one came in, I went to the door and opened it. There should still have been someone in the area, but there wasn't. I got a dreadful feeling.

No one ever saw anything. One young doctor used to work in the library until midnight. Suddenly I didn't see any lights on in the library any more. (I knew she must have stopped working there.) Others told me that she had seen the lights going on and off.

If it is unclear whether there are any apparitional aspects in the last report, it is unclear whether there are any physical effects in the next. At any rate, neither case directly associates a visual ghost with a physical act. The respondent in G087 is Professor C from G083, the townhouse case. When I suggested to him that the whole thing could have been an auditory apparition without any actual movement of doors, he agreed. If so, it would be a collective apparition, since his students also heard it. Should we be surprised that Professor C has had two such interesting experiences? It may be that certain psychic individuals are more susceptible to apparitions than others (cf. Chapter 12).

G087. The Late Student

A student who used to come to my tutorials [discussion section] died of a heart complaint in his second year, 1974-75, at age twenty-one. He died on a Sunday and was due to be buried on Friday afternoon.

He used to come to my Friday-morning tutorial and was always late, often ten minutes late. The Friday he was to be buried, the students (in the tutorial) were in tension, as if waiting for the student to appear. I felt it, too.

Then the outer door of the hall started constantly opening and closing, and the doors of the room (front and back) kept banging, rattling, although there was no wind. I said, "I must go to see who's banging the door." One student said, "Don't worry, Mr. C, it'll be all right after he's buried." The students believed he was wandering around.

It happened throughout the class, as if a strong wind were blowing through the building. The students were very perturbed and conscious of the noise. There was nobody there when I went out to check. We all left class at the end and didn't know if it stopped later.

The room is not used as a tutorial now, but it never happened before. People don't come through the hall door that incessantly, and as an inner door it wouldn't normally be sucked open and closed. It became louder and more frequent, an obvious opening and closing, maybe every five seconds. Then it stopped, and then started again, as if many people were going through.

The next case is also from a previously quoted respondent, the man in G001 (Chapter 1), and it took place in the same house. Although it is difficult to know where to draw the line between a haunting that has physical effects and a poltergeist that is completely physical and may have a living focus person at the center causing it, this part of what happened in that house has some classic poltergeist aspects (hurtling object, water appearing) and should probably be at least cross-listed:

P001, G088. Poker-Playing Poltergeist?

The house was built in about 1938 and was torn down ten years ago. We started to be quite nonchalant about the things that went on there, but one or two things were very frightening. A big clay eagle that hung on one wall smashed against the wall on the other side of the room.

Once, when I was playing poker, I heard something that sounded like a bird on the balcony outside the window. There was no bird there, but there was water all over.

One evening near midnight, when we were playing poker, we sent the servant to go get Cokes at the little store downstairs. We gave him the front-door keys; there were heavy locks.

The doorbell rang shortly after that. There he was, waiting to get in. Something had closed all the bolts from the inside.

Sometimes, rather strenuous physical effects seem to be perpetrated on people themselves. However, if no lasting marks or other evidence is left afterward, it is difficult to rule out a tactile apparition as the cause, as in G089, from a twenty-two-year-old woman.

G089. Haunted Hair

I was about twelve years old. One day I was washing my hands in my school's bathroom. Somebody pulled my hair (I had long hair) very hard. I yelled, "It hurts!" and looked up into the mirror and saw nothing behind me. I continued washing my hands, and somebody pulled my hair again. I said, "Don't do it," and ran out.

Bennett (1939: 233) recorded a much more ominous act. When staying at a cottage in Wales, a woman saw a man come across the room "until he came near to my face, and then placed his hands on my throat, and tried to strangle me; I endeavored to scream but could not do so until he had vanished." Even here, with a linked visual apparition, there is no evidence for a real choking, although the tactile perception is at least simulated. This is still different from actually being "thrown on the bed and choked" (cf. Chapter 8).

A fifty-nine-year-old woman reported the next case. Except for the footsteps, which might have been imagined by the gathering crowd after someone said they were there, this looks like a poltergeist.

P002. G090. The Sneaky, Green-Smoke Ghost

When I was living in Canton in my teens, my friends had a rice store, the first one on a long, pretty dark alleyway. I was playing with one of my friends in a courtyard outside when somebody yelled, "There's a ghost in the store! A *sip ching guai* [sneaky green smoke ghost]!"

I rushed in to look in the entrance and saw a pair of windows close by themselves with a crack like gunpowder. I saw green smoke coming up after it closed (as if it were burning). Somebody yelled, "It's going upstairs!" and we heard footsteps going up.

Twenty or thirty people were crowded in the alleyway. One box of clothes downstairs was actually burnt, although we saw no fire. Only the clothes inside the box were burned, not the box itself. All the people in the alley experienced it (the window, the sound, and the clothes). This kind of sneaky ghost is common in the village, but this is the only time I saw it.

One of the PK effects sometimes reported in a poltergeist is fires (Rogo, 1975: 178), including ones that are demonstrably paranormal in the sense that they are started from inside an object or burn only selectively (Rogo, 1979: 55). This seems to have happened here with the box that was not affected by the burning clothes.

Up to now, the cases that sound like possible poltergeists have contained no particular clues as to who might be a "focus person," a living individual who is always present when the physical manifestations occur and who is thought to cause them by psychokinetic (PK) means (Roll, 1972). P003 is exciting not only because it does indicate such a person (the woman in the report, who was nineteen at the time) but also because there may have been an ESP dream in another individual at the same time, possibly caused by a surviving spirit acting in conjunction with the living poltergeist focus person. Notice the idea of the spirit returning on a multiple of the seventh day up to the forty-ninth; the seventh and then the twenty-first days after death are most common.

P003. The Moving Pictures
On the twenty-first day after my cousin's death, an aunt of ours (neither his mother nor mine) had a dream that he came back

and visited all the extended family. That same night my picture fell off my bedroom wall, and the embroidery he gave me was twisted up on the wall.

I have a picture of myself on the wall over my head. On another wall there's the embroidery he gave me, along with a picture of the Holy Family. The Holy Family picture wasn't moved.

I interviewed the informant directly myself in English and in Cantonese. On further questioning, she explained that the embroidery stayed on its hook, but the bottom was rotated up to the right side. That and the picture that fell were both put on with string twisted *clockwise* around nails. For the stringed picture to have come off the nail, it would seemingly have to have been unwound as if by a force whirling through the bedroom in a clockwise fashion as seen from above.

The respondent said that she had never experienced any such physical effect before or since. However, when I asked her if she was the type to get angry with people when frustrated, she said, "No, I keep it inside." This has been found to be a common personality characteristic among poltergeist focuses. [77]

Even more important is the fact that she had an unusual emotional motivation in this case. Her "cousin" was really not genetically related because of an adoptive relationship in the family. In fact, he was her boyfriend, and the cause of death was thirty-five knife wounds to the head by his mentally disturbed brother.

Such a trauma (she is still distressed to talk about it many years later) might have led to an outpouring of her PK energy on the surrounding environment. An interesting point here is that the energy was selective, moving only things of mutual personal interest to the two of them: her picture, and his gift of an embroidery, but not the Holy Family picture.

---

77   Personal communication from parapsychologist Jerry Solfvin who has done extensive field research with poltergeist cases.

The fact that it occurred on the twenty-first day after death, a prime date in ancestor-worship culture, may have timed the release of PK according to her expectations. Perhaps the aunt's dream fit the same expectations independently. Alternately, the two occurrences might have been linked by ESP between the woman and her aunt, or the spirit might actually have contacted the aunt and had a hand in the movement of the frames on the wall. Louisa E. Rhine (1963) argues, however, that even with such a "target-person" as a spirit apparently involved as the reason for a "spontaneous physical effect" (poltergeist), it appears that the living subject actually causes the PK effect.

As the respondent who observed the next case is a thirteen-year-old girl, we have two prime suspects for a poltergeist focus: her and her sister (the accused). Teenaged girls are often identified as such, perhaps because adolescence is a rebellious age socially, and girls are under greater pressure not to show it. However, there is no information on motivation in this case, unless it is some kind of hostility against a nagging mother!

P004. The Teleported Basin

This happened in the winter last year. I remember my sister was the last one to take a bath at night. So she always had to hang the basin back on a nail on the wall in the kitchen after she was through. The nail is very secure, and the basin won't fall off the wall, even though it is very heavy. But every morning my mom found the basin in the bathroom. She kept thinking my sister must have forgotten to put the basin back after she was through. But it was like that every day, so my mom scolded my sister. But I was on my sister's side because I personally saw my sister hanging the basin up! But at night we would find the basin in the bathroom again. Strange!

P005 sounds like a poltergeist as well, reported by a thirteen-year-old boy, but it could also be a normal rattling of the flat. It is reminiscent of

G005, "The Noisy Ancestor" in Chapter 1, which might also have been a poltergeist, although the sound seemed apparitional.

P005. The Rattling Buddha

We put a Buddhist statue on the altar on the table. The statue is directly on the table, which can be stretched long and short. One week ago at 4 p.m., the table made some noises and was shaking. There were no electrical outlets or electricity in the surrounding things. But the statue was leaned against the wall. I used my hand to press on it, and it stopped all the noise.

If the next case, from a thirteen-year-old boy as well, is reliable, it sounds like either a poltergeist or a haunting.

P006, G091. Room Service

Last month, I was in a hotel in a foreign country. I heard some noise coming from the bathroom, and also the radio turned on and off. In the morning, I found my clothes all on the floor.

Mechanical devices like radios and televisions, clocks, sewing machines, etc., are frequently mentioned in poltergeist and haunting cases. Here is another, reported by a sixteen-year-old boy.

P007, G092. Unsolicited Advertising

It was one evening on a certain day. My sister and I were going out to eat. I turned the TV off, and we had just finished locking the door. Suddenly, we heard the TV making noises like "Cheap price! Cheap price!" We were very scared and looked in the house. We saw the TV set was still on.

Of course, a natural explanation for this one could be that people sometimes are sure that they have done something that they have done only in their minds, like turn off a TV set. Someone told me once that he was certain that he had taken a picture of his old girlfriend out of a photo cube that displayed several pictures on his desk. He *distinctly* remembered tearing it up. Later, his new fiancée was somewhat annoyed to see that he still had the other girl's picture in the cube! Nevertheless, he told me, "I must *not* have torn it up; to believe otherwise would make me doubt my sanity!"

The next somewhat dubious report (dubious not because it is paranormal but because I have never heard anything else very much like it) is from a thirteen-year-old boy. Assuming he is telling the truth, did he and his friend see a PK-propelled vehicle, an apparition (which would not be unheard of, except for the driverless part of the vehicle), or a normally driven cab whose driver was recklessly bending over to pick up something off the floor on the other side?

G093, P008. Ghost Cab
Half a year ago in North Point [district of Hong Kong Island] about 11 o'clock, I saw a cab without a driver running on a road. My friend and I both saw it.

Now, we come to some kinds of PK that are particularly "hard to swallow," although they seem to have some fairly good evidence for them in European and American studies. One of these is "apports," physical objects appearing or disappearing in thin air (Rogo, 1975: 197), as part of either a haunting or a poltergeist or a performance by a "physical (spirit) medium." Two thirteen-year-old girls report as follows.

P009. Lost and Found
If something was lost in my house, and we would search for it right away but couldn't find it, after a few days the lost item would appear on the table.

P010. Praying for a Pendant

I went swimming in Morrison Hill Swimming Pool once. After I finished swimming, I was going to change clothes. My pendant disappeared. I couldn't find it at all after a long search. So I started to pray. After I finished praying, I saw the pendant lying a little ways from me.

Admittedly, neither of these cases provides very solid evidence for apports, especially since no one actually saw the objects materialize, and some thief or prankster might have sneaked the objects back in place.

Another hard-to-believe PK phenomenon is "teleportation," the movement of objects, often large ones, from one place to another without being observed. The next two cases, the first reported by a thirty-three-year-old man and the second by a young woman, sound like possible sleepwalking to me, but neither of them thought so.

P011, G094. Rude Awakening

Sometime this year, when I was working as a night watchman on the dock, I was taking a nap on top of some boxes. When I got up, I found myself on the floor. I thought a ghost put me there.

P012, G095. The Teleported Tot

Once, when I was two or three years old, living in Hong Kong, I was sleeping on the residential upper level above the lower-level shop my parents had. In the morning, I woke up on the lower level. I was not in the habit of sleepwalking any other time. I think a ghost carried me down.

If there is any alleged PK phenomenon most especially deserving of suspicion, it is spirit photography. Nevertheless, Rogo (1974: 64-74) states that there have been some unusually good evidential cases, although the "history of psychic photography [has been] generally dubious." Some images on photographic film or plates have supposedly resulted from regular camera exposures of ghosts, whereas others have been created by PK force from a person's hands, for example, being passed over a container of previously unexposed film.

I saw one "ghost picture" in Hong Kong, brought to me by a friend at the Centre of Asian Studies at the University of Hong Kong. Her friend had taken a Polaroid picture at a picnic, which only sometime later showed an "extra" coming into focus in the background. Although I am uncertain what chemical changes might take place over time on instant film, it looked interesting at least. It appeared to be a Chinese man with a large head (perhaps too large for proper perspective) standing in the background, although the part below the shoulders was obscured by other objects. His face was in semi-darkness and looked pasty or "sickly," a kind of yellowish-green.

Finally, the only other word I have on ghost photography is this from a high-school senior.

Ghost Photo

At first, I [didn't] believe there is any ghost in the world. But about six years ago, I was saw a photograph that ...belonged to my primary teacher. It was [taken] at the entrance of the hospital. In the photograph, I saw a huge, white figure... standing among my teacher and her friends. My teacher said that she had asked the nurse in the hospital, [and] the nurse [recognized the figure and] told my teacher that the one in the photo [had died] the day before..

In this chapter, we have looked at hauntings and at physical effects that have been reported sometimes in hauntings as well as in poltergeist cases. Although apparitions and physical effects are sometimes both found in hauntings, they are rarely if ever part of the same act (such as a ghost breaking a glass).

The ESP theory of apparitions remains intact. The next chapter, however, deals with a special belief about ghosts in Chinese culture that provides still another challenge to the theory that ghosts are not physical.

II

Ghosts on People, Ghosts on Ice

2017: The 1982 edition of this book came out the same year as David Hufford's The Terror that Comes in the Night. *When I read his book I was very excited to see that he and I had come to the same conclusion about this type of ghost experience independently, although he had studied them much more extensively. I had merely read the literature on sleep and realized that many of my Hong Kong cases seemed to involve sleep paralysis.*

There is one other thing to be said about this chapter however. Parapsychological field investigators have often found temperature anomalies in hauntings, including cold spots that can actually be measured by temperature gauges. Perhaps there is something more than a "feeling of cold" related to a near-sleep state involved in some cases. I detected such cold spots myself on one such investigation. We measured isolated temperature swings of about 20 degrees (from 60s down to 40s) in certain parts of the house based on no obvious cause (like drafts). I couldn't spot these clearly without the thermometer.

Although I have not seen anything on this in descriptions of traditional Chinese culture, several people in Hong Kong told me about the concept of *bei guai chaak*, "being pressed by a ghost." Others who did not use the phrase itself nevertheless reported experiences of a similar nature. *Bei guai chaak* (let's call it BGC) involves a feeling of immobility, as if a weight were pressing down on the body. People sometimes say that they actually see a ghost on top of them. One young woman said that BGC can start with *bei guai jui*, being chased by a ghost (in one's dream); then you wake up and feel pressed by a ghost; you can't even move a finger.

This phenomenon certainly deserves looking into. If ghosts can produce such physical effects, it will put a crimp in the ESP theory of ghosts. In the first example, a sixteen-year-old girl reports having had numerous experiences of BGC (which she mentions by name). Although she has never actually seen the ghost, there have been accompanying auditory apparitions.

G096. Ten Times Pressed

I've had BGC. At night, just lying in bed awake, I feel heavy pressing on me. I can't move or open my eyes. I hear a lot of noise, like in the marketplace, but I can't tell what they are saying. The voices aren't clear. It has happened about ten times just like this. If I am able to open my eyes, it goes away and I can move. It can take a half-hour or longer.

I collected the next case by tracking down rumors of a haunted studio in a Hong Kong radio station. The technicians there interpreted the ghost as BGC. The man who told me the following is the only one I could find who actually claimed to have experienced something himself.

G097. Radio Voices

Two years ago, when I was sleeping on a bed in the studio, I felt a strange pressing and perhaps heard a person talking to me. I was sleeping lightly. I didn't know the language. It wasn't English or Chinese. It sounded like somebody upset, and I heard murmuring when I felt the weight.

I couldn't move or speak, but there was no actual weight. I woke up and tried to get up. It lasted about one minute. I tried to think of Jesus Christ, but then the force was actually stronger.

It calmed down when I thought about a Buddhist god. The force left me gradually. I could get up then. I tried to see if there was anything there, but no. Many people experienced it.

Notice that the technician said that there was no actual weight. Could there be a reason for not being able to move, other than a physical pressing? G098 sounds rather physical, however. It was reported by the same man who experienced G001 in Chapter 1 and P001 (G088) in Chapter 10.

G098. "Pushups on My Chest"

I was thirteen then... One evening, I felt the bed shake, and something leapt on me and hit me in the chest. It sounded as if it was somebody with asthma doing pushups on my chest. I said, "In the name of Christ, leave me alone," and it left. Another night, my brother screamed, having exactly the same experience. It's called BGC, being squeezed by a ghost or devil.

It is interesting, however, that although he labeled his experience as a case of BGC, he did not claim to have felt unable to move. This point remains uncertain.

So far, each case has involved an auditory and apparently tactile apparition. G099, from a thirteen-year-old boy, involves a visual apparition but still no glimpse of a ghost.

G099. The Mighty Powerful Person

One night, I couldn't sleep. I sensed some light in front of me. I wanted to open my eyes and look, but there was something pressing on my eyes. I couldn't open them. At the same time, I felt someone sitting on my body. I got scared and wanted to jump up, but no matter how I struggled I couldn't get up. I think it was mighty powerful. Because of my weight and height, I can usually push a person away if he is sitting on me, but not this one. This is really strange.

Next, a fourteen-year-old girl provides another example of a religious remedy for BGC to go with G097 and G098. She doesn't use the phrase BGC, however.

G100. Before I Wake
One day, when I was sleeping, I suddenly wanted to get out of bed, but I couldn't get up. I read the Catholic Bible in my mind, and suddenly I could get up and talk.

Another apparitional light is part of the following report from a seventeen-year-old girl. In contrast to G099, she thinks she is seeing the green light, at least, with her eyes open.

G101. The Green Ray
On a peaceful night, around midnight, I was pressed by a transparent shapeless strength. I felt short of breath, and the upper half of my body couldn't move. It was very painful. I wanted to yell and wake my family up, but I couldn't make any noise. I wanted to kick, but I couldn't even move my eyes. My eyes wanted to search for what power it was, but it was pitch dark, darker than it normally was, and I couldn't see anything at all.

My eyes reached the wall. I found... a ray of strange light (it was green) on top of my shadow (overlapping my shadow). The most unexplainable thing was how come I could see that and nothing else. Twenty to thirty minutes later, my body suddenly felt at ease and relaxed. Then, without knowing it, I fell asleep.

In G102, a twenty-nine-year-old woman gives our first example of a visual ghost, but it is not doing the pressing.

G102. A Blurry, Gray Figure

One year ago in Hong Kong, I was in the bedroom about 3 a.m. All of a sudden, I felt a heavy weight on me. I couldn't move. I opened my eyes and saw a blurry, gray figure standing next to the bed. It had long hair. I couldn't make out the face, but it was facing me. I was very afraid and closed my eyes. One or two minutes later, I felt the weight leave me. I opened my eyes and didn't see anybody.

Next, a forty-five-year-old woman actually reports a ghost on top of her. Not only can she not move (BGC), but she develops an illness according to the expectations of ancestor-worship culture.

G103. Pressed by a Plump Chinese

A couple of years ago, we rented a place in North Point. I was in the bedroom resting late one night, but I couldn't sleep. It was hot, and the door was partly open. A short, fat Chinese woman in her thirties floated into the room like the wind. She came to my bed and lay on top of me. She was face down on me, looking at me. I was very scared and couldn't move. I was semi-conscious and couldn't remember the rest. I got very sick for a couple of days, high fever and cold chills. My mother burned paper articles once after two days, and I got better.

Although the pressing ghost is a close relative in G104, from a thirteen-year-old girl, precautions are still taken in the form of a religious statue.

G104. Protected by a Buddhist Goddess

One night, my sister woke up in the middle of the night and saw my grandmother. She wanted to call her Grandma, but Grandma disappeared. The next day, my sister told my mom, and Mom put a Buddhist goddess in her bedroom. That night she didn't see her again. The next day, we put the Buddhist goddess statue in the living room. That night, in my dream, I was lying in bed, when somebody used his body to press on mine. I struggled fiercely and woke up from my dream. I saw my grandmother pressing on top of me. She was also drinking a glass of water. I used all my strength to push her, but she didn't respond. I wanted to yell but couldn't. Later, my grandma disappeared. She didn't look or stare at me. The next day, I told my mom about it, and she put the statue in my room from then on. I never saw [the ghost] again.

An eighty-three-year-old man, who says that he sees ghosts very often, told us the next account. Not only does he see ghosts on top of him; he claims to engage some of them in conversation.

G105. Paranormal Parimutuel

Sometimes, they lie on top of me; I feel the pressure. They just want to be close to humans. They always lie face down, but they don't look at me.

Once, I said to one, "You always bother me. Why don't you help me make money?" The ghost did; I'm not sure whether it was male or female. It gave me numbers of horses to bet on. I won.

There was no noise, but I saw the ghost's lips move. I read the lips to get the numbers. I think I heard the ghost in my mind; I'm not sure. I bet $48 H.K. on one offtrack-betting ticket on the quartet and won $10,000 [$2,000 in U.S. funds].

Up to now, every case of being "pressed by a ghost" has been experienced, understandably, in the prone position. However, one woman told me of being immobilized while sitting down. It occurred when she was staying overnight at her brother's house. The brother was supposedly showing signs of being possessed by the spirit of his friend, a doctor who had just committed suicide.

G106. Frozen in Her Seat

We had been up all night. Early in the morning, it was stuffy in my room, and I went out to the settee half awake. [Sitting there] I felt something pressing on my shoulder and couldn't move. It was a long time before I could; I tried very hard to move my left arm. It was just constant pressure that came all of a sudden. It left after somewhat of a struggle. Later, I asked where the doctor usually sat, and it was where I had been sitting.

Although I had never thought about anything like the BGC phenomenon before, I was surprised to be able to find some examples [78] of it in the West, once I looked for it. First, a seventeenth-century British example: "Being asleep in his Bed ... by something pressing upon him, he was awakened" (Glanvill, 1689: 455). Then the person saw an apparition, although the ghost was not said to be doing the pressing.

Here is one from the southern United States: someone seemed to be getting in bed with a woman house guest, who felt something cold as ice. "It lay right up next to me. I ran my hand down the bed and I could feel the pressure beside me, but I couldn't feel anyone. Once it seemed to be lying across my legs and I couldn't move. It was terrifying" (Roberts, 1979: 45).

In a third case, a woman reports what happened to her husband one night in their allegedly haunted house in Ohio. When he found himself able to speak, he told her that he had woken up "because he had felt a great weight, like a large animal, pressing down on his chest, making it almost impossible for him to breathe" (Mihalik, 1981: 92). Eventually, he was able to get free and look around the room, but saw nothing unusual there.

---

78   I cannot vouch for any of these three examples quoted from Western sources as a carefully recorded first hand report. Then again, they might all be genuine. At any rate, they are suggestive of the BGC pattern.

BGC and sleep

I collected fifteen cases of people in Hong Kong who had experienced one or more episodes of BGC. In every case, they had been either asleep when it hit or drifting off to sleep or waking up. This is true of the three Western examples I just gave as well. Even the woman who was sitting up (G106) had just gotten up "half awake" from a sleepless night.

Why don't ghosts do this to people when they are fully awake during the day? You may well say that it is impossible for ghosts to lie on top of people when they are walking around. However, couldn't they sit on their laps when they're sitting down, or wrap them in a bear hug when they're standing up?

And then it hit me: *bei guai chaak* is sleep paralysis! Although much about sleep is still a mystery, there is a correlation between sleep paralysis and the "hypnagogic" state, a condition of almost-sleep. Sleep paralysis has been observed occurring as "a benign, transient paralysis at the beginning or end of sleep usually associated with distressingly clear consciousness" (Rushton, quoted in Kleitman 1963: 236). It will be especially distressing and not so benign if you believe it is a ghost doing the pressing to keep you immobile (paralyzed)!

Ah, but what about the auditory and visual apparitions that thirteen out of fifteen people reported in addition to the paralysis? The hypnagogic state involves not only sleep paralysis but also "hypnagogic hallucinations," which may be visual, auditory, or tactile (Schneck, 1977)![79] Sometimes, hypnagogic hallucinations occur as people are about to fall asleep but before they realize it, "often smoothly continuous with the immediately prior waking events" (Dement, 1978: 77). This may explain why so many of all types of "waking" apparitions, not just BGC, occur when people are either close to sleep (43%) or in a quiet state (9%) in the Chinese study (and in Western studies as well).

---

79 These hallucinations are similar to the dreams of REM (rapid eye-movement) sleep, when the body is also essentially paralyzed except for the rolling eyes (Dement, 1978: 26). The perception of outside events is also cut off, which is why the woman in G101, for example, couldn't see things normally.

ESP may well be the spark that touches off the "hallucination" or apparition. Recent ESP research emphasizes that "altered states of consciousness" (ASC) like sleep are more conducive to ESP. It could be argued that the BGC cases are all simply hallucinations rather than apparitions (ghosts), because none of the fifteen cases is evidential. The most usual way to show that a case is evidential, however, is for it to be collective. Unfortunately, other people are not likely to be around in a waking state to share a BGC apparition, and none of the fifteen cases had others present. If some of the BGC cases really are apparitions, then the ESP spark could have been turned into the plausible "drama" of a ghost lying on top to go along with the condition of sleep paralysis.

There is a phenomenon in Western culture of the occult that sounds like BGC, namely the "succubus" or "incubus." The succubus in Medieval European witchcraft was a female witch, demon, or devil that had sexual intercourse with sleeping people. The incubus was the male equivalent. Not only does the feature of lying on top sound like BGC, but one wonders if the hypnagogic state might not imitate the full dream state (REM sleep) in which there are penile erections (Dement. 1978: 26). In the Chinese cases, however, the sex of the "pressing ghost" in a prone position was mentioned in only two cases, and both were female ghosts on female respondents. [80]

Ghosts on ice

Then I noticed something else about the BGC cases: four of fifteen involved a feeling of cold, or 27%, compared with only 6% of all of the apparition cases (ten of 176 were cold). Although the numbers are small, this surprising concentration of cold cases in BGC reports is high enough to be very significant statistically. [81]

---

80   One other cross-cultural comparison involving sex is possible. It has been found that males are four times as likely as females to experience sleep paralysis (Kleitman, 1963: 236). However, nine out of fifteen of the Chinese BGC cases were reported by women.

81   χ^2 = 12.6, p<.001. If "corrected for continuity," it is still 8.9, p<. 01.

I found this exciting, because I always wondered why people sometimes feel cold when they see a ghost. Maybe this connection with BGC would provide a clue. First, let's look at the four overlap cases, ones that have both cold and BGC. A twenty-seven-year-old man seems to have had quite a siege of it in G107.

G107. Strange Bedfellow

Every night for four months, every time I lay in bed I had a ghost pressing on my body. I got a cold chill and felt a heavy weight. I couldn't move or scream or yell. There was nobody else in the house anyway.

The next one, from a twenty-two-year-old woman, is an ancestor-worship case with a feeling of a presence but nothing visual.

G108. The Presence and the Chill

On the seventh day after my mother's death, I was asleep perhaps, but I knew what was going on. I couldn't open my eyes or move my body at all. I felt the presence of my mother (felt a presence and assumed it was my mother). I felt a cold chill. It lasted only a couple seconds, and then I could open my eyes and saw nothing. Nobody else was in the room. Nobody else in the house experienced anything either.

In G109, a fifty-year-old Chinese woman describes an actual apparition, not on top of her but associated with the BGC paralysis and the cold.

G109. The Westerner in the Gray (Flannel) Suit

In 1961, I went to Holland with my brother and sister-in-law. When I went to bed that night, I had my own twin room in the hotel. I locked the door. In the middle of the night, I felt a cold chill at the head of the bed, opened my eyes, and saw a man. He was a Westerner in his fifties with gray hair and a gray suit. I saw him very clearly from head to foot for a long time (about fifteen minutes). There was no movement at all and no noise. He stared at me and said nothing. He looked very sad. I have no idea who he could have been. I couldn't move or yell, but I'm a Buddhist and recited a Buddhist prayer inside. Then he disappeared all of a sudden, with no fadeout.

Sometimes, the cold or cool feeling is described as a breeze, as reported below by a fourteen-year-old boy. Note the numbness (sleep paralysis).

G110. Morning Breeze

A few years ago, I was sleeping at home on a holiday. It was about 6 to 7 in the morning. Suddenly, I felt a breeze. At that time, my mom was out grocery shopping, and my dad was still in bed. I slept on a cot in the living room. It was a hot summer day. I only had a very thin cloth covering myself. I looked and saw a woman with a big dress, like the type that nuns wear. But I didn't dare to continue looking. I wanted to look at her face, but I couldn't. I was very scared and my body became numb. I suspected that it was my real mother who died ten years ago because of a heart problem. I slept until my present mom came home and woke me up.

Why does the feeling of cold tend to be found in BGC cases? If BGC is associated with near-sleep and hypnagogic hallucinations, is it possible that coldness is related to sleep, too? One of the entire group of 176 Chinese ghost reports, sixty were close to asleep, thirteen were in a quiet state (like studying), sixty-seven were engaged in normal activity, and thirty-six didn't say what state they were in. *All ten* of the "cold" reports were from people in a near-sleep (eight) or quiet (two) state, but only 48%

of the non-cold reports that gave the relevant information (sixty-three of 130) were near-sleep or quiet! This is highly significant statistically. [82]

Why should people near sleep or just awaking from sleep feel cold? Body temperature is highest at midday and lowest in early-morning hours. Dement (1878: 18) says that if you stay up all night, you will feel chilly around 4 a.m., "even in a well heated room." This drop of about one degree in body temperature is part of the human circadian (daily) rhythm. It is interesting that many apparitions occur in the hours from around midnight to the early morning.

However, just getting into a quiet state, whatever the time of day, will have an effect on body temperature. "Most of the changes typically associated with falling asleep are the consequence of reclining and relaxing. Cardiac and respiratory rates will decrease, body temperature will fall..." (Dement, 1978: 26).

Although I cannot be certain about this particular link in the argument, it seems to me that coming into consciousness quickly when asleep (and moving into the hypnagogic state) may make a person feel cold. After all, remember Dement's comment that the circadian rhythm would lower your temperature enough to make you feel cold at 4 a.m. even if you had been awake all night. Those who are quiet but not asleep are already somewhat cooler than when active, and may feel colder yet when they drop into the hypnagogic state unawares but remain fully conscious.

Therefore, I suggest that both the feeling of cold and BGC (or sleep paralysis) are consequences of the hypnagogic state, in which hypnagogic hallucinations also occur. Yet there is another possible cause for feeling cold that ought to be considered. When I ask people to help me get some insight into the puzzling fact that many people have reported feeling cold when they see a ghost, the answer I usually get is that "they must be scared."

When somebody says, "Cold chills ran up and down my spine," you know that the person was afraid. Do the people who say they feel cold

---

82   χ^2 corrected for continuity is 8.1, p<. 01.

during an apparition feel cold because they are afraid? First of all, only 40% (four of ten) said they were afraid, compared with 36% (fifty-nine of 166) of those who did not feel cold. This is virtually the same percentage, although it is not a very certain estimate because there are only a few cases.

More importantly, *all six* of the people who claimed to have had a *visual* apparition in connection with the cold said that they felt cold *first*! Another man, who claimed to see ghosts on many occasions, made the general comment that he often felt a cold chill *before* seeing ghosts. In other words, they were cold before they saw anything to be afraid of. The cold appears to be part of the onset of the hypnagogic state. [83]

Although not all of the Western cases involving a feeling of cold seem to have the cold before the visual apparition (some have ghosts with cold hands, for example), the cases mentioned in Tyrrell's (1963: 81) discussion of the matter are associated with sleep and quiet states. "I awoke in a cold sweat." Or, in probably the best documented of all hauntings, "'I felt a cold icy shiver,' says Miss E. Morton as the ghost bent over her whilst she was playing the piano" (Tyrrell, 1963: 81). Playing the piano is not being totally inactive, but depending on the piece it may have the same kind of quiet concentration as studying, which shows up several times in the Chinese cases. In another part of the Morton case, five people standing outside their bedrooms with lighted candles felt a cold wind, but their candles were not blown. They had a collective feeling of cold, but it was subjective, and presumably they had been or were about to go to sleep.

Case G111, reported by a fourteen-year-old girl, involves the initial feeling of cold and an auditory apparition (or hallucination) but no BGC.

---

83   Tyrrell (1963: 81) himself suggests that "supernormal perception [may bring] about physiological changes which might lower the temperature of the body." At least, we agree that it is a real change in the temperature of the body and not of the outside environment. One woman in Gettysburg told me of being next to a man who felt cold when she did not. The next moment he saw an apparition, which she did not see.

G111. The Woman's Cry

One night, I was asleep when suddenly a breeze passed by. It scared me and woke me up. Then I wanted to go back to sleep, but I heard a woman's voice. It seemed as if she was crying. When I opened my eyes, I couldn't hear it. Then I closed my eyes, and I heard her voice again. From that time on, I have believed in ghosts.

Next, a thirty-year-old woman reports a crisis case with cold before a visual apparition.

G112. Quiet Goodbye

Some member of the family had just died. It was around midnight when I was awakened by a cold chill. I saw a shadow sitting by the side of the bed. I couldn't see the face, but I knew it was the dead person from the clothes and from his height. I closed my eyes and wouldn't look again. The next moment, I opened my eyes and it was gone.

The other cold cases without BGC have already been given in earlier chapters. In G043 (Chapter 6), a woman felt a cold chill while studying and looked up to see a glowing white figure floating along. In G051 (Chapter 7), a young man in a record store, looking at record albums in quiet concentration, felt a cold chill and looked round to see a pair of legs.

Previously, I pointed out that BGC cases might be suspected of containing merely hypnagogic hallucinations and no real ESP-based apparitions; none of the fifteen was evidential. Two of the ten cold cases are evidential (compared with 29% of all cases being evidential, not a big enough difference to claim significance), and even those are only loosely so, since each had two other witnesses allegedly to the same ghost but not at the same time.

In conclusion, both BGC (actually sleep paralysis) and the feeling of cold seem to be related to sleep or quiet states, more precisely to the hypnagogic state. Both phenomena are therefore better seen as characteristics of the receiver (percipient) than as characteristics of the apparition. Partly because of the fact that hallucinations are associated with the hypnagogic state, and partly because there are few if any evidential cases, it is questionable whether there are any ESP-based apparitions under such conditions at all.

On the other hand, the hypnagogic state may be an altered state of consciousness that is conducive to ESP communications. The Census of Hallucinations in Britain in 1890 asked if people had experienced apparitions "when believing yourself to be completely awake." One problem with this is that people cannot always distinguish the hypnagogic state from being completely awake (Kleitman, 1963: 236). The other problem is that if we refuse to study sleep-related apparitions, we may be shutting off a horizon in apparitional research.

12

Gifted Subjects and Yin-Yang Eyes

2017: As I look back on this chapter today, I think it is interesting that I suspected some people of exaggerating or making things up who had claimed multiple ghost experiences. To a certain extent I still think this, because I have observed that some people develop a reputation as psychic and then try too hard to act out that role, even if nothing is happening. These people make up a very small percentage of my sample.

On the other hand, by now I have had several apparition and haunting experiences myself, as well as experiences with spirit mediumship (Emmons and Emmons, 2003), and I know that I am not a fraud. I also do not consider myself a gifted subject, just somebody who has lived a long time and paid close attention.

There is one final problem of major significance to deal with as far as apparitions are concerned. Are some people especially good at seeing ghosts? According to the ESP theory, one would think so, just as some people are gifted subjects in laboratory tests of ESP, even if everybody has some such capacity. Presumably, the sender (either living or dead) of an apparition is one factor, but the receiver ought to be another.

According to Chinese culture as well, some people are thought to be especially good at seeing ghosts, but because of *yin-yang* (in Mandarin; in Cantonese it is *yum-yeung*) eyes. Yin and yang are the passive and active principles in Chinese traditional metaphysics and cosmology (see Chapter 3). A person with yin-yang eyes has the capacity to see not only the active, warm world of the living but also the passive, cold world of the dead.

Tyrrell (1963: 23) states that 66% of people reporting apparitions in the Census of Hallucinations had claimed only one experience in their lives. Although it is probably largely a matter of how the questions were asked, 84% of those in the Chinese telephone and school surveys who said they had encountered a ghost reported only one experience, 9% mentioned two, 2% three, and 5% eight or more. As some people no doubt failed to mention one or more experiences, it is difficult to estimate how close these percentages are to the real ones.

However, it is possible to look at some case studies of individuals who claim to have had numerous apparitions, in order to see if their experiences are any different from those of one-time receivers. The first subject came to our attention in the random telephone survey. He was an eighty-three-year-old traditional Chinese doctor who said that he saw ghosts all the time. Since he was very willing to talk to us, my wife, Chee, and I packed up the tape recorder and paid him a visit.

The doctor with yin-yang eyes

Dr. H, his wife, and various other relatives who happened to be in his apartment greeted us cordially. One wall was covered with containers of Chinese medicine.

"I never told anyone this," he said to his relatives as much as to us, since they also seemed surprised to hear a few of the things he ended up telling. As usual, the accounts here are translated from the Chinese.

G112. Canton Street Ghosts

The first time I discovered that I could see ghosts was in my teens in Canton city. I saw ghosts with white tops and black slacks. They were just walking on the street. I couldn't get a chance to see their faces, and they ran right into [through] the wall. There were two of them: a man and a woman. My hair stood on end. I went looking for them, but I couldn't find them. They looked just like regular humans, nothing special. It was 9 p. m.

G113. They Come and They Go

I can see ghosts all the time in the house here. I have a little shrine, where I worship the ghosts, too, any ghosts. I don't recognize any of them. I see them all of a sudden, and they disappear suddenly. Nobody else sees them. They are all different; I never see the same one twice. Most of them wear white tops and black slacks; I have no idea why. I never pay attention to them; they come and they go. I also saw a female ghost going into a woman's flat next door.

   We rented a room to a woman here. She moved out; maybe the ghosts disturbed her. She died a couple of years ago in the hospital, but I haven't seen her return.

Aside from the shrine, Dr. H mentioned one other ancestor-worship tendency regarding a ghost. Once, he saw a ghost on the street at night, after which his arm hurt very badly. He burned incense, and it stopped hurting. Another negative side to ghosts he noted was that he always sees them licking the skin of roast pigs; therefore, he never eats roast pork.

   Dr. H, however, certainly does not consider ghosts always to be dangerous or unhealthy, in spite of the general tendency for Chinese culture to define them so. He was the one who got the BGC ghost (G105 in Chapter 11) to give him the winning horse numbers on the "quartet." He went on to say that he bet on horses five or six more times. Once, the Jockey Club refused to pay him the $2,480 H.K. (about $500 U.S.) that he should have won on a $10 quartet bet.

   He showed us all the documentation, including letters from the Jockey Club that said that, although he had picked the right horses (5, 3, 2, 10), his ticket *application* had circled the wrong dollar amount of his bet. He

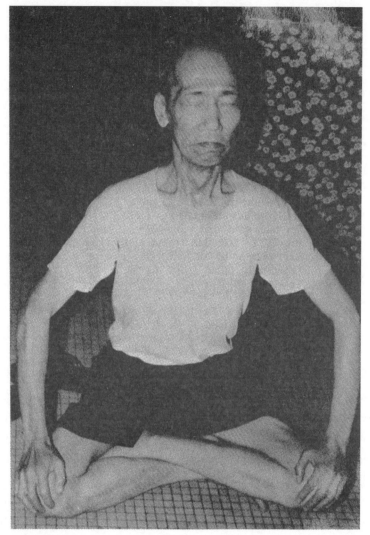

Dr. H

lost on a technicality, even though it was clear from his ticket how much
he had really bet.

In the next report, Dr. H sees multicolored clothing, a rare occurrence
(cf. Chapter 7), in contrast with the usual black and white. Note the time
of day (night), the time of lowest body activity and temperature for most
individuals.

G114. Multicolored Marchers

Once, I saw a bunch of real young ghosts marching in the house. I looked again and they were gone. They were young Chinese about eight to ten years old and had on assorted-color clothing. It was about 3 or 4 a.m.

G115. The Ghostly Nuisance

I used to see ghosts all the time in China when I was in my forties, and I would act as if I had seen nothing. When I was in the army, I went out at night one time to get a snack. The ghosts kept bothering me, and I couldn't find the place. They circled around me, but they didn't really pay attention to me. And when I really looked at them, I couldn't see them. They disappeared. They wore black and white again, and were both male and female. They wore pigtails; they were all like that, even in India. I haven't seen any Western ghosts.

The next case comes close to qualifying as a physical effect performed by a visual apparition (cf. G038 in Chapter 5). However, notice that Dr. H says first that he *jumped* up. Then he thought he saw ghosts helping him, as in the case of the "helping hand" (cf. G036 in Chapter 5) that seemed to be pulling on the blanket at the same time as the living person was. In other words, there is no evidence that the apparition itself was causing the effect.

G116. Dodging the Bullet

In two wars, I never got hurt. In Bangkok, a bullet almost went through me, but I jumped up. I saw Indian and Thai ghosts lift me up, throw me up to miss the bullet.

Dr. H says that he is not afraid of ghosts, even though he sees them almost every day. He knows they're there in the morning but pays no attention to them.

He has never known anybody else with yin-yang eyes. He said he thought that you can see ghosts only when you have no hair on your arms and legs, then showed us how hairless his arms and legs were, as he sat there in his white T-shirt and dark bermuda shorts. Ordinarily, he sees ghosts with his eyes open, except when he is meditating. Then he can see them with his eyes closed, very clearly as if his eyes were open.

Right at that moment, he showed us how he meditated, by getting down on the floor and sitting in a yoga position with his arms and legs folded. When I asked him if he was seeing anything, he answered right away, "Clouds and people walking on clouds: monks and nuns, fifteen or twenty people." After looking up and talking a bit, he went back into it and claimed to be seeing a different group of people.

Dr. H thinks that ghosts have helped him in his medical practice. When he was in his teens, he dreamt about one of the eight genies (in Taoism), who said to him, "Why don't you become a [traditional Chinese] doctor?" Then he went to college in China at age eighteen to study medicine, and he's been a doctor ever since. He also studies yoga.

Once, when he was sleeping, he saw the Earth God, who touched him. He burns incense every time he sees something like that. He has never been to the underworld. They just come to him.

He has ESP, too. When he looks at his patients, he can tell when they are going to die. Their ears look black to him. Once, he saw one of his patients while he was meditating. The next day, the person died.

He also told us something about his own unusual state and history of health. He thinks he has died three times, passing out for ten or fifteen minutes each time. They all thought he had died. Another peculiarity is that he claims to sleep only two or three hours a night.

My reaction to all of this was that it was a bit fantastic. Dr. H certainly seems like a nice person who would not intentionally distort or deceive. I was unable to see any significant vested interest in any monetary sense, such as with his Chinese medicine. He would be unlikely to expect us to advertise his psychic abilities as proof of his excellence as a Chinese doctor. After all, he is a doctor in the scholarly tradition and not a priest or spirit medium. However, I do think that he is proud of his role as a kind of mystic, a role not really very incompatible with the Chinese doctor role (as it would be if he were in Western medicine). I think that he tried to impress us with his excellent health and acuity for an eighty-three-year-old man, and his psychic ability is part of his overall presentation of self. This might have provided the motivation for some innocent exaggeration.

One thing that made me suspicious was the way so many unrecognized ghosts supposedly went in and out of his apartment (G113). In a "normal" haunting, even if the ghosts were people he had never known personally, he ought to begin getting some reruns, since hauntings are the ghosts linked to a place, not just a random group of wanderers!

I suspect that his ghosts are hallucinations, an explanation consistent with the fact that he sleeps only two or three hours a night, which might result in a lot of hypnagogic and even waking hallucinations, since he doesn't give himself much chance for the regular dreams of REM ("rapid eye-movement") sleep. On the other hand, judging from his horse-betting evidence and from the crisis clairvoyance he says he has when people die, maybe he does have strong ESP (even though on the telephone interview he claimed not to have had any ESP experiences, or anything other than ghosts). [84] If so, his "ghosts" may be clairvoyant images, which can be very realistic for some people, in which case the apparent apparitions in his apartment could be people seen from other locations, not haunting ghosts.

Another problem is the unusual ease with which he claims to call up images when meditating. He had barely gone into the lotus position when he was describing the monks and nuns on the clouds. There are also the culturally determined religious phenomena, such as his dream

---

84   As far as beliefs go, he said he believed only in feng shui, ghosts, and ESP out of a list of fourteen phenomena.

vision of the Earth God. But then, who am I to be suspicious of a doctor with yin-yang eyes?

The man from Canton

This is the forty-nine-year-old man who reported his encounter with the "Canton Tree Monster" (M001), which is probably the one tale that has stretched my credulity more than any other in the study. He gave several other accounts in his telephone interview that are more plausible and quite interesting, such as the ones I have called "The Ghost of the Big Black Cat" (G031) and "The Lucky Opium Smoker" (G023), both in Chapter 5. The latter, which referred to a person in white sitting on the bed and to the smell of opium, has a continuation in the following haunting report.

G117. Door Ghosts

I have seen a few figures all in white gowns at least five or six times in that house. They look like the one I saw on the bed. Sometimes, I'd close the door, and they would open it for me. Sometimes, they would lock it from the inside. Once, I knew that one of them had pinched me, but I couldn't see them then. The next day, I had a big bruise.

Here we have the recurring problem of physical effects (cf. Chapters 5 and 10).It is unclear at first whether these are simply PK features in a haunting, or the ghosts have been caught in the act. However, it then appears that they have locked him out (from the inside, where he can't see them), and finally he says that he didn't see the pinch but attributed it to them. Next, he reports another apparently atypical feature, touching a normal-feeling ghost body; whereas most touching is done by the ghosts, and when reached for, the apparition usually retreats or dissolves. [85]

---

85   Cf. section 2 on senses in Chapter 5, and section 1 on disappearing or fading out in Chapter 7.

G118. Rare Cuisine

I was coming home at night in Canton, when I was seventeen or eighteen. I saw a woman kneeling down in the patio area in front of the house. She was wearing a white top and bottom and looked as if she was cooking. There was a woman tenant staying with us then, so I went over and patted her on the shoulder (thinking it was her) and said, "Are you cooking this late at night?" She didn't answer me or turn around. The shoulder felt normal, yes. I didn't think it was very strange then, and went in the house and told my mother. My mother said, "The woman has gone to town." When I went out again she was gone. Therefore, it must have been a ghost. The gate was locked, and there was no way to get in or out. There were no traces of any cooking.

G119 is perhaps the most interesting of his cases, certainly the most consistent with the general pattern of hauntings. There are apparitional voices and noises (glass breaking with no evidence of real glass is common), collectively perceived, and a smattering of physical effects (door and light effects are also common).

G119. Laughter in the Kitchen

The first time I encountered a ghost was when I was fifteen. I was coming home to our very old house about 8 p.m., and I saw that the door was wide open. I thought maybe there was a thief, but there wasn't. I went in and closed the door and fell asleep. Later, I got up and was doing homework with my sister, who was seventeen years old then. My mother was there working on the job she had of making hemp at home. Then we heard a glass fall and break in the kitchen.

We looked into that room, but there was nothing (no sign of a broken glass). Two minutes later, all three of us heard a male laughing hysterically in that same room. My mother went in there to check, but there was nobody there.

So she went out to ask for help and locked the door, leaving us two kids behind. We were very scared, so I got a knife and we both locked ourselves in the bedroom.

Ten men came to help and yelled in that kitchen area, "Come out whoever you are, or else we'll shoot!" They were holding battery-operated searchlights (it was a huge house). Suddenly all the lights in the house and all the hand-held lamps went out. Just a little while later, all the lights went back on again. They searched and found nothing.

Except for the comments I have already made about the dubious features of this man's reports, I can think of no other insights or explanations in terms of falsification or exaggeration. I see no motive for him to share these experiences at great length on the telephone and to distort them consciously in the process.

As far as the tree monster is concerned, perhaps he saw some kind of normal animal in the tree, and got carried away with fright resulting in distorted perceptions (illusions). Although he scores a solid 5 on the ancestor-worship scale (out of a maximum of 8), he tells no fantastic ancestor tales. Moreover, he claims no experiences with any of the other thirteen phenomena listed, including ESP (like Dr. H, but in contrast to the third "gifted subject" in this chapter), and doesn't even believe in seven of the fourteen on the list. He says that he has seen spirit mediums and found them inaccurate.

The prolific psychic

The third and last gifted subject to be included in this chapter, a fifty-year-old college-educated woman, provided the greatest wealth of detail in the form of nine apparition experiences and five ESP cases. Moreover, as unique and interesting as they are, they are all internally consistent and generally quite plausible in terms of the theories discussed in this book.

Two of her cases have already been discussed: G009, in Chapter 1, "Destiny in Bangkok," which appears to be a precognitive apparition of the airline personnel killed in a hotel fire; and G109, in Chapter 11, "The Westerner in the Gray (Flannel) Suit," a case of cold combined with sleep paralysis (BGC). [86]

Here is the first of three ancestor-worship cases, a post-mortem apparition. She had an average score (4) on the ancestor-worship scale. Notice that some Asians (especially Koreans, although the respondent is Chinese) believe that the soul will return after three or one hundred days, not just multiples of seven up to forty-nine.

G120. A Father Looks in on His Daughter

Exactly one hundred days after my father's death, I was working with an electric saw, which I couldn't fix. I looked up and saw my father, who was very handy with tools, smiling at me. For a moment, I forgot that he was dead. He didn't move and made no noise. I saw him for just a couple of seconds, looked down, and when I looked up again he was gone. My brother and some other relatives were there, but no one else saw him but me apparently. I didn't say anything about it.

The next one could be a haunting type of physical effect, or a poltergeist involving PK from one or more living persons present.

G121, P013. The Curling Candles

As Buddhists, we believed that my mother's spirit would return after her death. At 9 p.m. we were waiting, and had two white candles [on the altar]. At 9:30 the two candles curled up by themselves like two cow's ears or like unicorns. Everybody saw it.

---

86   That this subject had a visual apparition evidently under the hypnagogic state makes me more likely to think that the hypnagogic state may be ESP-conducive, and not just hallucinatory.

Who would the focus or agent of the PK force be in this next case?

G122, P014. Sneaking a Nap

When my father had died, the children had to stay awake all night [waiting for his soul to return]. I was very tired after a couple of days [without sleep] and went up to the second floor to take a nap. When I was sleeping, the blanket came up and flew over my whole face. I went back downstairs, because we were not supposed to sleep for some days, I guess. I don't remember [how long].

Of course, a lack of sleep might make hypnagogic hallucinations easier, creating a kind of self-fulfilling prophecy. In G123, a haunting, she is in a quiet state, studying, as has been mentioned in several of the apparition cases.

G123. The Man in the Yellow Uniform

When I was in form II [eighth grade], in my teens, living in Macao, we had a very old, very big house. My bedroom was also very big. I was in my room studying for a chemistry test the next day, when I looked out the door into another room and hallway by a door to the roof. There I saw an old man in an olden uniform. He had his hair in a bun with a white cloth, and a pin sticking into the hair. His beard was very long and white, and he had a yellowish-beige uniform with black-and-white boots. I saw him walk out to the rooftop, but I was too scared to go out and see him. He didn't look at me, but just walked past my room. I heard nothing.

Thirty years later, when I was buying antiques, I saw a doll exactly like him, and I bought it. It has a kind face, like a lucky Buddha.

In G124, there is more mystery to the house in Macao, some of the peculiar noises often heard in hauntings, unless it was an animal they could not detect, perhaps.

G124. Dancing in the Ceiling

In the ceiling of our old house in Macao, we heard "horses running around" about fifteen minutes before midnight. We wondered if it could be mice. There was no floor above that ceiling. My father, mother, and brother heard it, too. I was in my teens. One morning, my brother heard it and fell down the stairway he was so scared. We even broke open the ceiling and saw nothing.

Apparitions of objects without any people are rare but not unheard of. This is the only example from the Chinese study. It might be better called a kind of clairvoyant vision of the "scrying" type, as in crystal-ball gazing, in which an object appears against a blank field.

E003, G125. The Chrysanthemum and the Rose

A few months later (after seeing the man outside my room), while lying in bed, I saw a black chrysanthemum on the wall, thirty inches in diameter, a shadow. We had none in the house. When my cousin slept in the same place, he saw a red rose. Years later, we discovered what the other had seen when we discussed it in Hong Kong.

In one more apparition case, this time in Hong Kong, there is a partial body, unlike the clear, colored image of the man in her house in Macao.

G126. Black Slacks

Ten or fifteen years ago I lived in Shatin [in the New Territories]. I had to pass the train station before I got to the house. They have often run over people there. I would pass over the bridge, stop the car, and walk over the tracks to get to my house. Once,

I thought a black dog was following me. I looked again and saw a person with the bottom half only, in slacks. It followed me each time I started to walk. When I turned around once more, it disappeared. It was only half a body, walking like a human. I got scared and ran home.

When asked why she had had so many experiences with ghosts, she replied that she thought she had "sixth sense" (ESP). It is interesting that she did not say yin-yang eyes. Notice that her ESP experiences, including the two below on World War II attacks, involve somewhat vague premonitions of danger rather than very specific messages. Also, all of them are precognitive (predict the future), as was her apparition of the airline personnel (G009).

E004. Escape to Macao

In Hong Kong in 1941, about two or three days before the Japanese attacked, I felt very confused and terrible. I told my father that I didn't know why, but something would happen. He said, don't worry. But we had to escape to Macao, which was neutral.

E005. Unexpected Attack

When I was going off to school one day in [Macao], dressed as a girl scout, I felt confused in the same way. I asked my father, "Why do I feel this way?" Two or three days later, planes attacked Macao unexpectedly to bomb gasoline supplies.

On the other hand, when most people were afraid during the leftist riots of 1967 in Hong Kong, she felt no necessity to leave. And things calmed down.

The next three cases involve a "let's-leave-this-place" feeling before falling objects on a smaller scale.

E006. Bingo!

Seven or eight years ago, I used to go play bingo with friends at the Kowloon Cricket Club every Friday night. One night, I was losing every game and said, "This is an unlucky seat; I'll sit across the table." A loudspeaker fell on that very seat, and the glass table was broken. My skull would have been cracked open.

E007. Timber!

My brother and I used to play at a lumber company that had imported lumber from Europe. We were jumping up and down on the lumber when I took my brother away from it, just before it fell down.

E008. Falling Fabric

I was buying some material once. It was yellow cloth, real thick, and as high as two people. My father told me to measure it; but I told my cousin, "Let's leave," just before the cloth fell.

Although I suppose that the last two ESP cases are not particularly amazing, her overall testimony is the most significant of the three from "gifted subjects." She claimed to have had experiences only of ghosts and ESP (the other two people claimed ghosts only), and said that she believed in six of the fourteen paranormal phenomena.

In general, it may be important that among the very few people I suspect of some at least unintentional exaggeration, two are in this chapter. Even if they have had some genuinely strange experiences, once they take on the identity of psychic person, they may try too hard to be convincing in that role.

13

New Materials about Ghosts

Added cases

Although I have not been able to return to Hong Kong for more interviews since 1982, I did use several methods for examining additional cases collected by others. This is more difficult than it might seem. Through our authors' website (ScienceandNewAge.com), Facebook and Twitter communications I managed to get only one (the one from Jim Kemp included below). There were five others in existing publications, and 35 more online (YourGhostStories.com).

There are many pitfalls involved in collecting apparition experiences, and I do not mean to be overly critical when dealing with these cases. I'm not saying that I could have done any better using the same methods.

The group of 35 online ghost reports were those listed as of February 8, 2013 on YourGhostStories.com for Hong Kong, China, Taiwan and Singapore. Clearly the administrators of the site are aware of the difficulties in collecting these submissions, and they use several controls to avoid sensational (especially sexual), fictional materials, including rejecting inappropriate material and requiring submitters to be over 13 years of age. You can easily read all of these cases by viewing them online at "Your Ghost Stories." Keep in mind that the democratic nature of the Internet makes it likely that many people submitting or reading these cases are more interested in entertainment than they are in social science.

In some ways the online cases are similar to the ones in this book. For example, 54% are visual (compared to 70% of mine), 23% are auditory (vs. 27%), 9% involve smell (vs. 1%), 23% are collective (vs. 25%), and 11% involve ancestor worship (vs. 14%).

One big difference is that 31% involve sleep paralysis (or *bei guai chaak*, "being pressed by a ghost," BGC) compared to only 9% of my cases. One reason for this may be that BGC is more startling to people (both experiencers and readers) and therefore more likely to be reported to the website. Another possibility is that if people are making things up to have a good story to tell, BGC may be an expected element in Chinese ghost stories. I had suspicions that 23% of the reports ("stories") were either made up or exaggerated. Also, three cases (9%) involved a physical effect, compared to 1% of mine, although we're dealing with a very small sample in the online cases.

My next case comes from an article by James McClenon (1990: 67) in which he compares the anomalous experiences of college students in China and the United States. A student in Xian, China reported seeing a female standing for a long time by the door while the rest of the family were asleep on the floor. When his father woke and turned on the light to go to the bathroom, the ghost disappeared but then reappeared again after the light was turned off. This is not a collective apparition, and indeed the student got no social support for its truth when he related the experience. Interestingly the apparition was visible without the light on, but not when it was on. This fits the "self-lit" phenomenon discussed in this book.

One report that I missed in my 1980 review of the literature was published by Hankey in the *California Folklore Quarterly* (1943: 305-306) about a Chinese village house for adolescent girls to stay before their marriage. "The girls' house was suddenly filled with tremendous banging, crashing sounds, as if heavy earthenware were being dropped and shattered. Even the beds rattled." Investigation revealed no cause for the noise. Later on townspeople came and saw a pot and a kettle falling down by themselves. After shamanic rituals were performed the girls moved back in and had no further experiences. Although this account might contain some elaboration after the fact (such as the physical effects after others arrived), the first part sounds very much like a similar apparitional crashing sound I had reported to me by students at Gettysburg College living in an allegedly haunted house off campus.

There are two other reports in the same folklore journal from Li (1945: 279-280). In the first a girl saw a figure walking in front of her through the family courtyard and called but received no response. The next day the family determined that there had been no one else there at that hour. Later it was discovered that a servant girl had committed suicide there. More on this case below in the section on Economic Importance.

Li's other report (1945: 279-280) involves a student seeing her friend Yu Mei (whose "face was distorted with deep lines of sorrow") approach down the path but then vanish. The next day a telegram arrived telling of Yu Mei's death the previous afternoon. This of course is a crisis apparition case, occurring within 24 hours of the death.

Next I am grateful to Jim Kemp, a semi-retired professor of Asian studies, who has allowed me to present the following account. Jim taught English as a second language in Taiwan from 1973-1977 while pursuing his own study of Confucian classics. One day in his ESL class of 20 advanced PhD physicists and engineers, he asked a physicist without warning...

" 'Do you believe in ghosts?' He deadpanned back in a monotone without hesitation, "Not in the daytime." This was not meant to be funny or sarcastic. And, a nervous reaction spread to the other students. I could feel they were very socially uncomfortable with the comment. Not only had they collectively lost a measure of "face" to the foreigner, after [in a previous class] denying ghost belief, but also they could not take back what had been spoken out loud, nor discuss it further. I wanted to pursue this as a curiosity, but I was flummoxed on how to do it.

"Only a few days later after the class had dismissed and the room was empty, the physicist came in to talk to me alone. 'My brother was possessed by a ghost. An adult had to stay home 24 hours a day with him. I did this many times as he is my younger brother. He is out of high school but was unable to go to college because of the ghost problem. (I took it to mean 19-21 years old and within the past year.) His demeanor was grave and uncomfortable.

" 'My brother would take off his clothes and get naked. He had violent and loud arguments with "someone" at night only he could see. The neighbors were alarmed and immediately wanted him exorcised. We refused. We are modern, educated, and Christian. We don't believe in such things. We even destroyed our ancestor tablets when we joined the church and were baptized. We were forced by the neighbors to do something as the episodes were becoming more frequent, more boisterous, and more angry, with a lot of dirty language.

" 'We took him to a Western educated doctor without result for several months of Western medication. [my guess an anti-psychotic] Nothing worked. We then took him to a Chinese traditional herb doctor for several months without improvement. Actually the episodes increased in frequency and ferocity. It was very difficult to control him without tying him up in a chair at times, always at night, never in the daytime.

" 'One night he was having an episode and three adults could not control him. He overpowered us and leaped naked out the second story window. He landed on the hood of a taxi passing by and rolled off the roof and down the trunk. He landed on his feet and ran off before we could get downstairs and capture him. He ran off and was gone in a dash. It took us three days of searching to finally find him in police custody, raving and refusing to wear clothes. He was like a wild man and very strong. When we got him home again a group of neighbors told us this was too much and too frightening to continue. They threatened legal actions if nothing were done.

" 'We didn't know what to do, nor how [to go] about the exorcism the neighbors demanded. They quickly volunteered to help us. We engaged a Taoist priest and a spirit medium (tang ki) to perform a séance and exorcism. We went to the City God Temple (Cheng Huang, a court official of the Taoist underworld [who] handles unruly ghostly affairs).

The medium underwent a trance and started talking with my brother. Not only that, but the ghost talked with the medium as well. She said that they [she and my brother] were married in the Tang Dynasty (618-907 CE). He [my brother] had been reborn many times, but she was still languishing in Earth Prison (hell) as a hungry ghost and she was jealous. He, in turn, wanted nothing to do with her. In the séance they struck a deal to provide her with paper clothes [effigies], paper ceremonial money, and other goods. If she came back to pester my brother, she would be sued in front of the City God for breach of contract and further punished. [Chinese hell tortures are quite horrid and graphic in Chinese folk religion.] The paper items were burnt according to custom and witnessed by the Taoist priest. Following this he has not had a problem for a year, or so.'

[Comments by Jim Kemp]: "I found this story telling on a couple of points. It was 'my brother' and not someone he heard about. He told me this in confidence and frank embarrassment. I was asked not to mention it in class, nor with other teachers. He said he was physically present during many of the episodes and at the temple ritual. Again, not family lore. His story was halting in places as he stumbled to recount the episodes and horror. I was very curious as to his motivation to confide in me a painful episode in his family's life. 'You are my teacher [he said]. You teach me English for me to succeed. I want your research to succeed as well.' I took the comment at face value without guile and still do 35 plus years later."

Now for my comments. This case illustrates several things. One is that scientists (both in modern China or Taiwan and in the West) are hesitant to discuss the paranormal, but of course they do have experiences. Next we can see clearly the Chinese cultural context and interpretation. Ghosts are usually feared, and there is a strong connection between ancestor worship, ghosts (apparitions), spirit possession and spirit mediums. Since this is really a possession and mediumship case without an apparition, it provides a good segue to the next two chapters.

Some of us have trouble accepting spirit possession cases like this one at face value and wonder if the person doesn't just have some psychological problem. I tend to think that way myself, although in the next chapter I present a couple of possible possession cases that I was involved in.

One time in the Spiritualist community of Lily Dale, New York a woman who seemed friendly and normal otherwise began to act strangely as if possessed by some nasty intelligence. I found it amusing that many spirit mediums, who would generally accept the possibility of spirit possession, thought that she was faking it to get attention. Some people tried to exorcise the spirit (or demon), but it didn't seem to take. Then I talked with her alone for a while because I was fairly well acquainted with her and thought I might be able to help. Part of the time she seemed normal, but then she would lash out violently and say something very nasty to me. It seemed so out of character, and I was partly afraid that she might really be possessed and do something dangerous. I have not seen her since and have often wondered what was really going on and how she made out after that.

My work since 1982

Part of me sees the 1982 edition of *Chinese Ghosts and ESP* as sufficient evidence for the universal ghost experience, because of the similarities between these cases and ones in the U.S. and the UK. Since then I have gathered more cases in the U.S. especially, but the main development in my thinking has been theoretical.

One piece was "Ghosts: The Dead Among Us" (Emmons, 2003) in the Sage *Handbook of Death and Dying*. There I pointed out all of the different ways that people frame ghosts. Normal science denies them without much serious consideration. Parapsychology took them seriously from about 1882 (the Society for Psychical Research in London) but then by the 1930s turned mostly to studies of psi (like ESP tests of card guessing) in the laboratory. Nevertheless ghosts are widespread in world folklore and have important cultural meanings (as in Chinese ancestor worship). Even in the West ghosts have been important as literary devices (as in Dickens' *A Christmas Carol*). Popular culture is full of them (Casper, Harry Potter etc.), and as pointed out earlier, almost half of Americans admit believing in them now in surveys. In my sarcastic conclusion I wrote, "It is difficult to take ghosts seriously in Western academe without becoming subject to ridicule. If scholars and scientists were not so haunted, we might construct a theory of cultural elaboration in which we could look for some basis for ghosts in experience, then see how this experience becomes framed variously by human cultural constructions. (Emmons, 2003: 94)."

That same year Penelope Emmons and I published *Guided by Spirit: A Journey into the Mind of the Medium* (Emmons and Emmons, 2003). "Ghosts" comes up eleven times in the index, partly because many of the mediums we studied had had ghost experiences, 69% of them (Emmons and Emmons, 2003: 184), which is about seven times the percentage of the general population who admit to ghost experiences. Clearly there is a connection between ghosts and spirit mediums (and possession, as I pointed out above), partly because of the culture of the spirit world, and partly because people who do spirit mediumship very commonly have other types of paranormal experiences as well. Also, 21% of the 120 spirit mediums (pp. 189-190) we studied had experienced apparitions of spirit friends (sometimes called "imaginary playmates") and/or of their spirit guides. For example, Penelope as a child often saw her "Turquoise Master," a male figure in a long robe who collapsed into a turquoise ball of light when other people besides Penelope were present (p.47). We also have a section on spirit mediums in China and other societies (pp. 269-274).

By 2012 we were ready to bring all of our paranormal studies together in *Science and Spirit: Exploring the Limits of Consciousness* (Emmons and Emmons, 2012). There are chapters on ghosts and on spirit mediums (pp. 102-112, 125-135), but the book as a whole considers how different types of evidence for paranormal consciousness fit into the question of whether there is life after death (survival), something I didn't deal with very much in the 1982 edition of *Chinese Ghosts*. This book (*Science and Spirit*) is worth reading for people who want to focus more on the theories and issues involved in apparitions and hauntings and spirit mediumship.

I should mention one other book: *At the Threshold: UFOs, Science and the New Age* (1997), even though it would seem to be more about the physical possibility of UFOs being either extraterrestrial or interdimensional. The main point of relevance is the discussion of witness reports (pp. 161-185), which sometimes seem to involve altered states of consciousness. Some researchers think that alien abduction experiences are at least partly psychic or spiritual, or that perhaps there are beings who have mastered these "paranormal" phenomena within their scientific framework.

Folklore, literature and popular culture

Chapters 3, 8 and 9 in the original edition of this book discussed the importance of ghosts in Chinese literature and folklore, and explained how folklore and rumor processes work. These factors are important culturally, but they also confuse what happens in ghost experiences due to the elaboration of elements to fit expectations. That is why I focused on collecting first-hand accounts that are less likely to be confabulated.

Nevertheless, it would be a mistake to ignore the traditional culture and popular culture elements. Here are some sources I have come across since 1982. Yu (1987) gives an excellent overview of "Ghosts in Traditional Chinese Prose Fiction," in which he emphasizes how ghosts were important throughout a very long history, there was often a blurring between fiction and nonfiction, there was often agnosticism or nonbelief in ghosts among the elite, and common themes included avenging ghosts, ghosts involved in justice or other moral issues, and amorous ghosts.

Campany (1991) deals more narrowly with Six Dynasties materials collected by the end of the sixth century CE, pointing out the overarching theme of relations between the living and the dead. These stories argue for the importance of ghosts (remembering the elite agnosticism mentioned by Yu) and advocate proper recognition and treatment of ghosts, who can also help or hinder the living (a point emphasized in chapters 6 and 15 on ancestor worship and spirit mediums in this book).

As for recent ghost lore in China, there is Bosco's (2007) study of "Young People's Ghost Stories in Hong Kong." Bosco does a brilliant job of analyzing the five most common ghost stories told by students at Chinese University from a folklore perspective. Bosco (2007: 797) argues convincingly that the symbolism in the stories "reflect[s] the tension between students' responsibility to study and their interest in sex and dating." Many of the students disagree with his analysis, but their defensiveness is not convincing, even though telling the stories may indeed also have less significant entertainment functions for many of them at least on a superficial level.

Interestingly Bosco (2007: 795) also states however that "some scholars…have taken such stories to be 'true' ghost stories, even using the stories to try to discover the underlying true universal (i.e., noncultural) nature of ghosts (see Emmons)." This reference to *Chinese Ghosts and ESP* (1982) fails to recognize that I made a distinction between first-hand ghost experiences and ghost stories (folklore), rumor and fiction. I never claimed stories like his to be true, and in fact none of his five most popular ghost-story motifs show up in my 176 first-hand reports! Joseph (Bosco), I hope you get a chance to read this; take a look at chapter 8 ("Ghost Lore and Popular Culture")!

Bosco is right however that we would still disagree about our approaches to ghosts in Hong Kong. He acknowledges that his research "does not prove there are no supernatural forces or spirits" (Bosco, 2007: 803), and he points out that some anthropologists like Susan Greenwood (2000) "strongly value the point of view of the native" and allow that ghosts might exist. He goes on to say (Bosco, 2007: 804) that his research "began with the … assumption that the spirits did not in fact exist, and asked why it was that students told such stories."

Bosco's point of view is a perfectly reasonable one and a safe one in normal science. However, he ought to recognize that I would never use his ghost stories as evidence for the "reality" of ghosts either! I prefer to respect a wide variety of approaches to the study of ghosts, including both folklore and paranthropology. Paranthropology is an anthropological/ sociological study of the paranormal in which people's first-hand experiences are taken seriously and examined for evidential elements, in addition to cultural explanations.

Another approach to ghosts is popular culture studies. I spent many good times in Hong Kong watching films about ghosts in the 1980s. Sek Kei (2001) includes a discussion of ghost films from this period. First there was the kung fu ghost story (e.g. "The Spooky Bunch" and "Encounter of the Spooky Kind," both in 1980). Sek Kei thinks that such ghost stories reflected Hong Kong Chinese anxieties in their relationship with the Mainland. However, some ghosts were good, as in "The Happy Ghost" (1984).

Following the anxiety theme, Delaplace (2010) discusses ghost stories collected in Mongolia from 2003-2008. This is a folklore and collective memory approach to understanding Mongolian depictions of the ghosts of Chinese immigrant merchants. Basically the accounts reflect fears of Chinese economic expansion.

Ghosts and the economy

One thing that the literary, folklore, and popular culture studies above remind us is that ghosts have had real practical meaning and application in Chinese lives. They have been important for matters of justice, morality, family and sexuality, politics and business.

I received the following email on March 4, 2013, forwarding a story from a news wire, dateline Beijing, China. "Four people have been jailed in China for digging up corpses to sell as brides for traditional 'ghost marriages' – where dead single men are buried with a wife for the afterlife – local reports said….A court in the northern province of Shaanxi sentenced the four to terms between 28 and 32 months…; they 'took advantage' of the 'bad tradition' of ghost marriages…." See the part about ghost marriages in chapter 6.

Another example of the economic importance of ghost beliefs can be found in an article by Rittichainuwat (2010) entitled "Ghosts: A Travel Barrier to Tourism Recovery." This study was a serious inquiry (based on surveys and interviews) into the loss of tourist revenue after the tsunami hit beaches in Thailand in 2004. It found that Chinese (and Thais) were much more likely than Westerners to avoid places where many people had been killed, especially near water, this based on stronger belief in ghosts in Asian than in Western cultures. This appears in the applied journal *Annals of Tourism Research*.

Although my article in *The Journal of Popular Culture* on *feng shui* (Emmons, 1992) is only tangentially connected to ghosts, it too shows that magic and other paranormal phenomena are taken seriously by Hong Kong Chinese when it comes to financial matters. For example, banks in Hong Kong used *feng shui* to place the safe in the right place or to shape the entrance in a way that would draw money in the door. Many Chinese restaurants in the world have a screen inside the entrance to block bad chi or ghosts from coming straight in (ghosts are not supposed to be able to turn corners).

Perhaps the best example of how ghosts have economic significance is the current real estate situation in Hong Kong. According to CNN online (Laje, April 22, 2013) a 2004 court decision in Hong Kong made it "compulsory for estate agents to report houses with a dark history." In other words, information about haunted properties (*hongza* in Cantonese) must be made available to potential buyers. In practical terms this has led to data bases (with no government oversight) listing information about apartments where people have died violent deaths, the assumption being that this would cause them to be haunted.

Websites like Squarefoot.com.hk sell such lists to realtors, according to CNN. In October, 2012 Squarefoot had 3,438 such entries. I examined Squarefoot's site on August 6, 2013 and saw lists of properties accompanied by addresses and the "case" for each, most of which were suicides, especially people who jumped or "fell" off the building. Here are some examples. "A 39-year-old woman committed suicide." "A 56-year-old woman was found dead at home" (not necessarily a violent or unnatural death, notice). "A woman in her 70s was burnt dead in her flat." CNN (Laje, 4/22/13) stated that prices for these "*hongza*" properties are 10 to 30% below the normal market value, and that owners of nearby properties complain that the *hongza* designation can affect the whole building or even the wider neighborhood.

However, *The Wall Street Journal* online (Chen and Ng, 1/14/13) stated that "The latest boom in real-estate prices has nearly wiped away Hong Kong's haunted-house discount." Their source, a Mr. Ng, says he doesn't believe in ghosts but has been buying up haunted apartments for over ten years and renting them to "expatriates, who tend to be less superstitious than locals." Over the past four years, says CNN, government data shows a nearly 60% increase in apartment rental prices. In the same period sales prices have doubled, and Mr. Ng has a dozen new competitors with the same business model. By now, according to Ng, the haunted-house discount has gone as low as 5%, and he could buy only one attractively-priced *hongza* in 2012.

This real estate phenomenon tells us a couple of interesting things. First, traditional Chinese attitudes about ghosts are still important, even in the practical world of business, just as in the case of *feng shui*, as I mentioned above. Also, if the haunted-house discount has declined, this may be largely due to demand from foreigners, especially Westerners, who are less likely to hold these beliefs.

I was surprised at the strength of traditional Chinese beliefs in the supernatural in 1980. For example, 72% of respondents to my survey of Hong Kong Island, the most modern part of Hong Kong, still practiced at least some ancestor worship. As we can see by this real estate situation, over 30 years later, ghosts still matter.

How long has this real estate pattern been going on? One of the ghost accounts referred to earlier, reported as occurring in the late 1920s in Beijing (Peking), involved the ghost of a girl walking through the family courtyard (Li, 1945: 278-279). "The [real-estate] agent admitted that the house had been vacant for a long time, because of the ghostly visitor [whom other people had seen previously]. Formerly, unpleasant people had lived in the house. They had mistreated one of their servant girls, and by persistent cruelties had driven the poor creature to suicide... My friend had seen her ghost. Needless to say, the haunted house was [then] abandoned."

The more things change, the more they stay the same.

14

Spirit Possession and Exorcism

2017: I have always been fascinated by the idea of spirit possession but uncertain about how to explain it. I don't disagree with anything I said in the 1982 version of this book. However I have had a couple of interesting experiences in my life to add. By the way, I see possession as closer to spirit mediumship (ch. 15) than to ghosts (ch. 3-12).

First, after my mother died in 1993, some of my apparent contact with her might be called spirit possession. Notice the theme of spirits inhabiting or influencing animals, especially flying ones (cases SP006 to SP008), which is common in many cultures.

I recall very clearly that one day I saw an ant in my bedroom behaving peculiarly, walking around by my bed. I then asked the spirit of my mother (mentally) to communicate with me by making the ant do certain things: first to climb up on my alarm clock, then go away from the clock, and then to crawl up on it again on a certain side, for example. I was amazed to see the ant do just what I had asked.

I know that there are several possible explanations for what happened, including far-fetched coincidence, my precognition, etc. But maybe it could be my mother possessing or controlling the ant. No one experience like this convinced me 100% that I was contacting my mother, but it certainly made me curious.

Numerous other times, including still today, I have asked my mother to help me get flying insects out of the house, because I try never to kill anything. I have seen it happen so many times that the bee or whatever will rather easily and quickly fly right out the open door or window, that it seems far beyond chance. Again there are other possible explanations, such as my communicating directly with the insect.

I realize that few people would take cases like the one above very seriously or consider them important to the discussion of spirit possession. I had another experience that is more to the usual point. As described in Guided by Spirit *(Emmons and Emmons, 2003: 74-76), I saw my wife Penelope apparently possessed (some people don't like that word and prefer "obsessed" or some other less dramatic word) by Joshua Chamberlain, the Union officer in the Civil War, on Little Round Top in Gettysburg in 1995, on the anniversary of the battle (July 1-3, 1863).*

Penelope experienced pains in the two places Chamberlain had been injured in the war, saw the battleground as he would have, and shared his thoughts, such as how he needed to get a letter to Sarah, which was the name of his mother and sister, I found out later. Penelope knew little or nothing about Chamberlain, although it is difficult to rule out cryptomnesia (hidden memories of something read in a book perhaps).

What makes the case much more evidential is that I got a call from a woman who had seen me on the TV show Ghosts of Gettysburg, *telling me about her very similar experience with Chamberlain's spirit, in a later year, also on the anniversary of the battle, a couple of hundred yards from where Penelope had been. Of all the hundreds of people who have contacted me about that TV program, she was the only person who recounted a possession experience, and it turned out to be the same soldier. Our book recounting Penelope's experience had not yet been published. I also*

found out later that Joshua Chamberlain had a habit of visiting the
battlefield on the anniversary of the battle when he was still alive.

From the point of view of parapsychology, there is something peculiar about the idea of a ghost taking over someone else's personality. Is the possessed person merely picking up the thoughts of another individual's "psyche" (which may survive the dead body) through ESP, and transferring them by speaking them in the first person, and perhaps even imitating the dead person's gestures? Or is there actually supposed to be a "psychic body," so to speak, a spirit that "takes over" inside the possessed person? I would find the former easier to believe, but generally the explanation seems to be the latter, in both Chinese and Western cultures.

Some parapsychological theory seems to be consistent with the "takeover" version. If one accepts Rogo's "phantom within" idea of apparitions (cf. Chapter 5), for example, then the same psychic body that leaves the physical body during an out-of-body experience (and may cause apparitions) may also locate itself within another person and take over. This is analogous to the idea that a haunted house is possessed by ghosts that refuse to leave because of some emotional attachment to the location. We shall examine cases of attempts to exorcise both possessed people and possessed places.

Some possessed people

It is interesting to see what kinds of behavior people attribute to spirit possession. Could some of these involve natural psychological phenomena, such as epilepsy or multiple personality? The first case here is from a twenty-eight-year-old man and the next from a fifteen-year-old girl.

SP002. The Possessed Neighbor

I saw a neighbor of ours possessed by a ghost. It was one of his enemies coming back for revenge. He got real sick, spat saliva out, and ran around like a mad person. He got better the next day.

SP003. Who's Talking to Whom?

I saw my brother talking to himself very softly, as if he were talking to somebody else. I went to ask him something, but he didn't respond, just kept on talking. Afterward, he didn't even know what he had said.

With the secondary-school students, I discovered a little subculture called *sun da* ("the god hits"), which is a combination of martial arts and calling up spirits (supposedly resulting sometimes even in spirit possession). First, there is an explanation of sorts for *sun da* from a thirteen-year-old boy, followed by an alleged possession case (SP004) facilitated by *sun da*, reported by a thirteen-year-old girl.

Sun Da

I'm not afraid to tell you. I've played *sun da*, a kind of *kung fu*. What I know is a branch of *sun da*. Before I was in the genie, I saw in front of my eyes little dots of white and green stuff. I asked my friend, the guy who taught me *sun da*, and he said that the white dots are genies, and the green dots are ghosts. The ghosts were flying in front of us, back and forth. I went up to the genies and saw them right away. There were three or four other people around me also practicing *sun da*, and they all saw ghosts, too. I learned this kind of *kung fu* when I was in primary school. I haven't played it for a long time. At home and in other people's houses, I see ghosts all the time.

SP004. The Contagious Ghost

One time, a girlfriend of mine, "A," was possessed by a ghost. She was crying one minute and laughing the next. And then she grabbed another girl's hand and said, "He's corning, he's corning." I asked some students [what was happening to her], and one girl said, "Yesterday [four of us] went to the cemetery in Happy Valley [district of Hong Kong] out of curiosity. One of the boys who knew *sun da* went there to practice. The other girl and I were watching on the side. We saw three women, but we didn't pay any attention to them. The next day (the day "A" was possessed by ghosts), the student who was practicing *sun da* told me that he had been possessed by ghosts. And when he returned to school, the ghost went into the body of "A." He also told me that the three women we had seen had gone through the students' bodies in the cemetery. He saw them. After I heard this, I believed it a little bit, because I saw how painful "A" was. After school, one boy helped "A" to ask the ghost to come out. He beat the ghost up, and the student was O.K.

One reaction I have to *sun da*, at least as practiced popularly in these descriptions, is that dots in one's vision are not the usual kind of evidence that there are ghosts present. More importantly in terms of social dynamics, *sun da* appears to be a catalyst in the kind of ghost fear among youth in Hong Kong that I referred to in the latter part of Chapter 8.

Although I have never been very worried about any harm that might come from psychic phenomena, I have seen people firsthand who have had psychological problems associated with "dabbling in the occult." Whether they would have had problems anyway I cannot tell.

One such person called me on the telephone three times in Hong Kong. The first time, he simply asked me how he could find out more about actually exorcising people. The second time, he was very agitated because the religious group I had sent him to did not match up to his expectations. The third time, when he called for yet another person to contact, he told me that he was desperate and that he had gotten himself in over his head, "fooling around with spirits." Evidently, he thought that he was possessed.

Before looking at SP005, from an adult woman, it would help to recall SP001 in Chapter1. In that case, an apparently possessed woman spoke as if she were her parents, once her brother held her middle finger to trigger the messages, and the spirits asked for paper effigies to be burned for them in the spirit world.

SP005. Guess Who's Coming to Breakfast!

In 1977, my brother was possessed in his house for one and a half days. The doctor thought he was schizophrenic, but I thought not. I'm a nurse.

His mother-in-law told me to come over there, because she thought that her daughter had used a knife and fork on him. He had blood on his face. It was early in the morning; I took a taxi to their house in Kowloon.

The two of them (husband and wife) had locked themselves up in a room. I knocked. He said, "You are the devil [ghost]; go away!" The ambulance people said that they would have to break down the door. I said, "Be patient, or he'll become violent. Wait five minutes...." In three minutes, we heard the bolt being pushed down. He opened the door.

When he came to, he seemed normal. He thought the ghost of their close friend, a doctor who had committed suicide over a week before by jumping out the window, had bit him on the lip. He had a one-centimeter-long cut on his lip. But his wife had bit what *she* thought was the doctor's ghost and actually bit her husband. Since it had happened early in the morning when they were having breakfast in the dining room, his mother-in-law thought that her daughter had used a knife and fork.

The next day was the Queen's Birthday [public holiday in Hong Kong, a British colony], so I stayed overnight. My brother told me that he sensed that his friend the doctor was in the bathroom and that the doctor wanted to pull the two of them down [have him die along with the doctor].

During the night I was there, he asked me to keep the door open to let the devil [ghost] out, but I was afraid of burglars. That morning my sister-in-law was not herself. She said, "You are a fairy sent from heaven to help us." She asked me to get her some tap water to drink, as if it were holy water.

Some Chinese say that if someone is possessed, you should press the middle finger, and the ghost will say what it wants. I used chopsticks to press on her finger, and someone else helped. She said, "I want a Rolls Royce with a chauffeur, radio, air conditioner, and some money."

The mother-in-law went to a Buddhist monk to have a paper Rolls Royce made and burned. After a while they were still afraid in the house, and it was suggested that they go traveling. Finally, they moved out and went to the YMCA in Waterloo Road. The minute they left the house, they were O.K.

He left me instructions about his affairs, noting them down systematically. Therefore, I didn't think that he was mentally ill. I thought him to have been possessed. Both of them seemed O.K. then. The Buddhist monk told him to stay away even for some months, and drew Chinese characters on the wall to drive away [exorcise] the spirit.

Early in the morning of the Queen's Birthday, the respondent experienced a feeling of "pressing" on her shoulder while sitting in the doctor's favorite spot (G106, Chapter 11).

Now let me relate another case of exorcism, a secondhand report but rather interesting. The unfortunate woman had been troubled by both mental and physical ailments. Notice that the spirits are actually exorcised from her surroundings rather than from her body--that is, she was not possessed.

She was pestered by a feeling of the presence of spirits, especially one male, and dreamed about them. She slept toward one side of the bed rather than the other where the ghosts were. She didn't see them or hear anything. Once, she dreamt that she was raped by the male. She even took a shower with some clothing over herself to keep the ghost from seeing her naked. She experienced *bei guai chaak*.

She was pestered by spirits in the hospital once, too. An in-law who belonged to a different sect of Buddhism prescribed some holy water (over which seven monks chanted for seven days and seven nights). To be polite and not offend the gods, she took it and sprayed some in an atomizer. Immediately, she felt the spirits leave that area of the veranda where they had been.

Ghosts are thought to be able to possess not only humans but also other animals, especially flying ones (birds and insects). Such motifs are found in the folklore of many societies (Thompson, 1966). In Chinese ancestor-worship culture, spirits of the dead may return on certain days as a bird, butterfly, or fly. The first Chinese case I ever heard was from a woman who called in the following when I was on Kirsty Hamilton's radio show.

SP006. The Walking Owl

The Chinese in Penang [Malaysia] believe that the dead one doesn't know he's dead until the seventh day, and then he visits, comes to say good-bye. On the seventh day after my father died, my servant told me that my father would come back. I said, "Ridiculous!"

That night, when we were in the sitting room, we heard a flap at the door, and in walked a fully grown owl! It went straight to me and turned its head just like my father did, because he had cancer and turned his head like that. Then it went down the corridor to the bed where my father used to sleep when he visited, and jumped right up on the bed! The owl just looked at me. I took the owl outside. When I let it free, it sat and hooted, and then went. I never again saw an owl.

The next animal-possession case is reported by the same man who experienced the "Smokey Ghost" (G001 in Chapter 1) and a poltergeist or haunting in Chapter 10 (P001, G088). I have heard other people tell me about the idea that a butterfly might be an ancestor, but sometimes the interpretation may be reincarnation rather than a temporary spirit possession.

SP007. The Forgiving Butterfly

The Chinese believe that the spirit will return to the house in the form of a butterfly. My grandfather's body was lying in a coffin in the sitting room, and there were eighty or ninety people in the house, including my father. My grandfather had disowned him after he had married an English woman, and they hadn't seen each other for twenty years. As my father was talking to the relatives, a butterfly came in and flew around and landed on my father's head, and then flew away. The Hakka [Chinese ethnic group] relatives said, "Your father has forgiven you!" I was twelve years old at the time.

The woman who told me the following is the same person whose pictures were disturbed in her bedroom in the poltergeist case P003 (Chapter 10), which she thinks relates to the same spirit.

SP008. The Fly

I went to Cheung Chau [Island, part of greater Hong Kong], for a school retreat once. That night, I felt very uncomfortable and couldn't sleep. There was a very oppressive atmosphere, but I did not have a feeling of immobility [I asked about BGC]. The next day, when we were sitting in a circle at the retreat, a very large fly sat on my knee. I shooed it, but it kept coming back. I was disturbing other people by the way I kept shooing it.

At about the same time, my cousin [actually only a cousin due to an adoptive relationship; he was her boyfriend] was stabbed to death by thirty-five knife blows around the head area by his mentally disturbed brother.

I think that the fly was his spirit coming back to me. Years later, I still see a large fly on the ceiling, very large for a house fly in Hong Kong, which I think might be his spirit. Flies and butterflies may be spirits.

Exorcism and the government

Without a doubt, the best-known haunting in the history of Hong Kong was that of Murray House (the Rating and Valuation Department building on Queensway, Central District), which was exorcised by Buddhist monks under government auspices on May 19, 1963. It has now become folklore, mentioned by many people I talked to in casual conversation. Even current newspaper articles frequently refer to it, often with distorted details (which show that they are working with the folklore rather than looking at the back-files of responsible journalism that generally characterized the articles that appeared in 1963).

Not only does the legend based on this case provide an exciting ghost story, for some people it serves as a proof of the truth of Chinese ghost belief, especially since even the British in control of the government took it seriously and "had it exorcised" (cf. Chapter 4). Actually, it would be more precise to say that they *allowed* it to be exorcised, in harmony with the idea that Chinese traditional beliefs should be respected. Let us examine the affair through government files (courtesy of Hong Kong Government Information Services) and newspaper articles written at the time, the best evidence available, except perhaps for direct eyewitness accounts (of which I shall present one in the next section).

SP009. Murray House

On May 4, 1963, the following government statement was released to the Hong Kong press: "Some Chinese staffs of the Rating and Valuation Department felt uneasy about some reported ghosts in Murray House, Murray Barrack. As a result, the Commission has sought S.C.A.'s [the Secretary for Chinese Affairs] advice on the matter."

The next day, articles appeared that described the alleged occurrences and tried to account for them (*Hong Kong Standard*,

Murray House

1963A; *South China Morning Post*, 1963A). Drawings, blueprints, and equipment in a dark room had allegedly been tampered with and stained. Laughter, other strange sounds, and unexplained shadows were also reported. Reasons given for the haunting were the building going on in the area, the fact that the department had just moved in a few months before, and the frustration of a previous clerk in the department (unlikely, since they had just moved into the old building).

On May 6, the government notified the press that "the Commissioner of Rating and Valuation ... met representatives of the Hong Kong Buddhist Association this [Monday] afternoon. A ceremony will be arranged in the near future to console any disturbed spirits in Murray House." It was also reported in the press that day that Murray House had been occupied by the Japanese in World War II, and that the Japanese police had tortured and killed people in the western part of the building, which was a detention center (*China Mail*, 1963a).

The government revelation of May 6 stimulated four articles the next day, including the announcement of the impending exorcism but no new details about the haunting. Two of the articles were satirical; one swiped at government bureaucracy by saying that the "ghost [had] a practical turn of mind... frustrated by certain delays emanating from that department" and therefore altered some of the blueprints (*South China Morning Post*, 1963b).

Criticism increased on May 9, when people who had lived or worked in the building came forward saying that they had never experienced anything paranormal there (*S.C.M.P.*, 1963c, d). "Sir, –What's all this poppycock about ghosts in Murray House?" one former resident wrote (*S.C.M.P.*, 1963d). "I think the whole affair is a serious reflection on the intelligence of our Civil Service.... Perhaps you would ask your reporters to find out if the costs of it are to be charged to the taxpayer." In fact, another paper reported the same day that the Hong Kong Buddhist Association would undertake the entire cost of the exorcism, about $1,800 U.S., to pay for the services of fifty monks and nuns (*China Mail*, 1963b). The latter article also revealed that "a Chinese newspaper has posted two reporters outside Murray House for the past two nights to await the appearance of the 'ghosts.' Their 11 p.m. to 6 a.m. vigil will be repeated again tonight." The affair was "hotting up," as the British press would say.

That night, the police broke up a crowd of about 300 people who broke through the gate in their excitement to get a look at the ghost (*S.C.M.P.*, 1963e). In the heightened awareness over ghosts, the *S.C.M.P.* (1963e) reported another ghost, which almost literally "came out of the woodwork": at a University of Hong Kong male residence hall, a ghost "suddenly emerged from a wall in (a student's) room and touched him on the leg as he was resting in bed."

The day before the big event, the Hong Kong Buddhist Association made the disappointing announcement that the public would not be invited inside the building for the exorcism after all, in spite of previous indications that they would be (*Hong Kong Standard*, 1963b). Only the officials of the association and of the Rating and Valuation Department, plus the press, would be inside. There would be three altars with fifty-six monks, but no nuns due to shortage of space, as the sexist decision went. Government files show that the department had been concerned about the safety of the verandahs with so many people interested in watching.

Pictures of the ceremony published in the papers afterward were all taken before it actually began, as a part of these regulations. They showed Buddhist monks sprinkling blessed water as they prayed and offering food to the spirits. Hundreds of people gathered outside the building, even though they were prohibited from going inside, and some people climbed walls and windows to sneak photographs (*Hong Kong Standard*, 1963c).

During the ten-hour rite, "wooden fish" clappers were used to call the spirits, and after the offerings were made to them on the floral-decorated altar, tablets with the names of people known to have suffered on the site were taken outside and burned to release their souls (*S.C.M.P.*, 1963f). The purpose of Chinese Buddhist "exorcism" is not really to wrench an evil spirit violently out of a person or place, but to help souls in a benevolent way to find peace in the Buddhist heaven.

Government files show that officials were generally pleased with the ceremony, although they were somewhat concerned over the tendency of foreign film companies to take close-ups of priests and monks who had "seemingly worried or care worn looks." The report of the Secretariat for Chinese Affairs states that someone "in the habit of seeing spirits at any time and place [evidently with yin-yang eyes; cf. Chapter 12], claimed to have seen many

Rev. Tai Kwong, Executive Director of the Hong Kong
Buddhist Association and monk who took part in exorcism of
Murray House

in the building." Also, after the first part of the ceremony, "the
procession and the sprinkling of vapors," some priests taking a
break "suddenly gathered at the far end of the corridor where a
spirit or spirits had been sensed. These incidents were not stunts.

They were very real to the people concerned." Later reports in early June published by the press said that no more ghosts had been encountered in the Murray House.

However, this precedent of the sanctioning of an exorcism by the government did not go without criticism, as already indicated. One letter to the editor of the *South China Morning Post*, before the ceremony, had sarcastically recommended the formation of a Ghosts Control Department and a Ghosts Resettlement Department (Nam Mo Lo, 1963). The government was not about to get in that deep. They had to walk a thin line between insensitivity to Chinese beliefs and violation of bureaucratic rationality. They even reacted rather defensively sometimes, as in the following release to a newspaper on January 14, 1969.

"You asked:

(1) What is Government's policy on ghosts?

(2) Does Government recognize that there are haunted houses in Hong Kong?

(3) Is Government concerned over the fact that rentals may be affected by ghosts?

Answer: The Government does not deal in the supernatural."

Treating this response as a kind of provocation, the *Star* (1969) printed it in the same form with a broken line around the outside for emphasis, and essentially accused the government of insensitivity to the problem: "Many Hong Kong residents are afraid of ghosts – but the Government doesn't worry about them ... [although] the loss of rental revenue is troubling many landlords.... "

The exorcist

I was fortunate to be able to interview a prominent Buddhist monk in Hong Kong with the help of my wife, who translated between Mandarin

Chinese and English. He had taken part not only in the Murray House exorcism but in many others as well.

On the subject of the Murray House, he said that workers there had often seen ghosts and therefore signed a petition requesting an exorcism. One phenomenon he mentioned that I had heard before was that a typewriter got caught inexplicably in a desk drawer, which they had to ruin to get out.

When he was in his robes, in the right frame of mind, he said that he was able to see ghosts at the exorcism, as could only one other man, one with yin-yang eyes. They saw shadowy, thin images, some with the upper or lower part of the body only; mostly Chinese, some Westerners, and some Japanese; some with gowns; some normal; and some with blood on their faces. They didn't tell anyone, he said, or they would have been blamed for starting rumors or for trying to trick the government, which was not very happy about the controversy. He did not seem to know about the people referred to in the Secretariat's report who thought they had seen ghosts at the exorcism.

After discussing several buildings he had helped exorcise, he began to talk about his work with individuals. For one woman in Wanchai (a district of Hong Kong), he wrote a character on a protective paper. When that didn't work, he wrote a curse on her door. He asks ghosts to come and eat the curse. Sometimes, he can see them coming.

Occasionally, he helps people talk with their ancestors, acting as a facilitator though not as an actual spirit medium. He asked one family if they wanted to speak with the grandfather. Some of them said yes. Then he put the grandfather's name on a piece of paper, which he screwed onto the ancestral tablet. When the paper was torn by the ghost, they knew he was there. They talked to him in their prayers.

We asked the reverend monk more about his own ability to see ghosts. Unlike Dr. H (Chapter 12), he did not claim to have yin-yang eyes but only to be able to see them when meditating with his eyes closed, in which case it appears as if he is looking at everything in the scene with open eyes. Some ghosts are very angry and frustrated. Some have a very strong will and beat up the weak ghosts.

One crippled ghost, he said, spoke through the body of a little boy with a bad leg who was watching the ceremony at the Murray House. The ghost said, "I came late, because I can't walk. They take advantage of me. I didn't get anything." Therefore, the monks who heard it burned some incense and gave food and money in his name only and threw more rice on the floor. When the ghost left, the boy's leg recovered. Only the monks could tell that there was a problem with his leg.

Regular ghosts look just like humans, he said, but evil persons become little devils, which look very ugly. He has seen little devils on the street, for example, every day when he meditates. He doesn't want to see them all the time, so he blocks them out. Only a few people can see them; it depends on how much you meditate and get into Buddhism. He has also seen the King of the Devils, who always comes to his exorcisms.

I am uncertain how to react to testimony about little devils or how to evaluate claims of easy apparitions with the eyes closed through meditation (although some clairvoyants claim to have such visions). As with Dr. H, I suspect that the role of psychic (or holiest of Buddhist monks in Hong Kong) does something to one's perceptions (assuming that they are telling the unvarnished truth). Whether these perceptions are merely hallucinatory or truly paranormal on some higher plane I cannot say. I *can* say that they are not typical.

Folk Taoist

Chinese religious traditions are so complex and borrow so much from each other that it is difficult to put them in neat categories (cf. Chapter 3). However, we interviewed one man whose orientation toward healing through exorcism is based on a kind of Taoism, which is more of a folk tradition than part of an organized religious group.

SP010. Ghosts in a Gourd

My mother got real sick one time when she saw the ghosts of her mother and father. She asked my older brother to come home and cure her. He rushed back and saw the ghosts. They were not my grandmother and grandfather but devils who looked like them. He exorcised them and she got better. He put them into a gourd.

The gourd that is used to trap devils (evil ghosts) is of a bottle shape with a double curve, something like a Coca-Cola bottle only fatter.

SP011. Soul of a Snake

I got sick when I was twelve years old. A voice came out of me saying, "Why are you beating me every day? Let me go!" I was possessed. I couldn't control it; my mouth turned blue, and my eyes were like a crazy person's.

I asked my older brother, ten years older than I, to come to Canton. When he put his hand on my head, the ghost started to cry. He asked the devil where he had come from. "From Indonesia [where they had lived previously], the soul of a snake." When it saw that my mother didn't believe in and didn't worship voodoo, it had to harm the family. My brother then trapped the snake among the lower spirits in the lower part of my body. Since the snake devil is trapped in my body, it hurts the devil every time I pray.

SP012. Possession, Soul Loss, and Recovery

My cousin from the same hometown was possessed by ghosts when she was eighteen or nineteen. She had seen a person dressed in Ching Dynasty clothes sitting in a sedan chair right outside her door. The next morning she was supposed to come over for breakfast, but she had died. She had blue finger prints around her neck. We asked what had happened; she had only had a headache.

My younger brother collapsed. When he woke up, he was holding her transparent soul. Even with his eyes closed, he could see it, the whole body. He put it back into her body, through the head, and she woke up. She said that people had tried to grab her and had taken her all the way to the underworld. She saw lightning and a guardian sent from the god, who grabbed her soul back. She got better and is still alive.

I felt a cold chill when I felt her soul approaching... I have trapped ghosts myself, and I have felt something running into my hand, like trapping a mouse.

The cousin's description of what she saw when "dead" sounds somewhat similar to the near-death experience (NDE) pattern in cases of people recovering from apparent death as studied by Moody (1976: 55-64), particularly in terms of "meeting others" and "the being of light." Otherwise, details like the blue fingerprints on the neck and the physical manipulation of the soul make this case, like the two before it, atypical as ghost-related reports go. And following the same principle as with Dr. H and the Buddhist monk, this man's strong attachment to a religious or spiritual perspective seems to have a profound influence on what he reports.

In the next chapter, we deal with another type of spirit possession: the regularized, formalized, and intentional possession undergone by spirit mediums.

15

SPIRIT MEDIUMS

2017: I really enjoyed researching spirit mediums in Hong Kong, and I still really like this chapter. Since 1980, however, I have had a lot more experience with this phenomenon, and my personal perspective has changed. In 1980 I was researching as a sociologist, anthropologist, and parapsychologist. I was basically an agnostic, and the part of this research ("Case study of a mun mai poh") that included messages to me allegedly from my aunt was a real shock to me. I tried to account for the evidential information I was getting in terms of parapsychology.

By the time Penelope and I had written Guided by Spirit: A Journey into the Mind of the Medium *(2003), I had become a Spiritualist and even a "student" medium myself. This experiential approach gave me a different point of view on the subject, although I have still retained a healthy skepticism and willingness to entertain alternative explanations. See* Guided by Spirit, *and also* Science and Spirit *(Emmons and Emmons, 2012: 125-135) for more information about studies of spirit mediumship, as well as some further reflections on the 1982 edition of* Chinese Ghosts and ESP.

A spirit "medium" is literally someone who occupies the role of go-between, standing in the middle between spirits and living humans. Just as in Western culture, a Chinese medium may try to become possessed by the spirit, speaking and acting like the deceased, or may provide indirect communication instead. One indirect procedure is to contact a "control," another spirit who either introduces the desired party or passes along the entire message. Even after the target spirit is introduced to the medium, the medium may simply repeat messages to the living rather than playing the part of the deceased. Automatic writing is also indirect, involving messages inspired by the spirit and copied down by the medium.

Cantonese trance mediums who speak their messages are known as *mun mai poh*, "ask-rice women" (or *mun mai gong*, "ask-rice men," in the rare instances that the medium is a man). Another speaking type is the *dang-ki* ("divining youth") described among Chinese in Singapore by Elliott (1964). A *fu gei sau* ("character writer"), on the other hand, does automatic writing.

When speaking completely directly, a medium may imitate the gestures, the dialect (Elliott, 1964: 135; Burkhardt, 1953: vol. 2, 147), and the sound of voice of the deceased. One woman in Hong Kong told me about an amah her family used to have thirty years ago in China, who would perform as a spirit medium. She imitated the voice and gestures of spirits of people she had never known, and spoke in dialects she did not know when out of trance.

Procedures for the mun mai poh vary widely. Some insist that rice be brought from the family rice bin (evidently helping the correct ancestral spirit find its way back through the family's offering), and that the sitter provide the medium with exact birth and death dates (sometimes, even time of day) plus the precise location of the grave. One woman told me that her family simply brought their rice to a medium in Hong Kong and said that the Wongs (surname, pseudonym) were looking for the Wongs, and up came the whole group of ancestors all at once. Incense and sacred paper offerings are fairly standard. Some Chinese mediums have the sitters form a circle, according to Elliott (1964: 136), but this is not typical in Hong Kong, where people sit in chairs in the vicinity of an altar or table where the medium goes into trance.

Some spirit mediums engage in minor forms of self mutilation, like cutting the tongue with broken glass (Kehl, 1971), or skewering the tongue or folds of skin on the cheeks or neck (Elliott, 1964: 54-56). This may serve to impress the audience that the medium is truly in a special trance state and protected from harm. The woman mentioned whose amah in China was a medium also said that she used to put burning candles and sticks of incense into her mouth without suffering apparent injury.

In addition to the variety of procedures, there is also more variety in the type of mediumship than indicated by mentioning just the mun mai poh and fu gei sau types that are most common in Hong Kong. In the last chapter ("The exorcist" section), I noted that a Buddhist monk acted as a facilitator of spirit contact by putting a piece of paper on an ancestral tablet. In SM001 below, a monk performs an unusual act of mediumship, reported by a forty-three-year-old man.

SM001. Spirit in a Bottle

The whole family had a Buddhist monk come to the house after my grandmother died. He was carrying a bottle with a stick in it. Without knowing anything about the family, the monk called the spirit of my grandmother through the stick. Then he was possessed and pointed the stick in the bottle at each person when talking about them. It was all correct.

The type and popularity of spirit mediums vary by location. Elliott (1964) found a thriving spirit-medium culture in Singapore in the 1950s, mainly the dang-ki type. Hong Kong's mun mai poh are said to be getting rare, although the ones I have discovered often have more clients than they can handle. When anthropologist Diana Martin asked her guides in China whether mediums were still active there in the late 1970s, the answer was, "'Perhaps in the backwoods – but isn't it ridiculous?'"(Walker, 1980). However, there has been less opposition to religion in China after the end of the Cultural Revolution (about 1976), and some of Martin's informants tell her that mediums are still common in China. In fact, these Hong Kong people had gone to mediums in China in the late 1970s. [87] The British colonial government in Hong Kong takes the same laissez-faire attitude toward spirit mediums that it does toward other traditional Chinese customs that cause no clear harm.

There are different patterns of recruitment for the different types of mediums. According to Elliott (1964: 46, 59), the dang-ki in Singapore are likely to be young males under twenty who are active in temple affairs and whose horoscopes predict that they will lead "blameless but unhappy lives, and… die young." Martin says that the women who become mun mai poh sometimes become mediums reluctantly after being cured of a spiritual-possession illness themselves; the gods allow them to *lengthen* a short life fate in exchange for providing spiritual services to others. [88] This notion, that there is a charitable aspect to the role of medium, is consistent with the fact that both mun mai poh and dang-ki are expected to work for donations of lucky money rather than for a stated fee (Burkhardt, 1953: vol. 2, 144; Elliott, 1964: 47, 48).

Perhaps the most important question is what function is served by spirit mediumship. Remembering the way Chinese have feared ghosts and attributed illness to them, even to one's own ancestors (cf. Chapters 3, 4, 6), one might wonder why anybody would seek out a spirit medium. Although there may be differences in emphasis for the various types of mediums (cf. Hsu, 1967: 171; Elliott, 1964: 109, 134, 135, 161), I think that they all involve some combination of the following concerns: illness, bad luck in matters of material success, and personal concern over one's relatives. There is really no paradox in the ambivalence toward the ancestors; even people who are afraid of them may have to contact them in order to keep them from causing trouble.

---

87   Personal communication from Diana Martin, August 29, 1980.

88   Diana Martin made this statement at a presentation to a class on "Health Care in Hong Kong" taught through the University of Hong Kong.

Who believes in spirit mediums?

Chapter 4 asked the same question about ghost belief. The startling contrast is that only 18% on the telephone survey claimed to believe in spirit mediums vs. 50% believing in ghosts (cf. Table 1 on page 325). Out of fourteen paranormal beliefs, spirit mediums rank only eleventh. Other related beliefs are closer to the top: #2 is ESP (49%), #3 is fortune telling (44%), and #6 is reincarnation (25%). Although I make a connection between ESP belief and the others due to the ESP theory of apparitions, there was not a big correlation in the survey itself. However, there was a fairly good correlation between belief in spirit mediums and fortune telling (probably because mediums often tell fortunes) and between mediums and reincarnation. [89]

It is clearly easier for Hong Kong Chinese to believe in ghosts and other psychic phenomena than it is for them to believe in spirit mediums. But as ghosts and spirit mediums are related phenomena, I would expect the same social background factors that supported ghost belief in Chapter 4 to support the belief in spirit mediums as well.

As far as religion goes, Buddhists and Catholics were the big ghost believers. Now, however, Buddhists stand alone on top: 29% of Buddhists on the telephone survey said they believed in spirit mediums, 16% of those with no religion, 15% of Catholics, and 14% of Protestants. After controlling for other variables (as explained in Chapter 4), Buddhism is still positively associated with belief in spirit mediums; no religion is negatively associated, but Catholicism and Protestantism are not significantly related one way or the other (cf. Table 2).

According to the prominent Buddhist monk I talked to, Buddhist organizations like his do not actively promote mun mai poh. He said that it was an "unrighteous way to do it," that he didn't believe in it,

---

89   Pearson's r, a statistic for measuring correlations, which ranges between +1.0 and -1.0, was the highest among the three Christian religious beliefs (over 0.8 for angels, devils, and life after death, taken any two together). However, otherwise only four correlations were over 0.3, including ghosts with spirit mediums (0.325), mediums with fortune-tellers (0.315), and mediums with reincarnation (0.308).

and that it was sometimes phony. This contrasts with the statement by one Buddhist who told us that all you had to do to find a mun mai poh was to "ask any Buddhist follower." Actually, it's not that easy, but some mediums do associate themselves loosely with various kinds of temples. As with feng shui, mun mai poh are supported by followers of "folk Buddhism," a conglomeration of Chinese beliefs that is broader than "official" Buddhist doctrine. Among Buddhists, 5.3% claimed to have had a convincing experience with a mun mai poh, compared with less than 2% for all the other religious-preference categories.

Next, we found that ancestor worshipers were more likely to believe in ghosts than those who did not worship ancestors. Not surprisingly, 22% of the worshipers said they believed in mun mai poh, compared with only 10% of nonworshipers. Controlling for other variables, including religious preference, ancestor worship is even more strongly associated with belief in mediums than Buddhism and "no religion" are (cf. Table 3).

Education had a slightly positive but statistically significant correlation with ghost belief. It has a slightly negative but not significant correlation with belief in mediums.

Age was found, surprisingly, to be negatively related to ghost belief, contrary to popular expectation. Three respondents on the telephone survey also said that older people believe in mediums, and two others said that it was traditional people. Surprise again! With other variables controlled, age is also negatively related to belief in mediums (Table 3). The relationship is about as strong as the ones for Buddhism and for "no religion."

A closer look at the percentages shows that there is not a smooth continuous decline in belief from the youngest to the oldest. Only 14% of those under age 18 said they believed, up to 23% in the 18-24-year-olds, and 24% in the 25-29 groups. After that, only 17% of 30-34-year-olds believe, and the rest of the older age groups fluctuate up and down" around an average of 17% as well. Although there are only fifty-three people in the survey over sixty years old, only *one* of them (2%) claimed to believe; this is the group one would probably expect to believe the most. This fluctuation in belief by age groups is very similar to the pattern for ghost belief, except that the under-18-year-olds have about the same percentage of *ghost* belief as the 18-29-year-olds. Perhaps the ghost lore in schools supports ghost belief, but there is nothing comparable in youth lore about spirit mediums, something they learn more about when married and responsible for their own families and ancestor worship.

I also found that the degree to which individuals think that they are westernized has no significant effect on belief in mediums. Therefore, it does not seem that young, Westernized adults should be expected to cause the (further) demise of the practice.

Finally, it was found that women were more likely to believe in ghosts than men were. Five people on the survey also commented that mun mai poh were for women only. This time, popular expectations are accurate: 26% of women but only 10% of men believe in mediums. After controlling for other variables, this association is as strong as the one for ancestor worship and belief in mediums (cf. "male" in Table 3). Judging by the sex ratio in the waiting room of the medium I observed personally, it is not surprising that 3. 4% of women but only 1.4% of men claim to have had a convincing experience with a mun mai poh. This difference is statistically significant; [90] although the sex difference in ghost experiences was not, it was still more common for women (cf. Chapter 5).

Diana Martin told me that most of her informants who had been to spirit mediums were impressed, especially people who had been nonbelievers beforehand. Although we did not specifically ask people on the survey if they were impressed, there were thirty-nine positive and thirty negative statements volunteered about mediums. On the positive side, thirty-one said that mediums they had seen were accurate in what they said about things they should not have known. Seven more said that their friends had found them accurate. And one person said that mediums were "scientific."

---

90   Corrected chi square = 5.62, p<. 02.

On the negative side, two said that they were not scientific or modern, five that they were superstitious, five that they were not accurate, one that they were guessing. Five people laughed or said that they were ridiculous. Twelve actually accused them of dishonesty, including seven who said that they cheated people out of their money, four who called them "phony," and one who said that they told lies. Two commented that they didn't believe because they were Christians, and one believer in mediums said that they did "black magic." Only five of the negative comments came from people who specifically said that they had visited mediums themselves, however.

Spirit mediums in action

Altogether thirty-seven out of 1,501 people reported significant experiences with a mun mai poh on the telephone survey, only 2.5%. However, only four out of 1,989 reported an experience on the secondary-school questionnaire! Most of the cases are not described in very great detail, the person typically saying only that the medium was accurate on statements about family relationships and activities. Let us look at some of the more interesting reports, beginning with one of the three cases in which the medium imitated the voice of the deceased, this one described by a sixteen-year-old boy.

SM002. Grandpa's Voice

I went to a mun mai poh once when I was very little with my mother to ask about my grandpa. She could do Grandpa's voice and gestures. She could also name everyone's relationship to him. The mun mai poh also knew that my grandfather died in the hospital and the cause of his death.

Next, a forty-five-year-old man recalls his youthful trip to the spirit medium.

SM003. Grandfather and the Basketball

I went with my parents when I was very young to ask the mun mai poh about my grandfather. She talked about our home – for example, where I put my basketball, and many small details about the environment of the house.

One peculiar thing I noticed is that spirits often act in these sessions as if they know about things happening currently. Perhaps this is logical, as the Chinese belief is that people continue to get older after death, and to live a parallel life in the other world, from which they sometimes return, as we know from Chapter 6 on ancestor-worship ghost cases. This report is from a thirty-year-old woman.

SM004. Right Up to Date

My mother and I went to a mun mai poh and asked about my father. The spirit knew about a lot of things that happened after his death: my new job, that I was getting married, and when.

Such reports may not seem peculiar by Chinese standards, but they help raise the question of whether the medium might not be using her ESP on the information currently in the minds of the sitters to reconstruct a plausible personality and set of statements. Or perhaps the spirit is using his or her ESP to add current information to things experienced before death.

Another example of a case that pits the survival theory against the super-ESP theory, this time in a way similar to that of the Chaffin will case (cf. Chapter 5), is SM005, reported by a forty-three-year-old woman. Did the spirit communicate the information or was the medium using her ESP? If it was the latter, then she could not have gotten the information telepathically from the sitters but only clairvoyantly, seeing the money directly. Another possibility is that this was a lucky guess, how lucky it is difficult to estimate without knowing what percentage of women in Hong Kong hide money under their beds.

SM005. The Late Will

My mother and I went to a mun mai pooh to ask about my aunt. We didn't know about any money, but we asked if there was anything she wanted to tell us. The spirit told us to look for her money that she had hidden under the bed. And we found it!

The next report, from an eighteen-year-old girl, makes the unique but interesting claim that a bystander was possessed by a spirit called up during a seance! An alternate explanation here could also be that the possessed person used ESP to create a plausible personality.

SM006. The Bystander Medium

My friend and I went to a mun mai poh. I saw my friend become possessed by a ghost. She appeared sick, talked, and fell down. As the ghost of my mother, she said things that were very accurate. They took her to a doctor to check out her brain, and it was O.K.

One other thing that we should not forget about the role of mun mai poh is the way she sometimes helps arrange ghost marriages (cf. Chapter 3, and case G045 in Chapter 6 for a ghost marriage set up by a matchmaker who was apparently *not* a medium). A thirty-six-year-old woman described the following.

SM007. Spirit Romance

Quite a few years ago I went [to a medium] with my friend, a woman who lived in the same flat and whose nephew had died. My friend had had a dream in which her nephew told her he had met a girl in the underworld. He also gave the girl's address and asked his aunt if she would go ask the girl's family if he could marry her. The aunt (my friend) was very puzzled about the dream and went [with me] to a mun mai poh who did not know her at all.

The mun mai poh [acting as the spirit] asked her if she had had such and such a dream [the same one] and also gave her the address in her dream. Then they went to that address and found that the girl had died just recently; her mother had just had the same dream. So they arranged the marriage and burned paper wedding clothes, house, and car. But the mun mai poh got nothing from the ceremony, wasn't involved. This was [long ago] in Hong Kong. The wedding was performed all at home.

Although some people who go to spirit mediums are rather easily impressed, the thirty-five-year-old woman who gave us the next experience illustrates how a mistaken detail can create skepticism in spite of an otherwise accurate performance.

SM008. The Flawed Performance

I think it's phony, because the spirit asked me to burn paper money to help her in the afterlife, which I don't believe in doing [the respondent scored zero on ancestor worship]. The spirit said that her adopted son is not reliable; watch out for him. The mun mai poh told how many children the grandmother had, and the fact that there was one adopted son and no other sons. This was accurate, because there was just the daughter. She knew the number of grandchildren, too. The spirit asked, "How come my granddaughter hasn't come to see me?" The medium did not make the mistake of thinking that I was a granddaughter.

In the following case, a session with a spirit medium was a prelude to a ghost experience (G127). After I had been interviewed about ghosts on a radio program in Hong Kong (the "Aileen Bridgewater Program"), I found that a woman had left her telephone number for me with the station. Although her experience had happened thirty years before, she was still upset by the strangeness of it. After her mother had died suddenly, her aunt had taken two of her mother's best friends to a mun mai poh to contact her within the first year after death. According to the aunt, my informant's mother expressed worry in the séance over her and the six older children, especially because she had had no opportunity to make any plans with them before her sudden death. This anxiety on the part of the spirit, or the corresponding anxiety in the living if they were the initiators, may have been the motivation that sparked the following ghost experience one month after the seance.

G127. The Worried Mother

That night, I felt cold and felt my bed sink down on one side. I didn't know what it could be. But the next day my auntie told me that she had seen my mother come into the house that same night and go up into her own room upstairs. Two dogs downstairs barked, growled, and wagged their tails. Then she heard my mother walking up and down in her room, and walking to all the other rooms upstairs to see us all.

Later on, the tailor said, "I saw your mother the other day. When I was standing down in the street, I saw her come into your room upstairs and smoke a cigarette." It had been her habit to do so. A week later, the tailor died, but my mother wouldn't harm him.

Every few years near her birthday, I feel the cold and the sinking on my bed. Three years ago was the most recent. It was the night of July 20, my son's birthday as well as my mother's. The dog howled at the door. Fifteen minutes later, the dog went to the door again, but nothing happened. That night I felt the bed again.

Case study of a mun mai poh

Now we come to my favorite single part of the entire study. I personally observed one spirit medium in Hong Kong on five separate occasions over a twelve-week period as she tried to contact a total of ten spirits. She also told some fortunes; which I'll save for Chapter 17. I further interviewed another researcher, who watched her contact eight more spirits at one sitting at the very end of the twelve-week period.

When my wife found out from the medium's assistant in a telephone conversation that she disliked publicity and wanted no photographs or tape recorders, I decided to go in the role of client and to take only enough notes when there in order to be able to expand details sufficiently afterward. I feel that this research strategy was an ethical one because I did perform the role of client honestly and adequately and never caused her any trouble. In fact, I came to be a favored customer and introducer of other clients (not that she needed any more!). Probably by the second or third visit, she strongly suspected that I was doing research, but we never discussed the subject.

One danger in participant observation is that the researcher may lose objectivity and "go native," as anthropologists say, causing a positive bias. I know that I lost my objectivity as I grew to like her; she even kidded the bystanders that I was like an adopted son! Later on, I was disappointed when some sittings were not very successful and was upset when some people questioned her ability to contact spirits. Fortunately, my after-session notes are very detailed, and I have been able to recover sufficient objectivity (I think) to describe and explain the pattern of phenomena that unfolded over those six sessions.

Tuesday, August 5, 1980:

That afternoon, someone recommended a spirit medium to us, and as soon as my wife, Chee, called to be sure that she was in that day, we were on our way to an apartment in a working-class neighborhood on Hong Kong Island.

There were eleven chairs in the waiting room outside the seance room, where a crowd usually gathers, but she was not expected to be in that day, and we were next. The assistant led us through a doorway and to the left past a stove area and bathroom to a small room where the medium, perhaps in her forties or early fifties, sat by a table in the corner.

On the table were a red bulb, a framed sacred writing in red, a statue of Sau ("Long Life"), incense, offerings of oranges and grapes, and a little pillow for her to lay her head on when going into trance. Since we had neglected to bring any rice in our haste, we provided one Hong Kong dollar ($0.20 U.S.) for each spirit instead, as instructed by the assistant. There was also some pastry and a cup near her, although we were told that she ate hardly anything all day once she went into trance in the morning.

The mun mai poh (whom I will give the pseudonym Sam Gu, "Third Aunt," a name that many mediums take in imitation of one name for the Buddhist goddess Kuan Yin, to whom they often pray for assistance) smiled but said that she was afraid of me. She had never contacted a spirit for a Western man before. When she asked if I believed, I said I thought I did. Then she thanked me for believing in her. Although mediums are not bothered by the government, as far as I know, I wondered if she thought I was investigating her.

I occasionally made remarks in Cantonese, but most communication was translated through Chee. The first spirit we tried that day, and others on other days, were English speakers who had lived and died halfway around the world. She might easily have refused to do it, but she did not.

I gave her my aunt's maiden and married names and how old she was when she died. Chee told her that she was my mother's sister. Sam Gu put her head down on the little pillow to meditate. She asked Chee if my aunt were tall, about Chee's height. Chee said yes, but actually she was a few inches shorter.

Sam Gu went on, "Her husband died long ago; she was a widow for a long time. [Her husband did die about twenty-five years before her.] She died of an illness, not just old age, died in a hospital. This woman has less than three children, a son and a daughter. She was pretty when she was young" [all correct].

"Yes, that's the one," Chee replied. "O.K.," Sam Gu said, "I'll ask her to come up." This was the end of the first stage, identifying the spirit, with the help of a genie (the assistant told us) who had died when she was three years old. The genie is Sam Gu's "control."

In the second stage, the spirit is "brought up" to speak through the medium in the first person, although Sam Gu never attempts to imitate voice or dialect (or language, since my aunt spoke in Cantonese, which she never knew, of course). Sam Gu's whole body shook, her head especially rocking back and forth. "She hasn't been asked to come up before, right? This is the first time." "Right."

Then Sam Gu made a gurgling noise, sat up, and said to Chee, "Hello, niece-in-law!" Speaking as my aunt, she smiled and looked and talked to us in her own normal voice, not appearing to be in any special trance state. "How long are you going to stay here? Are you going back to the States? I liked you [Charlie, although Sam Gu never used proper names] very much, better than my own son [not likely]. You didn't see me when I died, and you didn't go to the funeral [true; Chee did tell the assistant that before going in, but there seemed to be no chance for that information to have been relayed to Sam Gu in any natural way].

I shall skip a few less significant parts here, but not in such a way as to make her statements appear more or less accurate. Then she said, "My son's wife didn't treat me very well [so I had definitely heard at one point]. But I was very close to my daughter and visited her often [she was definitely very close to her, but trips were not frequent since she lived several hundred miles away].

"I was very close to your mother, who was a younger sister [they *were* very close, but the younger-sister part would have been a likely deduction, based on how old my aunt was]. I had quite a bit of money left when I died [very unlikely]. My son got all the money, because my daughter didn't want the money since she is very rich [this cannot be confirmed easily, but the daughter is probably quite comfortable by now, though certainly not upper class. She is definitely in better financial condition than the son, I should think].

"I had granddaughters, but not enough I didn't think [two by her daughter]. You [Chee] have one child, a son [right; and since he was not present, there was no clue to this]. I saw you [Chee] when you were pregnant, but didn't see the baby boy [another good hit, and the boy part shows an example of a spirit knowing about happenings after death, although the sex is only a fifty-fifty chance]. Your son is very cute and looks more like you [Charlie; most people say he looks more like Chee, but he is definitely high on cuteness, if I may say so!]. Your mother [Chee's] is taking care of the baby now [correct]; you should have brought him over to see me.

"You [Chee] have never met my daughter [correct], and should go visit her. I saw you [Charlie] growing up, and took care of you sometimes [incorrect on the last point].

"Your [Charlie's] parents' health is fine, but your mother has itchy skin and scratches all the time [at this point, Sam Gu imitated someone scratching the backs of her hands and her forearms; this gave me a creepy feeling, because it was such a precise statement about a nagging problem my mother has had; my parents' health is also fine in general]. She has had it for a few years now" [right].

Later, she called up the genie to recommend a cure. The remedy was something called "white soapy water," a substance that is neither really white nor soap, that is sold in the marketplace for making dumplings. Unfortunately, I was unable to get this before returning to the U.S. to try it out. The genie went on to say, "Your mother can't even put her hands in the water. In any weather, summer or winter, she can't do anything about it" [very true, although recently it has come somewhat under control].

Back to my aunt's spirit. "You don't go see your mother very often, because you both work" [true; Chee's vacations are harder to arrange than mine, and we make fewer trips than we would like]. She then went on to give our salaries, with five kibitzers standing in the hallway watching and listening! She was 15% to 20% too high, but I doubt that my aunt would have known that closely.

"Your sister [Charlie's] is not as tall as you, about up to her [Chee's] shoulder; very intelligent and a sweet looking kid [all very true]. She has a tall boyfriend [quite true at the time, although the young man I assumed she was referring to was *not* her boyfriend when I had seen him, my sister now tells me, although I guessed that he was!]. She is 18 [I then said no, 19; but this is really a good near miss, because she is my only sibling, and I would hardly seem to have such a young sister at my age, 37 at the time].

"I saw your [Chee's] mother and think she's a very kind woman [this is true – they did see each other when Chee's parents came to the U.S. for the first and only time in 1977; based on the knowledge already established by the medium that Chee's mother lived in Hong Kong, this is a very unlikely guess. I will bless you and look after you."

Then we tried to contact another spirit, this time a woman from China whom we had known in the U.S. Afterward, Chee and I told each other that we both had had a strange subjective feeling that she was being called up reluctantly. I imagined her thinking, "Why are you doing this?" We told Sam Gu her name, age at death, and when she died. At first, Chee told her the wrong Chinese name, because she was uncertain about it; we had always called her by her English name.

"Is she tall and fat?" Definitely not. "Is her name such-and-such?" We weren't sure. "Then it will be very difficult to contact her." We had gotten a wrong number! Then Chee told her the English name.

In the searching stage, Sam Gu said, "She died of an illness, a growth in her body [right]. Her husband is still alive [right]. She has not even three children, one son and one daughter in the U.S. [yes!]. They live in different places [true]. She tells me that you were just friends, that you lived very close to each other, and were very close friends, like brother and sister to her" [this is somewhat internally inconsistent; we were more than "just friends" but not quite like brother and sister; we lived about one mile away]. Chee said, "That's the one. "

Then she came up, and Sam Gu sat up and spoke normally as in the first case. "I call you brother and sister. When I was alive, I called you by your name, but now I call you brother and sister. We knew each other for a long time. We stayed in the same town. You're [Charlie] like an adopted son to me [her daughter had told us that she had considered another friend, call him Mr. I, like an adopted son; this plus the long-acquaintance statement were the first indications that I might be getting mistaken for Mr. I!].

"I was very bitter when I died, very painful [very true]. I couldn't eat [true]. You were in the states then, and you came to visit me, but you weren't there when I died [true]. You [Charlie] were a very good person. You came to see me when I was ill. My son didn't even come to see me [he didn't come very much, but he did come a couple of times when she was really sick; near the end, however, he arrived so late that she couldn't communicate with him very well].

"You brought me food when I was ill [again, confusion with Mr. I?; he brought her Chinese food that she craved from a town in the near vicinity].

"You know that my husband has a girlfriend. I'm very upset about it" [correct, but so far not such an unlikely guess]. Chee then said, "They have just known each other recently." "No," she objected, "he knew her before I died [there is some doubt here; she could not have known about her husband's girlfriend before she died, according to her daughter, who also doubts that the two met before her mother's death].

"She is after his money [this startled us, because both children had told us this very thing; they were concerned that their father, who had been tragically ill and had received neural damage, might not be able to protect his own best interests; the girlfriend, they said, had had a reputation for gold-digging!]. Even the house is transferred to her name [incorrect; the children *did* have the house transferred, but to *their* name in order to prevent her from getting it!]. Right after I died, he brought her to the house [no; he stayed in another state for some time after her death]. My house is very pretty [true].

"She is very rich herself and has a restaurant [not very rich; she does have a motel, but no restaurant]. She was married before, and her husband is still alive [true; she was divorced and widowed from another husband; one is still alive]. She has sons and daughters [sons, yes; we don't know about any daughters; however, the expression "sons and daughters" is often used to mean "children"]. A lot of people have seen them together [true].

"Did you know that I had a lot of money when I died? [true]. I had a small business outside [apparently inaccurate, but she did have a lot of stocks]. Your [Charlie's] mother and I were very good friends" [again, Mr. I's mother had met her in the U.S. and they wrote back and forth; she saw *my* mother only briefly].

Chee asked, "Do you remember Mr. I?" "Yes," came the response. "Do you know he's building a new house?" "Yes," she said, "about 2,000 square feet, very nice, just finished" [actually, he never built the house he had planned but moved to another state, into a house with about 2,000 square feet].

Chee then asked, "Do you know how your son and daughter are doing?" "Yes," she answered, "They're in two different places [right]. My daughter is very intelligent, a doctor [right, and certainly a rare occupation for a woman, if one has to guess!]. My son doesn't come back to see his father" [this was certainly our impression, too, although he did come back a lot especially in the first year after she died, although often to do business more than to be with his father very much].

"He's working in Baltimore now," Chee went on. "Yes, I know. He just graduated this year [right, with an M. A.]. He's not a doctor; he's an architect [right again!; another very good guess of occupation]. He makes big money now, over $2,000 (a month, U.S. funds)" [wrong, not that much].

Aware of the interesting problem of post-death information, Chee asked, "How do you know about all these things, being in the underworld?"

"I know."

After we returned to the U.S., we told Mr. I about all of this. He was impressed but somewhat ill-at-ease to hear it. Then he told us that he had had an experience himself one night when we were away in Hong Kong. Not accustomed to remembering his dreams, he was awakened by a realistic dream in which our Chinese friend had appeared in front of him, looking at him; then she had turned away and disappeared. Shaken, he wondered if she were warning him of something. He thought he had better drive carefully the next day, Saturday, on his trip to see his fiancée in another state. On Sunday, his future father-in-law had a stroke, went into a coma, and died a week later. Mr. I interpreted this as the reason for the dream.

Although this experience was a dream rather than an apparition, it might be considered a case of a deceased agent identifying the crisis of a third party. Louisa E. Rhine (1957b: 221-223) has found that, when apparitions of deceased agents (or "senders") relate to a crisis, 72% are crises of a third party, which occurs only 9% of the time with living agents. Her explanation is that culture sets limits on what supernormal abilities a living agent might be expected to have. However, we cannot eliminate the possibility that the deceased agent actually survives and acquires greater powers of communicating about third parties.

As far as Sam Gu's performance during this first session is concerned, we were definitely impressed. We had not expected anything like this, although we were open-mindedly curious. Although we usually told her whether she was wrong or right after each statement, we were very careful not to cue any new information to her beyond what I have indicated. She was wrong about several things, but the correct things seem to outweigh them heavily – that is, to beat chance by a wide margin. Of course, it is impossible to give precise probabilities for each statement, and the whole pattern of responses must be examined for a general impression. Not only did she do very well on the less startling statements overall, but she also came up with some very unlikely hits, such as the description of my mother's itchy skin, the issue of the allegedly gold-digging girlfriend (not all aspects of which were accurate, of course), and the occupations of the Chinese-American daughter and son. Even the pattern of errors that seemed to confuse me with Mr. I was fascinating. Because of the overall errors, however, I considered ESP to be a more likely explanation than spiritual contact.

<u>Saturday, August 16, 1980</u>:

On my next visit, I brought a Chinese man in his early twenties, call him Peter (pseudonym), a friend of my brother-in-law. Peter wanted to contact the spirit of the young bride of his friend in Colorado. She had died in Colorado in a car accident. Peter was staying with his parents in Hong Kong, having returned recently from the States.

This time, we experienced the usual crowd. Although we had an "appointment" over the phone, we had to wait from 2:45 in the afternoon to 6:15, sitting in the waiting room the whole time except for one hour when we went out for "tea." People had taken numbers; nearly all were women, but there were two or three men and a few children out of the two dozen people who came in and out. I was a curiosity. "If the Westerner keeps coming back, she must be good!" The assistant kidded me about wanting to "chit chat" with my auntie again. The Western emphasis on personal, emotional contact in a seance seems peculiar to Chinese, who are there on more practical ancestor and family business.

When we finally got in, we did only the one spirit. Peter gave her the name of his friend's wife. Going through the same ritual procedure as before, Sam Gu said, "I've found someone twenty-six years old, a boy." Wrong one.

Then she started to click. "She didn't die in China or in Hong Kong [right]. She died in America [right; he had not told her where she had died, but this might have been a plausible guess if she thought that Peter had spent time in the U.S. because he knew me]. She didn't die at home or in the hospital [right]. She died in a car accident [right!; she might have guessed that she had died in the hospital if in an accident, but she got even that aspect right]. I like you [Peter] very much. I did not like my husband [Peter doesn't know if this is true; at any rate, Sam Gu had not been told that the woman had a husband or that she was unrelated to Peter].

"When I died, my brain was smashed. Did you know that?" Peter answered, "Yes, I know." Peter told me later that he had seen the accident report. Her head had been nearly severed at the neck from the blow!

Then she said incorrectly that her husband had a house and girlfriend in the U.S. He did get a house in Canada after her death, and some would argue that this is not a miss, since "America" is often used by Cantonese speakers to include Canada as well. He did have a girlfriend, we found out later, but Peter didn't know how close they were.

Peter said to the spirit, "My best friend [her husband] said that you saved him in the accident." The spirit replied, "Yes, I held him. If not he would have died." [It is unclear what happened from the little that Peter's friend told him].

There was other inconsequential conversation. Peter thinks that she said (incorrectly) that I had taught the spirit in college (perhaps a logical guess about our relationships).

Peter was very impressed overall and gave her $20 H.K. ($4 U.S.) The assistant said that it should be $15 for the first time contacting a spirit. The medium said that $10 was enough, first or second time, it doesn't matter. After he gave her the money, she tried to give him $5 change, but he refused it. On the first visit, I had given her $50 H.K. ($10 U.S.) for two spirits and for telling two fortunes.

Saturday, August 30, 1980:
On my third visit, I brought a British woman who lived in Hong Kong and another woman who was her Cantonese-speaking friend. This time, we were first, and I was able to observe Sam Gu's fifteen-minute morning ritual. First, she burned incense outside the door, then on an altar in the seance room, praying at the same time.

At the table, as we sat there, she sang a haunting chant interrupted by little guttural grunts. She folded sacred paper, made offerings, and continued singing some more. At one point, she moved her neck, wiggled her head, and stopped singing. I wondered if the genie had entered. After two minutes in which her head lay quietly on the little pillow, she shook in starts, and a little voice came out, "Dje, Dje?" ["sister?", talking to the Cantonese woman].

The first spirit we tried was the British woman's husband. Although she was very impressed with the results, I found it very hard to evaluate. For one thing, Sam Gu does not speak any or much English, but there was a lot of chit chat in English going on during the seance that may have leaked clues to Sam Gu. I also thought that her statements were generally vague and repetitive. She was given fairly leading information upon which she built in the course of the discussion as well.

On the positive side, Sam Gu got very little wrong: she gave the wife's age incorrectly and said that there were five rather than ten years difference between husband and wife. There were a few good hits. She identified the cause of death as a burst blood vessel; in fact, he had a blood clot in the lungs and a stroke four years earlier. She correctly said that he had one son and one daughter. "You always have flowers for me. There's my photo by the ashes" [she had been told about the location of the cremated remains, and it might be logical to guess the photo if not the flowers].

Then we tried the Cantonese woman's father. Sam Gu was told his name, age at death, and the year. There was some unconfirmable information, then a good hit (that he had become a solicitor at a very young age), and then an issue that hit a nerve. She had actually been to Sam Gu eight years earlier, but thought it very unlikely that she could have remembered her out of her many thousands of clients. But Sam Gu told her the same thing about her father that she had before, something she had not believed.

"I made some money that you are still using for food, etc. I have left two houses for rental for you" [now she realized; there *were* properties held in trust, but she had gotten very little from them].

The spirit was angry with his third brother. "All my life I've helped him. Now for no apparent reason he's not even on speaking terms with my family. He has lost a lot of money in recent years. I'll see to it that he will lose more" [his daughter thought that it was unusual for him to be so bitter; I might add that it is an extraordinary thing for a medium to say with no clues to any problem in the relationship!; it was all true:

the uncle *was* making himself scarce, and he *had* lost a lot of money in a major investment recently; moreover, it was this uncle who seemed to be mismanaging the property held in trust, which the spirit claimed should be giving his daughter good income; now a strange transaction was in the works, with the property about to be sold to a group in which the uncle had an interest. Nothing could be proven exactly, but it looked like a conflict of interest].

<u>Sunday, October 12, 1980</u>:
Six weeks later, I brought an American man living in Hong Kong to see Sam Gu. A Chinese woman acquaintance of his met us there to act as interpreter. Let's call them Bill and Judy (pseudonyms). Judy had already been up to the apartment when we saw her in the street. Sam Gu had taken ill at 10 p.m. the night before and then went to see the doctor that morning. One woman had been waiting since 5 a.m. only to be turned away hours later. We had to try another day.

From then on, Sam Gu was ill off and on, according to her assistant. I suspected that this might have been an excuse used to cut down the crowds, because I later found her there when they said they thought that she would not be. However, she was never up to the quality I had observed in the first three sessions after that. Another factor may have been that the people I took from then on were generally much more skeptical.

<u>Saturday, October 18, 1980</u>:
Sam Gu had still been ill and had not been expected to come in that day to the room she rented in that apartment for her seances. However, it was too late to call Sophie and Linda (pseudonyms) by the time I found out that morning. We met for tea, and then called again just in case. She was there!

There was a big crowd. The assistant was trying to play gatekeeper, turning people away at the door by saying, "There are so many people. She's not been feeling well and doesn't want to do too many." Actually, she looked very well to me. I gave her six oranges I had brought her and was embarrassed when she gave me $10 H.K. in return in a lucky money envelope. Kibbitzers commented on how I knew what to do, such as putting a one-dollar piece on the incense burner in lieu of rice.

We tried Sophie's grandfather first (through Linda, our Chinese translator). There was endless fishing and wrong statements. For the first time, Sam Gu made excuses for herself, saying that the language difference made it difficult (although she had done well with two Westerners for me before). Most of it was vague. There were two interesting points, however. The spirit talked about some land in England and a lease to buildings on the land that he had left in his will, also about Sophie not living with a husband. Even these points were confused.

Then Sophie asked for her nephew, who was two months old when he died. This one involved even more erroneous fishing. The couple of hits could not redeem the mistakes. I doubt that this one, unlike any of the previous ones, was any better than chance guessing. In Sam Gu's defense, it might be pointed out that the interpreter falsely identified the nephew as an older (rather than younger) brother's son; she has no older brother. Moreover, the interpreter told us later that she was a disbeliever but frightened, hiding a cross on a necklace under her blouse! As far as the young age of the spirit is concerned, who during the time of the séance would have been two years old; his being able to communicate is not considered peculiar in the culture. I was disappointed, but it was to get worse.

Sunday, October 26, 1980:
Bill and Judy and I tried again. Judy and her sister arrived before us at 7 a.m. and were told that they had enough people already by 6 a.m. to last all day! Bill was determined, however, having taken his second long trip from across the harbor to see her. So I went up to ask. By now I was a V.I.P. and the assistant opened the door immediately when she saw me.

Nevertheless, we had to wait from 8:45 a.m. to 1:05 p.m. and stayed until 2:15 once it was our turn. The assistant was telling people on the phone that Sam Gu was taking a rest and not working that day. Perhaps she had never been sick at all, and this was just a ruse to keep the crowd down. I counted thirty people inside, including two men other than us.

When we went into the seance room finally, a woman just before us was paying Sam Gu $70 H.K. ($14 U.S.) to buy material to burn and to pray for someone. Bystanders started asking what these *guai-lo* ("foreign devils," Westerners) were doing here. Sam Gu told them that I often came and was like an adopted son to her. The bystanders said maybe he believes, maybe he's doing research, maybe Westerners are starting to believe. Sam Gu said that she had to translate (from the spirit) and that it was very troublesome.

Judy asked for her grandmother first. She was very clever not to reveal anything, including her attitude or evaluation of what was happening. Neither Judy nor her sister was impressed, I found out later. Although I agree that it was not very impressive overall, I still think that it seemed better than chance guessing and had some interesting hits. Since I had lost my objectivity due to my friendly relationship with Sam Gu, I was hurt that they were so negative when we discussed it over lunch. How ironic, I thought; the foreigner is feeling defensive about local Chinese being suspicious about something in their own culture!

Eventually, I realized what the problem was (other than my positive bias). I assumed that Sam Gu was using ESP rather than contacting spirits; therefore, I would suspect something paranormal even if she made several errors but did consistently better than chance. Judy, however, was testing the survival hypothesis only and would be disappointed at *any* indication that it was not really her grandmother!

Without going through the long seance in detail, let me illustrate. Judy criticized the fact that she used the wrong dialect's term for granddaughter and failed to call her by name, although the medium correctly identified her as a granddaughter without being told (a likely guess, admittedly). Also, the grandmother's spirit thanked them for burning ten (paper) camphor boxes filled with dresses for her, but Judy told me that actually they had burned only two. Two was too few to burn, but they didn't believe in burning paper effigies, so they did just two!

The best example of a hit in this sitting, I think, occurred when the spirit said that Judy's mother's health had not been very good. "She always has pains here and there. In her feet" [right]. Judy asked, "How should she cure it? Is it rheumatism or something else?" The spirit said, "It's not rheumatism. It's a problem with her nerves. Does the doctor say it's her nerves?" Judy replied that she had not gone to the doctor. However, at lunch her sister said that she *had* gone to the doctor, who said that it was something wrong with her nerves! And she does have pain in her heel. I thought that that was pretty good, but Judy shrugged it off as a likely guess. Although the probabilities are very hard to establish, I think that Judy and her sister, negative from the beginning, were so put off by the flaws they saw in the representation of their grandmother that they discounted even the good parts as guessing.

Bill tried to contact his mother and father-in-law. Neither of these was very impressive either, although they were probably a little better than Judy's grandmother. Although they both had several errors, they contained some good hits on family relationships, ages, and cause of death (she seemed to be good at causes of illness and death throughout my observations).

I wondered if more open and sympathetic sitters would have improved Sam Gu's performance on October 18 and 26. Altogether, I thought that nine out of ten spirit contacts showed better than just guessing ability. However, only the first three sittings struck me as highly suggestive of some paranormal talent.

Two days later, on Tuesday, October 28, another researcher, a Hong Kong Chinese named Cindy (pseudonym), observed Sam Gu for four or five hours as she contacted ten different spirits. On Wednesday, Cindy walked into my office at the Centre of Asian Studies to tell me about it.

"She's a total fake!" she said excitedly. "My faith went out the window, I feel disappointed and cheated, although I see she's obviously very popular among the women there. I thought it was really true, but I was let down. These people are really vulnerable!"

My ears were burning. She was talking about *my* medium! But actually I was getting used to the fact that Sam Gu seemed to have lost it, at least temporarily. It would be very instructive to hear how other sittings went with the usual clientele instead of with my atypical friends.

First, Cindy told me what happened when she had tried to contact her grandfather. The way she told it at least, it was not very impressive. In fact, Cindy said that there was nothing really surprising in the case. The "spirit" said that Cindy had a boyfriend and would be getting married soon to somebody a bit older. Cindy thinks that Sam Gu noticed her boss standing with her earlier and made the mistaken assumption that he was her boyfriend. "If it were really the spirit of my grandfather," Cindy said, "he would have asked me about my two kids!"

As far as the other sittings she observed were concerned, they were all similar in content. One was interesting, she said: a woman and her two kids and her mother were discussing things among themselves and with another couple, things that Sam Gu later used in the spirit conversation. People were amazed at what she said, not seeming to realize how she had been fed these cues. I pointed out that apparently nothing would shake the conviction of true believers in the subculture.

While Sam Gu was getting ready to call up a spirit, this little group were talking about what a jerk so-and-so was. When the spirit came up, they asked him what he thought of so-and-so. "He's a jerk," the spirit replied. That impressed them. "See! We don't like him, and the spirit doesn't either!"

Cindy was also surprised to see how petty and materialistic some petitioners were. One woman called up five spirits one after the other, threatening each one. "You make sure I get a spot in the Government Subsidy housing [in the lottery selection]! If I get it, I'll put you up on the altar. Otherwise I won't!"

Then I told Cindy my theory. A spirit medium uses all the cues that are available. I can't prove that there is no surviving spirit. But even if spirits are present sometimes, I think that ESP, logical deductions ("good guessing"), and cues leaked from the statements and gestures of the sitters are all part of the material that even an honest medium draws upon. ESP is exciting enough for me, let alone "authentic" spirits. But even a psychic is bound to have a bad day. What is she going to do, tell everybody to go home?

Everyone performs in roles and engages in "presentation of self" (Goffman, 1959) to make that performance look convincing. There is no simple distinction between honest and fraudulent performances. Using available cues and good guesses may not even be a conscious manipulation. At the other extreme, there are real con artists. Some fortune tellers and spirit mediums in Hong Kong, I am told, take clients' names and addresses ahead of time and do research on them before their appointments.

Cindy agreed with me that it was hard to call Sam Gu a real fraud. After all, Cindy said, she cleans her altars, prays on her knees for over an hour sometimes, and chants, etc., before starting. And charging $10 or $15 H.K. ($2 or $3 U.S.) per spirit is hardly exorbitant. Some mediums charge far more. I commented that she could triple her rates, cut the demand in half, and still make lots more money than she does now.

Although I had already heard about fraud and ESP as alternative explanations to the survival hypothesis in spiritualism, of course, I was fascinated to see how closely my findings and explanations fit other studies when I looked deeper into library sources on these points later on.

Elliott (1964: 137, 139) comments on Chinese spirit medium cults in Singapore: "To a European observer there is plainly room for much fraud." One method he mentions is the way some mediums keep going back several times, looking for the right soul, giving the sitters several opportunities to leak more information on the deceased. Sam Gu did go back a second time in a few cases but got little extra information, and in fact was given some incorrect information to begin with in one or two cases. At any rate, I took the information given to her into account when evaluating her performance.

Even Elliott (1964: 140) suggests the possibility of ESP in some of the more authentic-appearing cases: "The simplest explanation would be that the soul raiser is in some sort of telepathic communication with the circle in which she is performing." He goes on to say that, even if they have no psychic powers, good mediums are "a revelation in the skillful use of sociological knowledge." In short, they have excellent social skills, both in detecting cues and in their "presentation of self" in the role of medium.

British and American mediums show remarkable parallels with their Chinese counterparts. Based on his analysis of the classic medium cases, and on his own observation of mediums and automatic writers (including his own wife), Salter (1961) came to the same conclusion about Western mediums that I did independently from my study of Sam Gu.

First, on the matter of the role of the medium and her presentation of self: "No member of a profession likes to fall down on the job, and the subconscious, active during a trance, has a particular dislike of acknowledging defeat" (Salter, 1961: 125). Therefore, he says, bad days are a challenge, whether due to problems with the medium or problems with the sitter. Some techniques for compensating include "fishing" and looking for cues from the sitter.

Just as I pointed out to Cindy that there were many gradations from total honesty to pure fraud, I later read Salter's (1961: 129, 130) comment that "it is no slur on the integrity of a trance-medium if, having nothing paranormal in stock, he hands out to an expectant sitter anything lying ready in his subconscious.... All this may properly be described as 'trance-deception' and not as conscious fraud," unlike the practice of some mediums who actually collect information on sitters.

British investigators of spiritualism often came to the conclusion that in cases where normal explanations (fishing or fraud, latent memory, and guessing) were not sufficient, then telepathy from the living was (Salter, 1961: 114, 142, 145). In some cases, material in the seance was traceable to ideas currently a preoccupation of one of the sitters, or found in the same erroneous form in a newspaper.

Just as in my suspicions about possible negative effects from sitters, Salter (1961: 128) states that if a sitter is too silent or frigid, he won't encourage the medium. "For success he must acquire the art... of encouraging the medium at appropriate points without giving away facts. "

Another universal is that only a few mediums have been considered really competent under close scrutiny. Elliott (1964: 135) says that this scarcity of excellent mediums is a more crucial factor in the culture of the mun mai poh type in Singapore, rather than a drop in belief per se. It seems to me that a lack of competent mediums in Hong Kong (or perhaps lack of sufficient recruitment of mediums due to a lack of organized religious life beyond the family) is a factor in the decline in belief there. Around the turn of the century, in the height of interest in gifted mediums like Mrs. Piper and Mrs. Leonard, researchers scoured Britain and the U.S. for more, but found very few (Salter, 1961).

A note on reincarnation

Spirit mediums sometimes say that they cannot contact the spirits of ancestors who have died more than two years ago, because they may already have been reincarnated. Other mediums, like the one I observed, never worry about that. One might ask in general, what is the point of worshiping ancestors back several generations if they have left the spirit world to be reincarnated? The reason for such inconsistencies is that Chinese religion, in its eclecticism and tolerance, added the Buddhist emphasis on reincarnation to the more ancient Chinese practice of ancestor worship (cf. Chapter 3).

One other ambiguity, less significant than the above, lies in some of the spirit-possession cases (cf. Chapter 13). When animals are thought to be possessed by ancestral spirits, should they be considered reincarnations or merely temporary possessions by souls who will return to the spirit world?

Although reincarnation is expendable in the Chinese psychical-belief system, 25% on the telephone survey said that they believed in it, ranking it sixth out of fourteen paranormal beliefs (cf. Table 1 on page 325). Among those who made special comments, twenty-two were negative and nine positive. Among the negative ones, seven said that there was no such thing "these days" or "in this world, " four called it "ridiculous," and three said that it was a moral threat made up to convince people to do good.

One person said, "Ludicrous! Haven't you had any biology in high school?" Another, reflecting the same agnosticism as two other respondents, noted, "I'm not dead. I don't know."

The only comments about the social background of believers came from five people who said that "only Buddhists believe in reincarnation." As expected from the historical connection between Buddhism and reincarnation, Buddhism is the strongest social predictor of belief in reincarnation (cf. Table 2). The only other significant relationship between a religious preference and reincarnation belief after other variables are controlled is the negative one with "no religion." Before any controls, 49% of Buddhists believe, 20% of those with no religion, 19% of Protestants, and 12% of Catholics.

Although not technically considered a religion, ancestor worship is also significantly related to belief in reincarnation (cf. Table 3). Among ancestor worshipers, 29% believe, compared with 15% of nonworshipers. Incidentally, the highest correlation between reincarnation and any other belief is with belief in spirit mediums: 0.308. This is logical, as spirit mediums are involved with both reincarnation and ancestor worship, although I just pointed out above that reincarnation is sometimes thought to make it impossible to contact ancestral spirits after a time.

The only other significant factor is sex: 29% of women and 21% of men believe in reincarnation, which still holds after the controls (Table 3).

Age and education are conspicuously absent this time, as is Westernization, after other social variables are controlled. At least it should be said that belief in reincarnation does not appear to be especially under attack from youth, or from highly educated, Westernized people, contrary to what one might expect.

As far as experience is concerned, only seven people on the telephone survey, and none of the students on the secondary-school questionnaire, claimed any evidence for reincarnation. Five of the seven are women; and all seven are ones with "no religion" (surprising, considering the negative relationship with belief), although six are ancestor worshipers. Also surprisingly, none is a Buddhist. However, the forty-year-old man in R003 below claims to have an unusual interest in Buddhism.

R003. A Touch of Buddhism

My mother told a fortune-teller my date and hour of birth, and he told her what I was in a former life. I had been a monk twenty years before, and now I like to read Buddhist scriptures and go to monasteries to hear prayers, although I don't believe in Buddhism. I went to Anglican school, and my wife is Catholic, but I have no religion.

The next case, from a thirty-nine-year-old woman, also contains the notion that traits from former lives are preserved in the next. Remember, too, that the man who died and was reborn in another village at the same time (R002 in Chapter 1) had a physical similarity, a mole in the same place on both bodies.

R004. Cat with Two Lives

I love fish and scratch my neck all the time, and am very friendly to cats. My family tells me I was probably a cat before.

There is one other interesting case in Chapter 1 to recall: R001, "Soul of the Fair-Skinned Girl," in which a pregnant woman's husband dreamed of a naked woman floating in the window. The respondent interpreted the dream as an image of the soul that was entering her daughter, as both had light skin and as the dream coincided with the beginning of labor. If there was anything paranormal about the dream, it might also have been precognitive.

The final case below, reported by a forty-year-old woman, could also be an ESP experience rather than reincarnation. In other words, the deja vu feeling in the dream could be either clairvoyance of precognition rather than past life recall.

R005. The Beautiful Beach

I have dreamt of a beach with caves a lot. If is very pretty. I know every corner of the beach, but I have never been there. I know I must have lived there in my previous life. My dreams are identical every time.

Automatic writing

Finally, there is one other category of Chinese spirit mediumship, automatic writing, that is also found in various forms in the West. It is an *indirect* communication from spirits or gods, as pointed out earlier.

One type of automatic writing is *dip sin* ("saucer genie"), a popular practice in which people put a little soy sauce dish upside down on a paper with symbols and push it around unwittingly with one finger something like a Ouija board indicator. There are also various kinds of planchettes.

A more serious method is *fu gei* (literally, "character table"), practiced by people in the role of *fu gei sau* ("character writer"). There are numerous references to the various versions of *fu gei* (Elliott, 1964: 67, 140-145; Hsu, 1967: 170; Kehl, 1971). Generally, it involves a box of sand that is smoothed after each character or even after each stroke, and a wooden instrument, usually in a Y-shape, that is held by one or two people who make the point dart around in the box. Willoughby-Meade (1926: 358, 360) describes two unique variations on this pattern: a chopstick in a tray of flour, alleged to write in secret by itself, and the end of the shaft of a litter (sedan chair).

Lao Tzu's birthday

I was very fortunate to be able to visit a Taoist religious service on Hong Kong Island, at which fu gei was practiced. But it was just dumb luck that I went on the birthday of Lao Tzu, the founder or formalizer of Taoism in about the fifth century B.C. There were about thirty-eight people there that evening: twenty-two adult females, nine adult males, and seven children. Although I was somewhat apprehensive as an outsider at an exotic and impressive ceremony, people turned out to be very friendly and even open to photography of anything. The man conducting the service even stopped once to make sure my tape recorder was on!

People were impressed when they found out that I was a vegetarian. Lao Tzu said that you should try not to kill animals or eat meat, they pointed out. All the offerings on the altar before the portrait of one of the Taoist genies were vegetarian: fruits, pastries, fragrant wood, and so on. The food was destined to be eaten later on, the leftovers taken home in doggie bags. Incense sticks were lit one after the other, and the smoke spread like a thick, sweet blanket over the standing congregation.

To the right of the altar was a built-in board full of sand that pulled out of the altar. The fu gei sau wrote symbolic characters in the sand with a rapid scribble of a two-handled, T-shaped writing stick. After each character, he interpreted what character he had written and told it to an assistant sitting at a table near him. Another assistant wiped the sand smooth again with a wooden ruler-shaped piece.

First, Lao Tzu himself allegedly spoke through the fu gei sau. Then there was a question period, in which people submitted questions on folded pieces of paper (limit: three per person). Yellow ones (for illness) and white ones (for other questions) were burned on the altar, while the "Guardian Ho" came down and answered the questions through the fu gei sau.

I took two questions of my own to the altar: (1) "What will happen in my career for the next few years?"and (2) "How many children will I have altogether?" Both answers were very poetic and hard to decipher (just as reported for Singapore by Elliott, 1964: 145). To the first, the answer described a little boat on a dangerous river (possibly relevant to my career!), but the second stated that both science and the supernatural were very important. As these were written in Chinese characters, which

Worshiper before altar to Taoist genie

I cannot read, I had several bystanders helping me out by translating and giving their explanations of what they really meant.

I asked a young Chinese woman who had graduated from a state university in the U.S. if she were impressed with the appropriateness of

Offering of vegetarian pastries and fragrant wood on Taoist altar

Assistant burning a question on paper for Taoist automatic writing (fu gei)

Worshiper before altar waiting for response from spirit
through fu gei sau (in print shirt)

Fu gei sau preparing to receive message from Taoist spirit through automatic writing in sand

Fu gei sau writing message in sand

Fu gei sandbox and two-handled stick for automatic writing

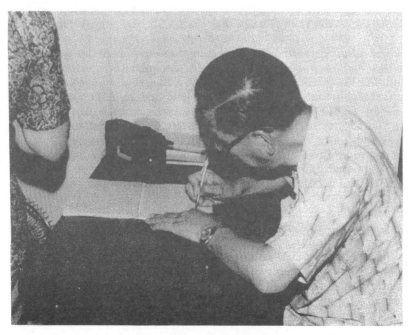

Recorder taking down spirit message from fu gei sau

the answers given to *her* questions. She seemed satisfied with all three of hers, although they seemed like general aphorisms to me. She also thought that it was amazing how the fu gei sau could crank out these literary-style poems on the spot. She didn't think that he could memorize them and then spit them out. He was not an especially highly educated person.

It's clear that the medium does not see the questions before he generates the message, although theoretically there could be an elaborate hoax with the fu gei sau sneaking a peek before the questions are burned and then remembering them when the persons' names are called out. Not knowing the questions on the yellow sheets (for illness) creates an odd situation. Clients must not only trust the efficacy of the herbal medicines that are prescribed through the medium, but hope that information about the correct ailment has been transmitted paranormally to match the prescription.

Mun mai poh, you recall, sometimes diagnose illnesses and prescribe herbal remedies (in addition to ancestral-worship remedies), perhaps with the help of a genie. Fu gei sau in the Taoist organization I observed also depart from their usual role during the sixth lunar month, when they contact the spirits of ordinary mortals instead of just genies.

16

ESP (Extrasensory Perception)

2017: One important thing to underline about this chapter is the fact that it shows the Chinese traditional tendency to connect ESP ("sixth sense") with precognition, knowing the future, as you can see from the specific cases included. In other words, ESP about the present or past is seldom reported. This may be part of the reason that I did not find it typical for Chinese to wonder if spirit mediums were using telepathy or some other type of ESP when they got information allegedly from a spirit about the present or past of the family.

For an updated treatment of ESP see Science and Spirit *(Emmons and Emmons, 2012: 92-101). For an extended discussion of our personal experiences with ESP and related matters, see* Guided by Spirit *(Emmons and Emmons, 2003: 45-139).*

Although this is the first and only chapter dealing exclusively with extrasensory perception, ESP has been a consideration in every chapter so far, especially as an explanation for apparitions. ESP turns up second on the popularity list of paranormal beliefs: 49% of the Chinese on the telephone survey said that they believed in it, just short of the 50% believing in ghosts, although slightly less than the 53% who believe in ESP in the U.S. (Table 1, page 325). And 19% claimed to have had one or more experiences with ESP, the most frequently experienced of the fourteen phenomena on the list.

Nevertheless, there is something peculiar about ESP in Chinese culture. Westerners have often claimed that Chinese are more psychic than Europeans (for example, cf. Burkhardt, 1953: vol. 2, 146). The only two respondents on the survey to comment on the matter, however, said that ESP was something Western, a view that receives some support in the next section of this chapter. One Western psychic in Hong Kong suggested to me that Chinese take ESP for granted as a normal part of life and therefore don't have a concept for it as a paranormal phenomenon. I don't think that this is quite right. After all, less than 0.4% on the survey claimed not to know what "sixth sense" (as we had to translate "ESP") is.

However, 72% of those who had experienced ESP gave examples that were precognitive (seeing the future) rather than telepathic or clairvoyant in the present. Although I know of no comparable survey in the West, this strikes me as an unusual emphasis on a narrow conceptualization of ESP. Perhaps many Chinese would agree with the two respondents who said that ESP is "the same as fortune telling" (telling the future = precognition).

In the West, the term "ESP" was coined by J. B. Rhine, the parapsychological researcher at Duke University who began in the 1930s to make psychical research more "scientific" by isolating psychic ability in laboratory experiments. At the same time, he largely removed psychic phenomena from their social contexts, like spiritualism, haunted houses, and fortune telling. Eventually, of course, ESP itself became part of American and British popular culture. In Hong Kong, however, ESP ("sixth sense") had to be introduced as an element of Western popular culture. Apparently, ESP has taken on a rather narrow meaning for many Chinese, perhaps becoming considered analogous to fortune telling as a way to make it socially meaningful rather than being seen as an abstract ability.

Who believes in and experiences ESP?

Unlike the comments on belief in ghosts and spirit mediums, there were virtually no statements from respondents to the survey on the social characteristics of believers in ESP. Eleven people said that only gifted people *had* ESP, more of a psychological factor. The only comment on social causes of belief was that "only Buddhists believe," which turns out to be untrue. This underlines the lack of a Chinese cultural context for ESP. One person said that the "*Reader's Digest* talks about ESP," someone else that it was on television, both popular-culture sources.

Are there any social correlates of belief in ESP? Yes. Table 2 on page 326 shows that Protestantism and Catholicism are somewhat positively related to ESP belief among Hong Kong Chinese. Buddhism is not significantly related after controlling for other variables, in spite of the fact that Buddhists are high on belief in ghosts and spirit mediums. Again, those with no religion are low on belief (just the opposite of the case in the U.S.; cf. Chapter 4 and Emmons and Sobal, 1981b).

As with Buddhism, ancestor worship is an unrelated factor this time, which emphasizes the lack of a home for the specific concept of "ESP" in traditional Chinese culture. The strongest factors, just as in the U.S. (Emmons and Sobal, 1981a), are education and age, even after controlling for other variables (Table 3). Although education was of minor significance in ghost belief and not significant in spirit-medium belief, there is a continuous increase in belief in ESP from 14% of those with no education to 66% of college graduates. As with belief in ghosts and spirit mediums, younger people are more likely to believe in ESP. This time, the change is more smoothly continuous: age groups under thirty are consistently at about 60% belief, declining thereafter to a low of 17% among those over sixty years of age.

"Westernization" (self-rating) is not significantly related after controlling for other variables, but the fact is that education and age are the only two that reduce the relationship with Westernization. Certainly, the younger and more highly educated are more Westernized than others

in Hong Kong. Therefore, Western culture really does have an impact on
the belief in "sixth sense."

As far as ESP experience is concerned, the same factors are significant
as with belief. However, it may be that believers are just more open to
labeling their experiences as ESP or revealing them on the survey, rather
than necessarily having more extrasensory communications.

In the following sections, let us look at some examples of ESP
experiences. I must say that in spite of the high percentage of people
claiming to have had an ESP experience, 19% on the telephone survey,[91]
the great majority of them were quite vague about details even when
asked for examples and particulars. A typical response would be, "I know
about things before they happen, and then they happen. I can't think of
a specific example right now." Moreover, the specifics that people did
give were generally not very strange or convincing on the surface. This
situation contrasts with the ghost reports, which were usually much more
concretely described, probably because apparitions are more startling and
memorable. The ESP cases included here are ones with greater detail than
most, selected to illustrate major types.

Feelings

The first three cases illustrate a common theme, that ESP often takes the
form of a physical or emotional feeling rather than some specific mental
message. They were reported by a forty-five-year-old and a thirty-two-
year-old woman, and finally by a thirteen-year-old boy. Recall that "The
Prolific Psychic" in Chapter 12 also received precognitive impressions
this way, as when she felt "confused and terrible" before the bombings in
World War II.

---

91   A surprisingly low 2.9% of the secondary-school students claimed to have
had an ESP experience. Although they generally described fewer experiences of
all phenomena than in the telephone survey (probably because they didn't want
to take the time to write them down), this is still lower than the number of
ghost experiences. On the telephone, there were almost five times as many ESP
as ghost cases.

E009. Uncomfortable

When bad things are going to happen, I feel very uncomfortable.

E010. The Unlucky Shiver

I feel a cold chill, I shiver before something unlucky happens.

E011. The Lucky Murmur

When they were drawing prizes at a function, my mother and I simultaneously had a "heart murmur." Then they called my number, and we won a prize.

Twitching eyes

Nine people specifically referred to a system of eye twitches that are supposedly harbingers of good and bad luck. There are, however, variations on the theme. Some people simply said that a twitching eyelid meant bad luck. Another said that a twitch in the right eye was bad, but one in the left eye meant nothing. Someone else thought that an eye twitch was good, but a moving eyebrow bad.

This phenomenon takes on the character of a cultural system of divination in some cases, more than simply an idiosyncratic way of receiving precognitive ESP messages. My wife, Chee, says that a twitching above the right eye is supposed to mean celebration, below the right eye anger, upper left sadness, and lower left happiness. Alternately, she says, both uppers can mean that you will have food to eat, and the lowers that you won't get to eat. Her own version, which she seems to believe in a little bit, is that uppers are good, lowers are generally bad, as in the food system. (She gives herself the bonus of making the lower left mean happiness, as in the four-quadrant system!)

Symbolic dreams

Thirty-five people on the telephone survey said that they had had precognitive dreams. Since dreams in general are often symbolic, as Freud emphasized, for example, it is not surprising that precognitive ones are also less than completely literal sometimes, as in this case from a thirteen-year-old girl.

E012. The Chase
I dreamt of being chased by a lion once. The next day I was chased by a dog.

I got the next report secondhand from an interview with the "folk Taoist" (cf. Chapter 13), whose mother allegedly had a clairvoyant or telepathic dream, a death crisis case with some symbolic elements in the sense that she did not realize that her daughter-in-law was supposed to be dead in the dream. It is possible that the message from the deceased was equivalent to a last farewell in a death-crisis apparition.

The Hay Pile
My mother had this dream in Indonesia the same day her daughter-in-law drowned. She saw her lying all wet on a hay pile, saying to her, "Thanks for the letter and the money. I'll write soon." Later, she found out that they had put her drowned body on a pile of hay. The daughter-in-law was an unloved wife [who was rejected in favor of a concubine]. She committed suicide in the river.

Relatives
It is a well-known finding that ESP is often strong among people who are close to each other, especially when some incident of high emotion is taking place. In E013, a traumatic dream is shared by a pair of twins who seem to have the kind of telepathic communication that some have argued is often found among identical twins. The fourteen-year-old boy who wrote this on his school questionnaire did not say if he and his brother were identical or fraternal.

E013. Twins

I have experienced something concerning sixth sense. When I was eight or nine, I was in the third grade. My brother and I are twins. That night, in the middle of the night, I fell asleep and had a dream. I dreamt that I was playing with my cousin in his house, and suddenly somebody with a knife jumped in from the window. I got very scared and ran and hid underneath a chair. Then I woke up very frightened.

The next day, at dawn, my brother woke up and told me he had had a dream. He told me in detail about his dream, and it was exactly the same as my dream.

Another thing, from the time I was very little to now I have had some ESP incidents. Sometimes in my heart I was singing a certain tune, and my brother suddenly sang it out. These things happened a lot of times. I don't think it is just coincidence.

Next, a fifteen-year-old boy reports a precognitive dream that is symbolic of a family tragedy.

E014. Crying for Grandpa

This cannot be considered a strange phenomenon. But it *is* pretty strange. One night, I had a dream. I dreamt of crying next to a corpse. It was my grandpa's. Surprisingly, the next day my grandpa died. This is in connection with sixth sense maybe.

Although some ESP messages are good ones, as with the prize in E011, certainly the great emphasis in the Chinese cases in on ill omens. The forty-year-old man in E015 is not alone in this regard.

E015. Sick Again

My wife gets mad at me for thinking about such things. For me, ESP is mainly about bad things. Three times in my office, I

thought about my daughter getting sick. She got sick the same
night every time. I told my wife about it only once.

Accidents

The emphasis in ESP cases on paranormal communication about dangers
to oneself, relatives, or friends makes me wonder if ESP is some natural
adaptation established long ago in human genes, or farther back on the
evolutionary trail (considering the evidence of ESP in animals). A twenty
-six-year-old man in E016 thinks that his ESP kept him away from the
scene of danger, but the twenty-one-year-old man in E017 experienced a
somewhat different outcome.

E016. Construction Death

I didn't go to work one day this year because I felt like there was
a rock on my heart. That same day a fellow worker got killed on
the site.

E017. Off the Track

Last year, when my friends and I were going on a picnic, I had
a feeling that we should take a train instead of a bus. I felt like
something bad would happen to us. We planned to take the train,
but missed it and had to take the bus. The bus had a problem just
as it was about to go down a hill and had a minor accident.

Hospital cases

Continuing with a related bad-luck category, E018 is from a sixty-year-
old woman patient, E019 from a forty-three-year-old male doctor, and
E020 from a twenty-eight-year-old female nurse.

E018. Hospital Blues

I knew I was going to be real sick and would have to spend a lot
of money. I ended up in the hospital.

E019. "Calling Dr. …"

Once, I thought about a patient and was called fifteen minutes later to the operating room to attend to that patient, who had just been in a car accident.

E020. A Turn for the Nurse

I sometimes know whether a certain patient will get worse by the way I feel in the morning.

War

This next case, reported by a fifty-nine-year-old man, is similar to a story I heard at a party in Hong Kong about a woman who kept having dreams about where the Japanese would attack next when she was living someplace in Asia during World War II. In one symbolic dream just before a bombing, she saw bird's eggs falling out of a nest and exploding on the ground.

E021. Early Warning

During the war, I could sense when a place would be dangerous, and I would tell people not to go there. Then there would be an explosion there. Some people thought I was crazy, so I didn't say it too much.

Gambling

One common type of ESP case that is not completely ominous involves gambling. Some 8% (twenty-three of 279) of the ESP reports on the telephone survey specifically mentioned gambling. One person went so far as to say that "only gamblers believe in ESP." People never said that they used clairvoyance or telepathy on the cards or on other participants during a game or event; but they often stressed that they would know beforehand (precognition again), especially the night before, whether they would be lucky at mahjongg, the lottery, or horse betting. Unfortunately, no one gave very specific examples. A few people mentioned two-digit numbers that came to mind in a dream, for example, and that turned out to be winners for them on the lottery, but even these one-in-a-hundred chances are not that rare to be impressive without keeping a long record of tries.

A few people said that they had used their ESP on the dice game in the casino at Macao, a Portuguese colony forty miles west of Hong Kong on the south coast of China. On two different occasions, I have done the same thing myself! However, I tried to combine PK and ESP. First, I concentrated on either "big" or "little" (a total on three dice of eleven and above or ten and less). As the dice are scrambled under a black cover before the bets are placed, and revealed by raising the cover after all bets are on, it is possible to try to get an ESP impression of whether the desired outcome was registered on the dice before betting. Before I bet, I did some dry runs, just standing there to see if I was "on," or to see whether I was more disposed to get big or little. Then I bet. Both times I won about two-thirds of the bets, instead of the expected amount, just under half (the house takes all bets when triplets are thrown, one chance in thirty-six), and won money, of course. I was not able to make a sufficient number of bets for the results to be statistically significant. The reason that I tried the experiment to begin with is that I had done a long PK experiment with dice many years before as an undergraduate, in which the results were highly significant.

Schools and teachers

A frequently reported category of ESP experience among younger respondents has to do with school traumas. Seventeen said that they knew ahead of time something about questions on their exams or results of exams. Six more claimed to have known that their teachers would not show up on a certain day! Although not part of the survey, the woman in P003 (Chapter 10) and in SP008 (Chapter 13) told me the following precognitive dream.

E022. The Delayed Grades

I had a dream that everybody else got their grades in the mail except me, and to get them I had to see the sister who was principal of the convent school. A couple days later, in fact I *didn't* get my grades.

I went to ask about them in the office and was told to go look for the principal. I found her in the playground near the school building, in exactly the same place I had seen her in my dream! It frightened me.

"What's for supper?"

ESP messages about food would seem to be anticlimactic, to say the least, after the list of dangers and traumas we have just been through – but perhaps not as hunger approaches late in the afternoon, especially considering the importance of food in Chinese culture! E023 and E024 are from thirty-five- and thirty-one-year-old women.

E023. The Menu

I often know ahead of time what the family is going to eat for supper.

E024. Chinese Carry-Out

When I want to eat something, my husband usually buys it and brings it home that night (without me telling him).

Evidently, the woman in E024 is sending telepathic messages to her husband (unless he guesses what to buy by normal means). The respondent may be the sender in E013, "Twins," as well.

Déjà Vu

The literal meaning of the French phrase *déjà vu* is "already seen." It is used to refer to the strangely familiar feeling of having already been in a place where apparently you have never really been. The confusing part is the implication that the paranormal phenomenon is the encounter with the familiar place or activity. What really needs explaining, however, is where the original memory came from. When you remember a precognitive dream, the connection falls into place, as in the next case from a sixteen-year-old boy.

E025. Familiar Scenery

I've experienced sixth sense. In my dream, I saw a road in a construction site where construction was going on. I also saw a green hill on my left. When I woke up, I still remembered the scenery.

A few months later, my friend and I went to Bride's Dam to have a barbecue. As I was riding my bicycle, I saw this place exactly like what I saw in my dream; except that in my dream I was riding a little car, but then I was riding a bicycle. Other than that, there were similar things happening.

In the next report, a twenty-one-year-old woman describes a precognitive waking impression that has essentially the same function as the dream in the previous example.

E026. Housing Speculation

One day, I went out and accidentally saw a house. I thought that I would live there one day. My parents ended up buying the house later and living in it.

Paranormal perception in China

Although I have emphasized that the idea of ESP as an ability in individuals, apart from some social role like fortune-teller, is Western rather than Chinese, there is at least one Chinese type that is becoming well known in both China and Hong Kong. Some children in the People's Republic of China allegedly have the ability to read through their ears or other parts of the body (*South China Morning Post*, 1980). Not only have stories on this phenomenon appeared in the Hong Kong press, but I also heard citizens of the PRC talk about it when I visited the country in late 1980.

Personal confirming experiences

It is one thing to read studies of paranormal phenomena, but it is quite another thing to have firsthand experiences. The experiences themselves can be more *personally* (as opposed to intellectually) convincing than any statistically significant findings can. Except for the dice experiments, I have never considered myself particularly psychic. My wife, Chee, however, has done quite a few things in my presence that make me as certain of ESP as I think I ever could be of anything so puzzling or intangible.

In the summer of 1976, Chee and I were sitting in her parents' condominium in Hong Kong talking about mental telepathy. We decided to try it. I picked a two-digit number and asked her to guess it, say 47. She guessed it! One chance in 100. Well, let's try that again, I said. She got my second and then my third number (say 81, then 16). Admittedly, such a test is not acceptable by the standards of experimental research. I might have somehow been predisposed to pick certain numbers in ways she might have guessed, for example. But as a confirming experience, this was enough to shock me. The chances (barring some bias, which I doubted) were $1/100 \times 1/100 \times 1/100 =$ one in one million. It shouldn't have happened, but it did, a challenge to my materialistic, scientific view of the universe. I could not bring myself to ask her to guess another number at that moment.

On some other occasions, she has failed to show any ESP whatsoever. This is the trouble with ESP. Even gifted subjects cannot always perform. Nevertheless, it has certainly been my impression that Chee is far beyond the chance level overall, and that she *has* performed on many occasions, although she dislikes controlled situations or the feeling that she is being tested.

I once tested her, however, with results that astonished me. I was just asking her to try out a design for me that I wanted to use for a class demonstration of ESP-testing. Out of our about 200 record-album covers (with which she has a very slight acquaintance because she never plays the records), I used a random procedure to select four. In another room, she concentrated while I looked at the covers, and she drew her impressions. The similarities were remarkable. Just to take one example, for the Beatles' *Abbey Road* album, she drew four figures going over a path (very similar to the cover) and even wrote "Beatles" below her drawing.

Then I tried precognition, making her draw her impressions *before* I even knew how I was going to devise the randomizing procedure for selecting four more albums. The first one she drew, was a head-and-shoulders view of a man in a suit, tie, and formal hat. The first album I ended up selecting by a flip of a coin and throw of a die was the "Frank Sinatra story," with a photograph of Frank Sinatra on the cover just like what Chee had drawn precognitively.

I have witnessed many other examples of her ESP. These may suffice to illustrate the Chinese gifted-subject case that did more than any other to interest me in doing this study to begin with!

17

Fortune Telling

2017: There are a couple of curious things about this chapter. One is that more than twice as many people in the study said that they believed in fortune telling compared to spirit mediums, both of which are associated with ancestor worship. Perhaps the reason for this is that more people actually go to fortune tellers (and in general it may cost less), but the direction of cause and effect is not clear (between belief and consultation).

Also, now it can be told: her predictions about me turned out not to be very accurate. I did not experience an upswing in wealth between the ages of 40 and 44, I am still working at age 74, and I am still waiting to be rich. I did not buy property in Hong Kong, unfortunately. She was much more accurate, though not completely, about my past. This might suggest that her knowledge about me (and perhaps her spirit mediumship as well) was based partly on telepathy, because I knew both types of information myself, about me and the spirit people.

Although there is a fairly high correlation between belief in fortune telling and belief in spirit mediums (0.315), and spirit mediums often tell fortunes, Hong Kong Chinese are nevertheless much more likely to believe in fortune telling: 44%, which puts it third on our list of fourteen para-normal beliefs (cf. Table 1 on page 325). It also ranks second in experience at 7.7%. [92] By contrast, only 18% believe in mediums, ranking eleventh. Moreover, there were very few negative comments about fortune telling volunteered on the telephone survey, only eleven, including three who said it was not accurate, and two who thought that it was a way to cheat people out of their money (see the harsher judgment of mediums in Chapter 15). However, a fairly large group (38) indicated that they didn't take it seriously, saying that it was "just for fun," or a hobby or pastime.

Who believes in and experiences fortune telling?

As with belief in ghosts and spirit mediums, Buddhists have a significantly high level of belief in fortune telling, and, as usual, those with no religion a significantly low level of belief even after controlling for other variables (cf. Table 2). Buddhists are most likely to believe (53%), followed by Catholics (47%), those with no religion (42%), and Protestants (37%). [93]

As expected, ancestor worship is positively related to belief in fortune telling, showing the effect of traditionalism and probably the connection with spirit mediums, although it is not as strongly related as Buddhism after controlling for the other variables (cf. Table 3). Among ancestor worshipers, 47% believe, compared with 39% of non-worshipers. For some reason, however, the ones with average scores on ancestor worship are more likely to believe than the ones with very high or very low scores.

Only two people commented on the social correlates of belief in fortune telling, both of whom said that it was for women. There is a slight but significant difference, 52% of women and 48% of men, which

---

92   Only 0.4% (eight of 1, 989) on the secondary-school questionnaires claimed a fortune-telling experience. In addition to a general lack of writing about their experiences, the students have probably had less opportunity to contact both fortune-tellers and spirit mediums. Cf. also footnote 91 in Chapter 16.

93   Although Protestants rank lower in belief than those with no religion, their low level of belief is explained by other factors and therefore is not significantly below the average of 44% after other factors are controlled.

holds up after the controls (Table 3). There is an even more significant difference in experience, 9.5% for females and 5.8% for males, [94] which is also logically connected with spirit mediums, whom women are much more likely to visit than men are (cf. Chapter 15).

Education is positively related to both belief and experience. Among previously discussed beliefs, education was most significantly correlated with ESP, and somewhat with ghosts, both positively. Although the correlation with belief in fortune telling is not as strong as with ESP, it is increased by controlling for other variables (Table 3). The most notable aspect is the very low belief, 23%, among those with no education. After that it increases, somewhat inconsistently up to 57% for those with some college education, but declines again to 38% for college graduates.

Age is the only other significant factor, negative with both belief and experience. As usual, younger people believe more (Table 3), but the relationship is the weakest it has been for any of the beliefs so far. There are some inconsistencies; as with belief in spirit mediums, the very youngest don't believe as much in fortune telling as the young adults. Among the under-18 group, 45% believe, then 50% of the 18-24-year-olds, and 54% of the 25-29-year-olds. From 30 to 59 years of age, it fluctuates within the high 30% to high 40% range. Then there is a sharp decline to 21% for the over-60 group.

Divination (plus present and past)

By definition, fortune telling is divination, discovering the future through some occult means. However, Chinese "readers," like their Western counterparts, often read the past or present in addition to the future. In fact, 59% of those describing their own fortune-telling experiences on the telephone survey (sixty-eight of 115) specifically stated that they were told things about the present or past, and only 31% (thirty-six of 115) said that they were told about the future. Of course, some cases fall into both categories, and there was probably more of a tendency to mention

---

94     $\chi^2 = 6.65$, p<.01.

statements about things that had already occurred, as respondents were relating mainly statements from fortunetellers that could be confirmed. Nevertheless, the majority of the readings had at least some discussion of present and past, as in FT001, from a twenty-two-year-old woman.

FT001. Shoulder Mole

I went to a fortune-teller and told him my time and date of birth. He told me about my family background, etc. He also said that I had a mole on my shoulder (which was true).

From the point of view of parapsychological theory, we would expect accurate readings of such past and present facts to be telepathy between sitter and fortune-teller or perhaps clairvoyance on the part of the fortune-teller alone. Of course, the mole-on-the-shoulder statement seems not to be a very long-shot guess considering the commonness of moles among Chinese people. Next, a forty-year-old man reports an actual prediction, a long-range one at that.

FT002. The Second Son

During the Japanese occupation, I went to a palm-reader with my mother. She had given another son to some other people. The fortune-teller said that this had happened but that she should not be sad because she was meant to be served by just one son. If he would see her other son, she would be close to death. Ten years later, the second son appeared. Within a month, she died. Before she died, she told me [reminded, since the respondent had evidently been too young at the reading to remember] what the fortune-teller had said.

Who tells fortunes?

It is convenient to divide Chinese fortune telling into three levels: at the lowest is the self-reading by an individual or small group, then the fortune-teller, and finally the spirit-medium who often tells fortunes in addition to contacting spirits. Only the last two are specialized fortune-telling roles.

Although the fortune-teller per se (nearly always a man) is the only one who exclusively tells fortunes, it can be argued that spirit mediums carry the art to a higher plane in terms of Chinese culture, as they are thought to be possessed or inspired by some spirit. Elliott (1964: 39) comments that it is a short step from fortune telling to mediumship: there is thought to be some divine inspiration behind the occult information in fortune telling in any form.

It may be remembered from Chapter 15 that there are two types of Cantonese spirit mediums: mun mai poh (women) and fu gei sau (men). The former tell fortunes both in the regular manner (for example, by looking at palm and face) and by communicating information from spirits while possessed during a seance. The latter tell fortunes by communicating the answers to sitters' questions through the words they write in the sand.

In FT003, we have an example of a self-read fortune by a thirteen-year-old boy using cards of some type. I cannot say how serious he is in his comments, but I have my doubts!

FT003. Are You Sure, Cards?

One day, I played fortune cards. I wanted to know the weather on the day of the picnic. The answer was: two days later the sky would clear up. I also wanted to have the outcome of the picnic foretold. The answer was: this will be a meaningless picnic.

I asked three times, and the answers were the same. Finally, the cards said, "Please don't ask me again. If you don't believe me, why bother to ask me in the first place?" I can't explain it. Up through the day of the picnic, the fortune cards really predicted everything. I don't know how to explain it.

Next, an eighteen-year-old man describes his own amateur fortune telling, which might be considered somewhere between the self-reading stage and professional fortune telling. His self-proclaimed techniques may not be very different from professional ones, however.

FT004. Tricks of the Trade

Sometimes, I tell fortunes for fun. I use my ESP to try to figure out what people are thinking. I also use tricks like noticing someone falling and then in the fortune telling him that he had an accident that day.

Methods

Whatever the actual source of information a fortune-teller taps (ESP, spiritual inspiration, normal knowledge, logical guessing), some procedure is generally used ostensibly to focus the flow of information (a crystal ball, cards, etc.). Usually, the focus is vague (like tea-leaf patterns), allowing many interpretations, or randomized (like the fall of the dice) to leave the decisions to chance. The most popular method mentioned in the telephone survey was examining the palm (forty-four times), which often goes along with examining the face at the same times (mentioned nineteen times). FT005, from a thirty-six-year-old woman, involves palm reading.

FT005. Poverty in the Palm

I'm not stupid or illiterate, but I believe. I went to two different palm-readers. Both knew I was very poor when I was little, although it wasn't obvious at the time [of the readings] from my clothing. They were accurate about my character, too.

The second-most-popular method in the telephone survey was drawing straws or sticks (twenty-one times). This is commonly done in a temple, especially on Chinese New Year, a time for divining the future a year at once in many cultures. About a hundred sticks are shaken in a bamboo vase until one falls out on the floor. The stick number is then matched to a message held by the temple keeper (Elliott, 1964: 38, 39). Next, a thirty-seven-year-old man refers to this method.

FT006. New Year's Straw
I always draw a straw on New Year's Day. This year, it told me to invest and that I'd be healthy and make money. It came true.

All other methods were only seldom mentioned. The Chinese astrological system, requiring date and time of birth, was specifically noted five times. Cards and handwriting analysis got only two mentions each, and coin flipping (self-reading) one. In spite of the popularity of the *I Ching* in the West, it was not discussed at all by the respondents.

One other method involves shaking dice in a hollowed-out turtle shell. Although no one referred to it on the survey, I have seen fortune-tellers on the sidewalk with this apparatus. Turtle shells have a long association with divination in Chinese history (Chan, 1969: 9, 10). Hookham (1969: 34) describes how symbols were written on shells and on shoulder-blades, which were then heated until they cracked. These sacred symbols on turtle shells are associated with the origins of writing in the Shang Dynasty or earlier. Reading patterns of cracks on bones as a system of divination is found in many other cultures as well.

What do you want to know?
An inventory of the topics discussed in the fortuneteller readings reported on the survey reflects major values of Hong Kong Chinese. From the amateur fortune telling that I have done for fun with tarot cards in the U.S., I would say that the only difference seems to be that there is still a greater emphasis on the family in Hong Kong. Forty-six mentioned that their fortunes included something about marriage and family matters. These statements are often limited to identifying family relationships and numbers of children and serve to impress the sitter that the fortuneteller has paranormal knowledge of the sitter's background.

Second most frequently mentioned were the nineteen fortunes that referred to career progress and wealth, "fortune" in the narrow sense, certainly a main preoccupation in materialistic Hong Kong. Another eighteen had to do with health.

Already, we see a reflection of the three major values: *Fok, Lok, Sau*, (Blessing, Fortune, and Long Life), which are personified in the set of three statues of old men displayed in most homes and Chinese restaurants. *Fok* often carries a small child in his arms, *Lok* is a man of prosperity, and *Sau* carries a long-life peach.

After the three major values, character or personality (nearly always of the sitter) was discussed fifteen times, school and exams four, and love life two. Whereas the stereotype of Western fortune telling contains the popular statement about a woman meeting a "tall, dark, handsome man," Chinese young people in the courtship years do not typically go to fortune-tellers to find out about their love life. Although age in general is negatively related to experience with fortune telling, teenagers actually had less-than-average experience. Also, many of the younger ones were just describing times they had tagged along with their mothers on a visit to the fortune-teller.

Impressed?

Although I suppose that at least some of the fortune-telling experiences may have been amazing at the time, I remain generally unimpressed. Neither the fortune telling nor the ESP cases have very much detail, in contrast to many of the apparition experiences.

One difficulty in trying to truth-test fortunes is that future events predicted in them may still happen at a much later date. Many people noted this on the survey.

However, it is also interesting to see how easily impressed some people are with apparently flimsy evidence, for example with very vague predictions, as in the case of the thirteen-year-old girl in FT007.

FT007. Bad Luck Before Good

Two years ago, my mom took me to a fortune-teller. He said that before I was fifteen I would run into unlucky things. After fifteen, everything would be smooth. Recently, my house was robbed, and we lost a lot of money. So comparatively speaking, I believe in fortune telling.

By "comparatively speaking," she evidently means compared with the other thirteen paranormal phenomena listed on the questionnaire. She claimed to believe in only two others: astrology and UFOs, both to a lesser degree than Chinese fortune telling.

Sometimes, the predicted event is not amazing because it is not a very low probability, perhaps is even more likely to occur than not. Although I don't know how much the twelve-year-old girl in FT008 means by "a lot of lucky money," nearly all Chinese children in Hong Kong get money in red envelopes from their elders on Chinese New Year.

FT008. Lucky Lucky Money

Once I was playing fortune-teller cards, and they told me that I'd make a lot of money that day. I did, because it was Chinese New Year and I got a lot of lucky money.

Next, another twelve-year-old girl is given what sounds more like good advice than a prediction!

FT009. The Soothsayer and the Scholar

A male fortune-teller told me to write my first name. Through my handwriting, he was able to answer my question about whether I would do well in my exams. The fortune-teller said that if I studied hard I would do well, and it came true.

The following report, from a twenty-seven-year-old man, drew laughter from people in the background when he gave it over the telephone.

FT010. Still Poor

The fortune-teller told me that I'd be wealthy in my old age. And so far I'm still poor!

Even cases that involve more specific detail are not very long-shot statements and, to the extent that they come true, may be partly self-fulfilling prophecies. It seems plausible that the thirty-three-year-old and forty-seven-year old women in FT011 and FT012 respectively may have been somewhat influenced in their actions by the predictions.

FT011. Adventures Abroad

When I was in high school, I went to a palm-reader who told me that I wouldn't stay in Hong Kong but would go overseas to study, and I did. I would get married overseas and have two children. This was all correct.

FT012. Emigration by Divination

The straws told me that I would not be in China long, and what year I would leave. I did leave then, and now I'm here.

There is one more factor to be mentioned that might make predictions seem better than they are. Among believers, there is probably a tendency to forget statements that lie unconfirmed. One high-priced fortune-teller in Hong Kong, however, has an unusual practice in this regard, I am told. He tape-records the session, gives the tape to the client, and says, "if this turns out not to be true, you can come back and tear the sign off my door!"

Personal observations

The high-priced fortune-teller I just referred to charges from $40 U.S. on up for a reading. I never observed any fortune-tellers in that range. In general, I decided to concentrate my efforts elsewhere, because I was told that some readers are associated with Hong Kong's underworld (crime, that is, rather than the home of the spirits!).

However, I did observe "my" spirit medium (Chapter 15) telling three fortunes for $2 U.S. each, and a well-known Western fortune-teller who charged $10 U.S. each in 1978, now $12 I hear. Although the latter is not very relevant to this study of Chinese phenomena, I saw her do two fortunes using playing cards in a way that seemed to be just a framework for her attempts at ESP rather than any strict formula. She kept reshuffling and resorting the cards for me and said little about me that seemed significant. Her reading of my sister-in-law came much more fluently and looked at least suggestive of some paranormal ability.

One of the three fortunes told by the spirit medium, Sam Gu, was short, vague, and erroneous enough to rate as no better than chance. She told it on August 30, 1980, not one of her notably bad days.

The other two were long, fairly specific, and apparently accurate enough to be very interesting although not startling. These were readings of my wife and me, both on my first visit, August 5, 1980. She looked at my hand and face, pushing my hair away to get a better look at my forehead. She worked her way chronologically through my life, commenting on good and bad years financially for my family and discussing my years of schooling and work.

Overall, it was a good enough fit to seem much better than chance guessing, although I could not attach accurate probabilities. For example, she said that I started working part-time at eighteen when I was still studying. Actually, I worked three summers from ages sixteen to eighteen, the last one between my freshman and sophomore years in college. At age twenty-two, I really started working, she said. This is correct, because I took my first serious job in a Chicago bank at age twenty-two, although I unexpectedly returned to graduate school a few months later. She said that I left home at age twenty-six or twenty-seven, but in fact I left at age twenty-one, when I graduated from Gannon College in my hometown of Erie, Pennsylvania. But she was right on the money when stating that

I studied until I was twenty-eight; I got my Ph.D. in 1971 at age twenty-eight.

Some of her predictions will have to wait for confirmation at a later date. Five fascinated bystanders were listening in the hallway nearby, calling in translations of some of Sam Gu's country-dialect expressions, putting them into standard Hong Kong Cantonese. "When you're between forty and forty-four, you'll be very rich. If you throw a rock on the floor, it'll turn into money! You can do no work and just wiggle your feet."

Such talk may become a self-fulfilling prophecy, as it gives me encouragement to act aggressively in activities like writing this book!

"Ages fifty-three to fifty-nine will be bad years. You'll lose money. Don't let people invest your money for you. At sixty-four, you won't have to work any more. You'll die when you're eighty."

Then she proceeded to give me advice. Come to Hong Kong. The food is bad in the States (from a Chinese point of view, of course!). She predicted that I would buy a house in Hong Kong between ages forty and forty-four and have a maid.

One final comfort: since I have a beard, I won't starve. I'll be able to eat even when I'm dying. We shall see.

My wife's reading was shorter and less specific, concentrating more on physiognomy as a reflection of personality traits. Less was confirmable, at least in the present. Those thing that were verifiable were mostly quite accurate, but cannot be revealed because of their personal nature. I can say, however, that she correctly stated that Chee has many brothers and sisters, of which two are brothers. Chee has two brothers and three sisters. For the future, Chee is supposed to have a nonserious illness at fifty-one, a big one at sixty-three, and die at seventy-one.

At any rate, Sam Gu's performance, as recorded in detail in my notebooks, was much more revealing and impressive than the short statements from respondents on the survey in regard to fortune telling just as it was in regard to spirit contact in Chapter 15.

18

CONCLUSION

2017: I substantially agree with the following conclusion from the 1982 edition. However, here are some added points from my current perspective.

Part of this study showed correlations between paranormal beliefs (in ghosts, ESP, spirit mediums, reincarnation etc.) and social background factors like age, education and gender. Only a new large-scale survey like the one conducted in 1980 could discover whether there have been changes not only in the levels of these beliefs but also in how all these variables relate to each other. For example, we would like to know not only whether ghost belief has increased or decreased in Hong Kong, but also whether its relationship to amount of education has changed. The perhaps surprising finding in 1980 was that people with low levels of education were the least likely to believe in ghosts, making it seem unlikely that recent increases in educational levels would bring about a decline in ghost belief.

Religion (or spirituality) and popular culture in recent decades may have brought about changes in ghost folklore, if not experiences, and it would be interesting to do further research in these areas. In this 2017 edition I have shown that ghost belief is still a big factor economically, in terms of tourism and real estate (see the section in Chapter 13 about hongza, haunted properties, and the haunted-house discount).

In the 1982 conclusion I referred to ghost folklore as a moral social control system. As pointed out in Chapter 13, Bosco's (2007) recent study of young people's ghost stories demonstrates this very well in terms of the theme of studying vs. sex.

The 1982 conclusion also emphasizes the methodological importance of looking for patterns in a large number of cases, rather than investigating in great depth a few particular cases. This is something I have elaborated on in recent conference presentations. Fortunately it is still possible to get a fairly good sample of cases through ethnographic interviewing without doing a large survey. At the same time, parapsychologists who investigate individual cases thoroughly are still making a useful contribution to understanding the phenomenon.

On a theoretical level I concluded in 1982 that parapsychologists should keep looking for some kind of ESP receptor and transmitter in the brain. This would be discussed as a neurophysiological approach today. What I would add to this now is that perhaps there is no actual ESP center but rather a holistic blend between the brain and consciousness beyond the brain. In other words, perhaps we should look to a quantum physical explanation of paranormal communication that rests on nonlocal connections between things in different places and times, rather than on some actual movement of information through space (Emmons and Emmons, 2012).

One thing really has not changed since 1982: my statement that "evidential apparitions (ghost experiences that lack a simple normal explanation) ... will require radical rethinking of scientific theories of the nature of humanity and perhaps of the universe."

When I first began this journey through the Chinese world of the unexplained, I didn't know quite what to expect. Perhaps the most significant surprises along the way turned out to be certain stunning similarities to the West.

One set of similarities demonstrated that essentially the same social-background factors help predict belief in paranormal phenomena both in Hong Kong and in the United States. Generally speaking, for most phenomena, believers tend to be young and highly educated; this is contrary to the stereotype in both cultures that the old and the uneducated are "superstitious." The major difference between the Chinese and the American date lies in the effect of religion. In the U.S., those who claim "no religion" are very high on belief in nonreligious paranormal phenomena; just the opposite holds true in Hong Kong. My guess is that the American use of the "popular occult" as a "functional alternative" to mainstream religion (Emmons and Sobal, 1981b) has not taken root among nonreligious Chinese in Hong Kong, where faith in capitalism and upward mobility is still strong and where there seems to be no movement to revitalize or import new religions to find meaning in a troubled secular society.

There is no doubt that Hong Kong has been inundated with Western popular culture. Television-program and movie-theater listings in the newspapers, fast-food establishments in the streets, and clothing fashions on the inhabitants make this all too obvious. And, just as in the United States, educated youth among Hong Kong Chinese are the most vigorous consumers of popular culture and the most open to change. However, Westernization has not swept aside traditional Chinese beliefs in the paranormal. There is still fairly strong belief in such phenomena as ghosts, Chinese fortune telling, and Chinese geomancy (*feng shui*), even among those who consider themselves highly Westernized. Indeed, Western and Chinese versions of the paranormal seem to coexist side by side on Hong Kong's newsstands.

Christianity, really an aspect of Westernization, is positively related to several paranormal beliefs, especially to some considered by the Chinese to be mainly Western: angels, devils, life after death, and ESP. However, there are no significant *negative* relationships between either Protestantism or Catholicism and any of the fourteen beliefs included in the survey. Again, Westernization has encouraged belief in Western mysteries but has not discouraged belief in traditional Chinese ones. The suggests that Hong Kong Chinese feel comfortable with becoming bicultural, just as Chinese have traditionally accepted and blended many religious philosophies without taking any too seriously.

Another set of surprises came in the cross-cultural testing of paranormal experiences. Fortunately, the topic I was most interested in among the fourteen (see entire list in Table 1 on page 325), ghosts, yielded the best cases. I knew from the beginning, of course, that ghost belief was central to Chinese culture. As Chapter 3 explains, ghosts are not only part of the cosmology of yin and yang or of underworld and this-world. They are also socially important as ancestors, ghost relatives who are part of family worship and are thought to influence the health and welfare of their descendants. Neglecting one's ancestors is not only immoral but dangerous. Especially when ghosts return shortly after death or during the Hungry Ghost Festival, they must be satisfied with offerings of food and incense.

Therefore, a major question in terms of cultural effects on ghost experiences was whether the folklore of ancestor worship, with its strong expectations of physical effects performed by returning spirits, would result in firsthand reports of apparitions performing physical effects. As Chapter 6 shows, even the disturbances reported at family altars turned out never to be specifically linked to apparitions. Sometimes handprints were found on the rice, sometimes apparitional noises were heard or ghosts were seen around the altar. However, not one respondent reported catching a ghost in the act of disturbing the altar! This is perfectly consistent with parapsychological theory of ghosts as ESP-generated rather than physical. In Western studies, although physical effects (PK) may occur in hauntings, they seem not to occur simultaneously with the apparitions themselves, or very rarely so.

This means that the central aspect of Chinese culture about ghosts – ancestor worship – does not in fact result in firsthand reports that are inconsistent with the ESP theory. Instead, the reports support the view that there is a universal ghost experience found cross-culturally. There was, however, another ghost concept in Chinese culture that threatened the ESP theory by describing an apparently physical effect: *bei guai chaak* ("being pressed by a ghost," Chapter 11). Analysis of these cases, which also have their parallels in cases reported in the West, points to a natural physiological/psychological explanation. I have argued that BGC is sleep paralysis in the hypnagogic state, associated with hallucinations and sometimes with the feeling of cold, due perhaps to a lowering of body temperature during sleep or near-sleep. Some or all of the "hallucinations" may actually be ESP-induced apparitions, but none of the BGC cases in this study is "evidential," and this point must remain open.

As mentioned above, physical effects (PK) are found in hauntings separate from the apparitions themselves. Some cases of this type plus some possible poltergeists are discussed in Chapter 10. Only one or possibly two of the Chinese reports connected an apparition directly with a physical effect (G037 and G038 in Chapter 5).

Although the question of physical effects is the main theoretical issue that needed to pass the cross-cultural test, a broader perspective also shows that the generalizations in parapsychology about apparitions studied in the West may be applied to the Chinese cases as well. The following are some of the concepts and categories used in Chapter 5 to illustrate such similarities: crisis, post-mortem, and haunting cases; visual, auditory, tactile, and olfactory senses involved; the feeling of a "presence"; collective apparitions; and evidential cases.

Nevertheless, there has never been much emphasis in parapsychology on the precise nature or appearance of apparitions, visual ones in particular, although they have been categorized by sensory modality (visual, auditory, etc.). Consequently, the more I noticed that "weird" features were showing up in the Chinese cases as we collected them, the more suspicious I became that we were getting highly imaginative accounts influenced by ghost lore. Glowing figures with horrible faces and partial bodies did not fit my preconception of a "normal" apparition. After all, the best cases found in the West seemed to emphasize a realistic appearance, unlike the ghosts of popular horror stories.

Therefore, I created a list of "abnormal features of perception" (Chapter 7) based on the Chinese cases: disappearance or fading out, insubstantial image, glowing (self-luminescence), white and dark clothing, sickly or horrible look, partial body, abnormal walking, and abnormal sound. To my surprise, on closer comparison, all of these features have been reported in Western cases as well! Moreover, I have argued that they are a logical result of the lack of realism and completeness to be expected from ESP in general and from apparitions in particular.

Again, Chinese folklore turned out not to be responsible for molding and shaping a peculiarly Chinese type of firsthand ghost experience, as might have been suspected. Why not ignore the folklore and popular culture of ghosts altogether then, once this point has been established? As Chapters 8 and 9 reveal, analyzing the ghost lore not only produces insights into the social system but also has implications for the methods used by parapsychologists who study apparitions.

Both Western and Chinese ghosts are commonly portrayed in the folklore as moral agents of social control, making their physical powers useful for administering rewards and punishments. Although both malevolent and benevolent ghosts exist in both traditions, Chinese ghosts seem to be more malevolent than Western ones. Some common ghost-lore themes in Hong Kong reflect feelings about the Japanese occupation during the Second World War; fears of hospitals, car accidents, and bathrooms (among schoolchildren especially); and the ambitions of college students for success.

As far as parapsychological methods are concerned, the cases in which I was able to observe the folklore process in action and to trace a rumor or legend to its source illustrate how easy it is for distortion to creep into secondhand reports, even without intent. My advice to those who would use secondhand reports (cf. footnote 32 in Chapter 5) in studying apparitions is to exclude them from any statistical treatment of ghost reports that are supposedly authentic experiences.

Although the firsthand reports in this study give an overall impression of much greater validity than the hearsay ones do, it should be emphasized that the precise authenticity of any one of them cannot be guaranteed. As in the various studies by Louisa E. Rhine of spontaneous ESP cases (including apparitions) collected from various sources, this study has been directed toward looking for statistical patterns in a large number of self-reported cases, rather than toward intensive investigation into a few cases.

Another caution should be observed in the matter of gifted subjects (Chapter 12). Apparition experiences are rare, and so, apparently, are people with multiple experiences. Although there seem to be some genuinely gifted subjects, I also suspect that some of them take on the role identity of "psychic person," which may affect their perceptions or at least their presentation of self to others in discussing their powers.

In all of this analysis, the ESP theory of apparitions predominates. However, Chinese in Hong Kong do not seem to make the connection between ESP and ghosts, or between ESP and either spirit mediums or fortune telling, since the correlations between the belief in ESP and the belief in these others are not high. They do see the obvious connections between ghosts and spirit mediums and between spirit mediums and fortune telling (cf. Chapters 15 and 17), a conclusion supported by the correlations among these beliefs.

Although the belief in ESP is high (Chapter 16), "sixth sense" is viewed as more of a Western concept. Hong Kong Chinese nevertheless tend to equate ESP with precognition, as evidenced by the examples they gave of their own experiences on the survey. In spite of this narrowed folk definition of ESP, ESP experiences (excluding apparitions) were much more frequent than ghost experiences, just as in the West (cf. Chapter 5).

In Chinese culture, of course, ESP is not the explanation for the interrelated phenomena of ghosts, spirit mediumship and possession, and fortune telling. It is the surviving spirits themselves. Even fortune telling is thought to involve some kind of divine inspiration from the spirit world (Chapter 17). In Western culture, too, this has been a traditional explanation, as can be seen in the word "divination" itself or by the ancient Greek use of oracles, like the one at Delphi.

Modern parapsychology is ambivalent over the survival hypothesis, which claims that spirit mediumship and apparitions of the dead are links to surviving spirits. Survival is generally considered unproven if not unprovable, although there are some intriguing arguments in support of it. Therefore, the tendency is to prefer ESP without survival as the more parsimonious explanation in lieu of more compelling evidence.

The same may be said of the Chinese data. Although my case study of a spirit medium (Chapter 15) yielded some impressive material, ESP is probably a sufficient explanation. Telepathy between the medium and the sitters would explain nearly all of it, with perhaps some long-distance clairvoyance between the medium and the situation in the United States as a supplement. Those sitters who were disappointed during partially successful sessions were skeptical because they had expected actual contact with a surviving spirit. The erroneous, out-of-character statements made by the "spirit" during the session were too numerous to sustain such a view in their minds.

Overall, parapsychological theory based on apparitions in the West has been found strikingly appropriate for dealing with Chinese apparitions as well. The related phenomena of PK, spirit possession, spirit mediumship, ESP, and fortune telling also have remarkable parallels in the two cultures. I do not feel that we are any closer to resolving the "survival vs. ESP" question as a result of these findings, but my conclusion is that psi (psychic phenomena) in general has passed through the social/cultural filter as a result of this cross-cultural test.

It would be exciting to study the paranormal in still other non-Western cultures with the same methods, especially African and other Asian cultures. Even if similar psychic parallels are found, as I now expect to be the case, such studies may help to uncover new explanations. For example, the Chinese ghost cases led me to hypotheses that account for cold chills and paralysis (Chapter 11) and to a systematic treatment of "abnormal features of perception" (Chapter 7). Further studies should lead us even closer to a scientific understanding of some apparently universal mysteries.

Whether these mysteries will turn out to have explanations that are completely continuous with the rest of our understanding of the natural world is impossible to say. At the moment, psychic phenomena, for example, are not fully accepted as legitimate subjects for scientific inquiry, largely because they do not appear to fit the scientific, materialistic view of the universe, let alone any particular testable paradigms.

In my opinion, there are ample cases of what *seem* to be authentic, evidential apparitions, and of other forms of ESP and PK as well. However, psi is a tender and rather infrequently observed phenomenon, not easily generated in stimulus-response fashion. Parapsychology will not be fully accepted until it is capable either of replicating psi easily or of explaining the ESP and PK processes. The latter will probably require the discovery of at least an ESP receptor in the brain that then stimulates images and impressions in the conscious mind. In the case of PK, there may be a "transmitter" in the brain that produces or interacts with psychic energy outside the body.

In the meantime, cross-cultural studies of psychic and other paranormal phenomena help answer a very important question: to what extent are popular conceptions and reported experiences of the paranormal due to cultural expectations, and to what extent do they reflect a universal reality independent of the influences of a particular culture? Although they have not been a focus of this study, UFOs, for instance, received little or no support in the survey, just a few unimpressive firsthand experiences, in spite of a high level of belief in UFOs (42%). Negative findings cannot disprove paranormal claims, but they may suggest some revisions in thinking and testing. Positive cross-cultural findings, on the other hand, provide good reason for thinking that there is really something there that needs explaining.

If, for example, the explanation for an allegedly paranormal phenomenon turns out to be a natural physiological/psychological pattern as in the case of BGC ("the pressing ghost"), then how fascinating! If some of them turn out *not* to be "natural" phenomena in our current understanding of the term, as evidential apparitions seem not to be, then they will be more than merely fascinating. They will require radical rethinking of scientific theories of the nature of humanity and perhaps of the universe.

TABLES

Table 1: Percentages who believe in various paranormal phenomena; Hong Kong Chinese vs. Americans

Paranormal Belief	Hong Kong	United States *
1. ghosts	50 % (N=1479**)	12% (N=1435)
2. ESP	49 % (N=1454)	53% (N=1453)
3. fortune telling	44 % (N=1488)	N. A. ***
4. UFOs	42% (N=1437)	N. A. (57%)***
5. feng shui (geomancy)	35% (N=1433)	N. A.
6. reincarnation	25% (N=1469)	N. A.
7. life after death	24% (N=1467)	65% (N=1462)
8. water monsters	21% (N=1346)	15% (N=1420)****
9. angels	21% (N=1378)	56% (N=1465)
10. devils	21% (N=1378)	41% (N=1447)
11. spirit mediums	18% (N=1438)	N. A.
12. Western astrology	17% (N=1468)	31% (N=1431)
13. witches	7% (N=1456)	10% (N=1429)
14. faith healing	6% (N=1469)	N. A.
15. precognition	N. A.	31% (N=1431)
16. déjà vu	N. A.	31% (N=1431)
17. clairvoyance	N. A.	25% (N=1416)
18. Sasquatch (Bigfoot)	N. A.	14% (N=1419)

* Based on a 1978 national-sample Gallup poll (Emmons and Sobal, 1981b).
** N refers to the number of respondents who answered the question.
*** N. A. stands for "not available in this study." However, another Gallup poll showed that 57% of Americans believed in UFOs in 1978 (Public Opinion, 1978: 39).
**** The Gallup poll asked about the Loch Ness Monster specifically, but "water monsters" as designated in Hong Kong were usually equated with Loch Ness by respondents.

Table 2: Correlations (Pearson's R) between religious preferences and paranormal beliefs; Hong Kong telephone survey, 1980†

	Religious Preference			
	Buddhism		No Religion	
	Zero	Variable	Zero	Variable
Paranormal Beliefs	Order	Controlled	Order	Controlled
1. ghosts	.09***	.08**	-.12***	-.14***
2. ESP	-.06***	-.04	-.07**	-.10***
3. fortune telling	.13***	.13***	-.07**	-.07**
4. UFOs	-.11***	.01	-.01	-.04
5. feng shui (geomancy)	.14***	.12***	-.09***	-.09***
6. reincarnation	.27***	.22***	-.13***	-.14***
7. life after death	-.13***	-.03	-.45***	-.44***
8. water monsters	-.09***	-.04	.06*	-.03
9. angels	-.17***	-.07*	-.44***	-.43***
10. devils	-.18***	-.08**	-.43***	-.42***
11. spirit mediums	.13***	.09***	-.07**	-.09***
12. Western astrology	.00***	.03	-.06*	-.09***
13. witches	.02***	.03	-.04	-.05*
14. faith healing	.04***	.06*	-.07**	-.09**

	Religious Preference			
	Protestantism		Catholicism	
	Zero	Variable	Zero	Variable
Paranormal Beliefs	Order	Controlled	Order	Controlled
1. ghosts	-.02	.00	.09***	-.14***
2. ESP	.10***	.07**	.09***	-.10***
3. fortune telling	-.05*	-.05	-.07**	-.07**
4. UFOs	.09***	.05*	-.01	-.04
5. feng shui (geomancy)	-.04	-.02	-.09***	-.09***
6. reincarnation	-.04	-.01	-.13***	-.14***
7. life after death	.49***	.44***	-.45***	-.44***
8. water monsters	.02	.02	.06*	-.03
9. angels	.49***	.43***	-.44***	-.43***
10. devils	.48***	.42***	-.43***	-.42***
11. spirit mediums	-.02	.02	-.07**	-.09***
12. Western astrology	.03	.03	-.06*	-.09***
13. witches	.02	.02	-.04	-.05*
14. faith healing	.05	.06*	-.07**	-.09**

*p<.05   **p<.01   ***p<.001

Table 3: Correlations (Pearson's R) between social characteristics and paranormal beliefs; Hong Kong telephone survey, 1980††

| | Social Characteristic | | | |
| | Age | | Education | |
Paranormal Beliefs	Zero Order	Variable Controlled	Zero Order	Variable Controlled
1. ghosts	-.13***	-.1***	.06*	.06*
2. ESP	-.24***	-.17***	.27***	.18***
3. fortune telling	-.07*	-.06*	.04	.09**
4. UFOs	-.28***	-.20***	.32***	.18***
5. feng shui (geomancy)	.07**	.08**	.05	.12***
6. reincarnation	.01	-.02	-.08**	.01
7. life after death	-.03	.01	.28***	.16***
8. water monsters	-.20***	-.15***	.16***	.08**
9. angels	-.03	-.01	.25***	.11***
10. devils	-.03	-.00	.26***	.11***
11. spirit mediums	-.08**	-.09***	-.08**	-.04
12. Western astrology	-.23***	-.22***	.04	-.04
13. witches	-.08**	-.06**	.07**	.06*
14. faith healing	-.03	-.04	.00	-.03

| | Social Characteristic | | | |
| | Male | | Ancestor Worship | |
Paranormal Beliefs	Zero Order	Variable Controlled	Zero Order	Variable Controlled
1. ghosts	-.09***	-.08**	.16***	-.17***
2. ESP	.07**	.05	-.06*	0.04
3. fortune telling	-.10***	-.10***	.10***	.06*
4. UFOs	.19***	.16***	-.12***	-0.02
5. feng shui (geomancy)	.01	.00	.13***	.12***
6. reincarnation	-.10***	-.07**	.19***	.11***
7. life after death	-.07*	-.07**	-.25***	0.02
8. water monsters	.14***	.12***	.00	.06*
9. angels	-.06*	-.06*	-.27***	.00
10. devils	-.06*	-.05*	-.27***	.00
11. spirit mediums	-.17***	-.14***	.18**	.14***
12. Western astrology	-.06*	-.04	.02	.03
13. witches	-.03	.03	.03	.05
14. faith healing	.07*	.07**	.00	.01

*p<.05 **p<.01 ***p<.001

† HOW TO READ TABLE 2: Each number is a correlation coefficient. The larger the number, the stronger the relationship. Negative numbers mean that people with that religious affiliation are less likely than others to believe in that paranormal phenomenon. In the "Zero Order" column, no other variables are taken into account. In the "Variables Controlled" column, the effects of the following variables have been eliminated: age, education, sex, ancestor worship, and Westernization. The asterisks indicate that the correlation is statistically significant, and show the probability that the finding is an accident of the sample of people interviewed. Three asterisks show the highest level of significance: probability (p) of this result is less than (<) one in 1,000 (.001).

†† HOW TO READ TABLE 3: Each number is a correlation coefficient. The larger the number, the stronger the relationship. Negative numbers mean that people who score high on that social characteristic (or who are male in the one case) are less likely than others to believe in that paranormal phenomenon. In the "Zero Order" column, no other variables are taken into account. In the "Variables Controlled" column, the effects of the following variables have been eliminated: Buddhism, "no religion," Protestantism, Catholicism, Westernization, and all three of the other social characteristics in this same table. The asterisks indicate that the correlation is statistically significant, and show the probability that the finding is an accident of the sample of people interviewed. Three asterisks show the highest level of significance: probability (p) of this result is less than (<) one in 1,000 (. 001).

BIBLIOGRAPHY

Alexander, Marc
1975   *Phantom Britain: This Spectre'd Isle*. London: Frederick Muller.
Bennett, Sir Ernest
1939   *Apparitions and Haunted Houses: A Survey of Evidence*. London: Faber and Faber.
Björkhem, John
1973   "Did Harry Price return?" Pp. 150-160 in Andrew MacKenzie (ed.): *A Gallery of Ghosts: An Anthology of Reported Experience*. New York: Taplinger.
Brunvand, Jan Harold
1968   *The Study of American Folklore: An Introduction*. New York: Norton.
Burkhardt, V. R.
1953   *Chinese Creeds and Customs*. 3 vols. Hong Kong: South China Morning Post.
Census and Statistics Department
1978   *Hong Kong By-Census 1976: Tertiary Planning Unit Tabulations*. Vol. 1: Hong Kong Island. Hong Kong: Census and Statistics Department, Hong Kong Government.
Chan, Wing-tsit (ed.)
1963   *A Source Book in Chinese Philosophy*. Princeton: Princeton University Press.
1969   *The Great Asian Religions: An Anthology*. London: Macmillan.
Chaney, David C., and David B. L. Podmore
1973   *Young Adults in Hong Kong: Attitudes in a Modernizing Society*. Hong Kong: Centre of Asian Studies, University of Hong Kong.
Charlton Publications
1979   *Ghost Manor*. #46 (October). Derby, Conn.: Charlton.
Chin, Steve S.K.
1979   *The Thought of Mao Tse-Tung: Form and Content*. Hong Kong: Centre of Asian Studies, University of Hong Kong.

China Mail

1963a "Government to deal with ghosts in two buildings." (May 6).

1963b "Ghost hunt won't cost government anything." (May 8).

1965 "NT fishermen flee in terror." (March 23).

Christie, Anthony

1968 *Chinese Mythology.* London: Hamlyn.

Comber, Leon

1972 *The Strange Cases of Magistrate Pao: Chinese Tales of Crime and Detection.* Hong Kong: Heinemann Educational Books (Asia).

DC Comics

1979 *Ghosts: New Tales of the Weird and Supernatural.* Vol. 9, # 76, 82 (May, November) New York: DC Comics.

De Fleur, Melvin L., William V. D'Antonio, and Lois B. De Fleur

1971 *Sociology: Man in Society.* Glenview, Ill.: Scott, Foresman.

Dement, William C.

1978 *Some Must Watch While Some Must Sleep.* New York: Norton.

Doré, Henry, S.J.

1918 *Researches into Chinese Superstitions.* Translated from French by M. Kennelly, S. J. 5 vols. Shanghai: T'usewei Printing Press.

Economic and Social Commission for Asia and the Pacific

1974 *The Demographic Situation in Hong Kong.* ESCAP Country Monograph Series, No.1. Bangkok: United Nations.

Elliott, Alan J. A.

1964 *Chinese Spirit-Medium Cults in Singapore.* Monographs on Social Anthropology, No. 14. Singapore: Donald Moore.

Emmons. Charles F., and Jeff Sobal

1981a "Paranormal beliefs: testing the marginality hypothesis." *Sociological Focus* (January): 49-56.

1981b "Paranormal beliefs: functional alternatives to mainstream religion?" *Review of Religious Research* (June): 301-312.

Endacott, G. B.

1966a "Chinese ghosts." *The Mandarin* (June): 27, 29.

1966b "The Hungry Ghosts Festival." *The Mandarin* (June): 31.

Fleischman, Sid

1971 *McBroom's Ghost.* New York: Grosset and Dunlap.

Freedman, Maurice

1971   *Chinese Lineage and Society: Fukien and Kwangtung.* London School of Economics Monographs on Social Anthropology, No. 33. University of London (Athlone Press).

1977   "A report on social research in the New Territories of Hong Kong, 1963." *Journal of the Hong Kong Branch of the Royal Asiatic Society* (vol. 16): 191-261.

Fuller. John G.

1969   *Aliens in the Skies.* New York: Putnam.

Glanvill, Joseph

1689   *Saducismus Triumphatus: Or, Full and Plain Evidence Concerning Witches and Apparitions.* 1966 reprint. Gainesville, Fla.: Scholars' Facsimiles and Reprints.

Goffman, Erving

1959   *The Presentation of Self in Everyday Life.* Garden City, N.Y.: Doubleday/ Anchor.

Greeley, Alexandra

1977   "Those strange night visitors." *South China Morning Post* (November 20).

Green, Andrew

1973   *Ghost Hunting: A Practical Guide.* London: Garnstone.

Hallam, Jack

1976   *Ghosts of the North.* Newton Abbot: David and Charles.

Hart, Hornell

1956   "Six theories about apparitions." *Proceedings of the Society for Psychical Research* (vol. 50): 153-239.

1957   "Mrs. Rhine's conclusions about survival: a critique." *Journal of Parapsychology* (vol. 21, September): 227-237.

1958   "Do apparitions of the dead imply any intention on the part of the agent? -- a rejoinder to Louisa E. Rhine." *Journal of Parapsychology* (vol. 22, March): 186-226.

Heenan, Edward (ed.)

1973   *Mystery, Magic, and Miracle: Religion in a Post-Aquarian Age.* Englewood Cliffs, N. J. : Prentice-Hall.

Hong Kong Standard

1963a   "Murray Building ghost is haunting government clerks." (May 5).

1963b   "Exorcism at Murray House not ghost hunt." (May 18).

1963c   "Old Huang pacified." (May 20).

1977   "Fort ghost scares Stanley amahs." (September 16).

Hong Kong Star

1969   "Expensive ghosts." (January 19).

1977a   "Fungshui fear by residents." (September 22).

1977b   "Major who saw a ghost at Stanley Fort." (October 7).

1978   "Night ghosts went dancing in Wanchai." (April 19).

1980   "The ghost chasing incident in New Territories, Tuen Mun, Tai Hing, New Village." (July 29): 4.

Hookham, Hilda

1969   *A Short History of China.* New York: New American Library.

Hsu, Francis L. K.

1967   *Under the Ancestor's Shadow.* Stanford, Calif.: Stanford University Press.

Johnson, Elizabeth L.

1977   "Patterned bands in the New Territories of Hong Kong." *Journal of the Hong Kong Branch of the Royal Asiatic Society* (vol. 16): 81-91.

Kehl, Frank

1971   "Chinese ghost festival in urban Hongkong." 25 min., 16mm., color film. Hong Kong: Centre of Asian studies, University of Hong Kong.

Kingston, Maxine Hong

1976   *The Woman Warrior: Memoirs of a Girlhood Among Ghosts.* New York: Knopf.

Kleitman, Nathaniel

1963   *Sleep and Wakefulness.* Chicago: University of Chicago Press.

Kramer, Nora (ed.)

1960   *Arrow Book of Ghost Stories.* New York Scholastic Book Services.

Lethbridge, Henry

1978   *Hong Kong: Stability and Change: A Collection of Essays.* Hong Kong: Oxford University Press.

McHugh, J. N.

1959   *Hantu Hantu: Ghost Belief in Modern Malaya.* Malayan Heritage Series, No.3. 2nd ed. Singapore: Eastern Universities Press.

Mihalik, Emma

1981   "A toast to our ghost." *Fate* (February): 90-92, 94.

Ming Pao Weekly

1980   "Talking about ghosts." (June 29).

Moody, Raymond A., Jr.
1976 *Life After Life.* New York: Bantam.
Nakamura, Hajime
1964 *Ways of Thinking of Eastern Peoples: India--China--Tibet--Japan.*
Honolulu: University Press of Hawaii.
Nam Mo Lo
1963 "Allo-so." *South China Morning Post* (May 11).
Pao-p'u tzu
1966a *Alchemy, Medicine, Religion in the China of A. D. 320: The Nei P'ien of Ko Hung (Pao-p'u tzu).* Translated by James R. Ware. Cambridge, Mass.: MIT Press.
1966b *The Wai P'ien of Ko Hung (Pao-p'u tzu).* Translated by James R. Ware. Cambridge, Mass.: MIT Press.
Potter, Jack M.
1970 "Wind, water, bones and souls: the religious world of the Cantonese peasant." *Journal of Oriental Studies* (vol. VIII, no. 1): 139-153.
Public Opinion
1978 "UFOs ... and tennis grows." (July/August): 39.
Rhine, Louisa E.
1953a "Subjective physical effects and the psi process." *Journal of Parapsychology* (vol. 17, June): 77-114.
1953b "The relation of experience to associated event in spontaneous ESP." *Journal of Parapsychology* (vol. 17, September): 187-209.
1956 "Hallucinatory psi experiences: I. An introductory survey." *Journal of Parapsychology* (vol. 20, December): 233-256.
1957a "Hallucinatory psi experiences: II. The initiative of the percipient in hallucinations of the living, the dying, and the dead." *Journal of Parapsychology* (vol. 21, March): 13-46.
1957b "Hallucinatory psi experiences: III. The intention of the agent and the dramatizing tendency of the percipient." *Journal of Parapsychology* (vol. 21, September): 186-226.
1957c "Letter to editor on Dr. Hart's critique." *Journal of Parapsychology* (vol. 21, September): 237.
1962 "Parapsychological processes in ESP experiences: Part I. Waking experiences." *Journal of Parapsychology* (vol. 26, June): 88-111
1963 "Spontaneous physical effects and the psi process." *Journal of Parapsychology* (vol. 27, June): 84-122.

1978 "The psi process in spontaneous cases." *Journal of Parapsychology* (vol. 42, March): 20-32.

1981 *The Invisible Picture: A Study of Psychic Experiences.* Jefferson, N. C.: McFarland.

Roberts, Nancy

1979 *Southern Ghosts.* Garden City, N. Y.: Doubleday.

Rogo, D. Scott

1974 *An Experience of Phantoms.* New York: Dell.

1975 *Parapsychology: A Century of Inquiry.* New York: Dell.

1979 "Arsonist or poltergeist?" *Fate* (August): 52-56.

Rogo, D. Scott, and Raymond Bayless

1979 *Phone Calls from the Dead.* Englewood Cliffs, N. J.: Prentice-Hall.

Roll, W. G.

1972 *The Poltergeist.* Garden City, N. Y.: Doubleday; reprinted Metuchen, N. J.: Scarecrow, 1976.

Saint Fist Society

n.d. *Everything Under Heaven: Number Two Book of the Strange; What Happens After Death.* Cantonese-language version only. New Territories, Hong Kong: Shui Kee.

Salter, W. H.

1961 *Zoar, or The Evidence of Psychical Research Concerning Survival.* London: Sidgwick and Jackson.

Schneck, Jerome M.

1977 "Hypnagogic hallucinations: Herman Melville's *Moby Dick.*" *New York State Journal of Medicine* (vol. 77, No.3, November): 2145-2147.

Sin, Daniel

1977 "Spirits of Stanley Fort." *Hong Kong Standard* (November 18).

South China Morning Post

1963a "Ghosts haunting Murray House and the Old Tamar." (May 5).

1963b "Go bump in the night." (May 7).

1963c "Disturbed spirits." (May 8).

1963d "Haunted house." (May 8).

1963e "Unruly crowd waits for Murray Barracks' ghost." (May 9).

1963f "Ceremony to exorcise 'disturbed spirits' at Murray House." (May 20).

1980 "Reading through her ears...." (October 23): 8.

Taillepied, Father Noel

1933 *A Treatise of Ghosts.* London: Fortune Press.

Thomas, W.I.

1928   *The Child in America: Behavior Problems and Programs.* New York: Knopf.

Thompson, Stith

1966   *Motif-Index of Folk-Literature.* Revised edition, 6 volumes. Bloomington: Indiana University Press.

Tin Tin Daily News

1980a   "Ban Ban is playing a ghost in a movie." (July 11).

1980b   "Strange incidents in the space era? Two workers fainted in _____ Hospital after seeing ghosts." (September 17): 1.

Truzzi, Marcello

1972   "The occult revival as popular culture: some random observations on the old and nouveau witch." *Sociological Quarterly* (vol. 13): 16-36.

Tyrrell, G. N. M.

1946-49 "The modus operandi of paranormal cognition." *Proceedings of the Society for Psychical Research* (vol. 48): 65-120.

1963   *Apparitions.* New York: Macmillan.

VanGulik, Robert

1963   *The Haunted Monastery: A Chinese Detective Story.* London: Heinemann.

Walker, Judy

1980   "Garrulous ghosts." *South China Morning Post* (November 8): 73.

Western Publishing Company

1979   *Grimm's Ghost Stories.* # 49, 52, 53 (March, September, October). Poughkeepsie, N. Y. : Western Publishing.

Willoughby-Meade, G.

1926   *Chinese Ghouls and Goblins.* New York: Stokes.

Wolman, Benjamin B. (ed.)

1977   *Handbook of Parapsychology.* New York: Van Nostrand Reinhold.

Added for the 2017 edition:

Alfano, Sean

2009   "Poll: Majority Believe in Ghosts." CBS News online, February 11.

Bosco, Joseph

2007   "Young People's Ghost Stories in Hong Kong." *The Journal of Popular Culture* 40, 5: 785-807.

Campany, Robert F.

1991 "Ghosts Matter: The Culture of Ghosts in Six Dynasties Zhiguai."
Chinese Literature: Essays, Articles, Reviews 13, December: 15-34.

Chen, Te-Ping and Jeffrey Ng

2013 "Hong Kong's Real Estate Boom Conjures a Scary Development." *The Wall Street Journal* online, January 14.

Cooper, Callum

2011 "The Ka in Ancient Egypt." *Paranthropology: Journal of Anthropological Approaches to the Paranormal* 2, 3: 43-45.

Delaplace, Gregory

2010 "Chinese Ghosts in Mongolia." *Inner Asia* 12: 127-141.

Emmons, Charles F.

1982 *Chinese Ghosts and ESP: A Study of Paranormal Beliefs and Experiences.* Metuchen, NJ: The Scarecrow Press, Inc.

1992 "Hong Kong's Feng Shui: Popular Magic in a Modern Urban Setting." *Journal of Popular Culture* 26, 1, summer: 39-50.

1997 *At the Threshold: UFOs, Science and the New Age.* Mill Spring, NC: Wild Flower Press.

2003 "Ghosts: The Dead Among Us." Pp. 87-95 in Clifton D. Bryant (ed.), *Handbook of Death and Dying.* Thousand Oaks, CA: Sage Publications.

Emmons, Charles F., and Penelope Emmons

2003 *Guided by Spirit: A Journey into the Mind of the Medium.* N.Y.: Writers Club Press.

2012 *Science and Spirit: Exploring the Limits of Consciousness.* Bloomington, IN: iUniverse.

Hankey, Rosalie

1943 "Ghosts and Shamanism in Kwangtung." *California Folklore Quarterly* 2, 4, October: 303-308.

Hufford, David J.

1982 *The Terror That Comes in the Night: An Experience-Centered Study of Supernatural Assault Traditions.* Philadelphia: U. of Pennsylvania Press.

Laje, Diego

2013 "How Secretive Databases Control Hong Kong's Haunted House Market." CNN online, April 22.

Laursen, Christopher

2012 "Surveying Hong Kong's Abundant Spirits." Christopherlaursen.com, July 7.

Li, Lillian

1945   "Two Chinese Ghosts." *California Folklore Quarterly* 4, 3, July: 278-280.

Lyons, Linda

2005   "One-Third of Americans Believe Dearly May Not Have Departed." Gallup-online, July 12.

McClenon, James

1990   "Chinese and American Anomalous Experiences: The Role of Religiosity." *Sociological Analysis* 51, 1, Spring: 53-67.

2002   *Wondrous Healing: Shamanism, Human Evolution, and the Origin of Religion.* DeKalb, IL: Northern Illinois U. Press.

Nesbitt, Mark

1991   (and later volumes) *Ghosts of Gettysburg: Spirits, Apparitions, and Haunted Places of the Battlefield.* Gettysburg, PA: Thomas Publications.

Newport, Frank

1999   "Seven Out of Ten American Families Will Be Giving Out Treats This Halloween." Gallup News Service, October 29.

Newport, Frank, and Maura Strausberg

2001   "Americans' Belief in Psychic and Paranormal Phenomena Is Up Over Last Decade." Gallup News Service, June 8.

Rittichainuwat, Bongkosh

2011   "Ghosts: A Barrier to Tourism Recovery." *Annals of Tourism Research* 38, 2: 437-459.

Sek Kei

1994   "Achievement and Crisis: Hong Kong Cinema in the 80s." *Bright Lights Film Journal* 13, January 13.

Speigel, Lee

2013   "Spooky Number of Americans Believe in Ghosts." *Huffington Post* online, February 2.

Squarefoot.com.hk. August 6, 2013.

YourGhostStories.com. February 8, 2013.

Yu, Anthony C.

1987   "'Rest, Rest, Perturbed Spirit!': Ghosts in Traditional Chinese Prose Fiction." *Harvard Journal of Asiatic Studies* 47, 2, December: 397-434.

Glossary

Agent. In an apparition, the person who is sensed by another, considered also by Tyrrell (but not by L.E. Rhine) to be the sender or initiator of the apparition.

Apparition. Paranormal sensory experience of a person or situation, generally thought by parapsychologists to be generated by ESP.

Automatic writing. Communication with a spirit through the writing of a medium.

Bei guai chaak (BGC). "Being pressed by a ghost." Chinese ghost experience that seems to be sleep paralysis.

Buddhism. A religion imported from India, based on teachings of Gautama Buddha (sixth and fifth centuries B. C.), emphasizing mysticism but adapted to indigenous beliefs in China.

Clairvoyance. "Clear sight." A form of ESP in which a person knows information directly without the help of another mind (cf. Telepathy).

Confucianism. A Chinese philosophy, based on teachings of Confucius (sixth and fifth centuries B. C.), emphasizing loyalty to nation and family, agnostic on spiritual matters.

Dang-ki. "Divining youth." Type of verbal spirit medium, found among Singapore Chinese.

Déjà vu. "Already seen." Unexplainable sensation of having experienced a situation before, perhaps through ESP or reincarnation.

Evidential case. Apparition that seems not to be merely hallucinatory, based on evidence of multiple witnesses (collective) or of paranormal knowledge from the experience.

Experimental case. Apparition in which agent consciously tries to appear to percipient.

Extrasensory perception (ESP). Knowing without the normal use of the five senses.

Feng shui. (also spelled *fung shui*) "Wind and water." Chinese geomancy, magical art of harmonizing with supernatural forces in the environment.

Folktale. Story in oral tradition that is not claimed to be true.

Fu gei sau. "Character writer." Automatic-writing medium who uses a stick to draw Chinese characters in sand.

Guai (also spelled *kuei*). Ghost or evil spirit in Chinese culture.

Hallucination. Imitation sensory experience. Used by L. E. Rhine to refer to apparitions.

Hypnagogic state. Condition of near-sleep involving conscious hallucinations.

Karma. Indian religious concept of moral credits accumulated in series of incarnations.

Legend. Story in oral tradition that is claimed to be true.

Ling wun. Soul or spirit.

Mah-jongg. Chinese gambling game using small tiles, played somewhat like gin rummy.

Motif. Theme, or recurring element or idea in folklore.

Mun mai poh. "Ask-rice woman." Type of verbal spirit medium found in Hong Kong.

Percipient. In an apparition, the person who senses another person or object.

Precognition. "Knowing ahead." A form of ESP in which a person knows information about a future event.

Psi. Parapsychological term for psychic phenomena, including both ESP and PK.

Psychokinesis (PK). Causing physical effects without the normal use of machinery or human motor ability.

Retrocognition. "Knowing backward." A form of ESP in which a person knows about events in the past.

Shen. Good ghost or superior spirit in Chinese culture.

Super-ESP. The theory that there is no limit to ESP in time or space.

Survival hypothesis. The idea that the soul or spirit of a dead person can cause apparitions or communicate through spirit mediums.

Taoism. A Chinese philosophy and religion, thought to have been formalized by Lao Tzu (seventh and sixth centuries B. C.), emphasizing mysticism and distrust of formal social order.

Telepathy. "Communicating at a distance." A form of ESP in which information from one person's mind is obtained by the mind of another.

Yang. Active, male principle in Chinese cosmology. Cf. Yin.

Yin. Passive, female principle in Chinese cosmology. Cf. Yang.

Yin-yang eyes (also spelled *yum-yeung*). Ability of a person to see ghosts on a regular basis.

ABOUT THE AUTHOR

Charles Emmons is a sociologist/anthropologist at Gettysburg College (Pennsylvania, USA) who has studied paranormal phenomena for 35 years. He combines an open but skeptical social-scientific approach with (more recently) an experiential, intuitive view from his personal experiences as a Spiritualist.

His books include *Chinese Ghosts and ESP* (1982), *Hong Kong Prepares for 1997* (1987), *At the Threshold: UFOs, Science and the New Age* (1997), and coauthored with Penelope Emmons: *Guided by Spirit: A Journey into the Mind of the Medium* (2003) and *Science and Spirit: Exploring the Limits of Consciousness* (2012). He is active in the research groups Exploring the Extraordinary, and The Society for Scientific Exploration.

EXPLORE ASIA WITH BLACKSMITH BOOKS

From retailers around the world or from *www.blacksmithbooks.com*

Living & Working Series

LONDON'S SECRETS: BIZARRE & CURIOUS

ISBN: 978-1-909282-58-2
£11.95, 320 pages
Graeme Chesters

London is a city with 2,000 years of history, during which has accumulated a wealth of odd and strange sights. This book seeks out the city's most bizarre and curious attractions and tells the often fascinating story behind them, from the Highgate vampire to the arrest of a dead man, a legal brothel and a former Texas embassy to Roman bikini bottoms and poetic manhole covers, from London's hanging gardens to a restaurant where you dine in the dark. *Bizarre & Curious* is sure to keep you amused and fascinated for hours.

LONDON'S SECRETS: MUSEUMS & GALLERIES

ISBN: 978-1-907339-96-7
£10.95, 320 pages
Robbi Atilgan & David Hampshire

London is a treasure trove for museum fans and art lovers and one of the world's great art and cultural centres. The art scene is a lot like the city itself – diverse, vast, vibrant and in a constant state of flux – a cornucopia of traditional and cutting-edge, majestic and mundane, world-class and run-of-the-mill, bizarre and brilliant.

So, whether you're an art lover, culture vulture, history buff or just looking for something to entertain the family during the school holidays, you're bound to find inspiration in London.

LONDON'S SECRETS: PARKS & GARDENS

ISBN: 978-1-907339-95-0
£10.95, 320 pages
Robbi Atilgan & David Hampshire

London is one the world's greenest capital cities, with a wealth of places where you can relax and recharge your batteries. Britain is renowned for its parks and gardens, and nowhere has such beautiful and varied green spaces as London: magnificent royal parks, historic garden cemeteries, majestic ancient forests and woodlands, breathtaking formal country parks, expansive commons, charming small gardens, beautiful garden squares and enchanting 'secret' gardens.

LONDON'S SECRETS: PUBS & BARS

ISBN: 978-1-907339-93-6
£10.95, 320 pages
Graeme Chesters

British pubs and bars are world famous for their bonhomie, great atmosphere, good food and fine ales. Nowhere is this more so than in London, which has a plethora of watering holes of all shapes and sizes: classic historic boozers and trendy style bars; traditional riverside inns and luxurious cocktail bars; enticing wine bars and brew pubs; mouth-watering gastro pubs and brasseries; welcoming gay bars and raucous music venues. This book highlights over 250 of the best.

see www.londons-secrets.com